SHERIDAN MARITIME CLASSICS

T0021023

THE LONG WAY

BERNARD MOITESSIER

TRANSLATED BY WILLIAM RODARMOR

SHERIDAN HOUSE

GUILFORD, CONNECTICUT

An imprint of The Rowman & Littlefield Publishing Group, Inc.
4501 Forbes Blvd., Ste. 200
Lanham, MD 20706
www.rowman.com

Distributed by NATIONAL BOOK NETWORK

British Library Cataloguing in Publication Information available

Library of Congress Cataloging-in-Publication Data available

ISBN 978-1-4930-4278-4 (paperback)
ISBN 978-1-4930-4279-1 (e-book)

♾™ The paper used in this publication meets the minimum requirements of
American National Standard for Information Sciences—Permanence of Paper for
Printed Library Materials, ANSI/NISO Z39.48-1992.

Printed in the United States of America

Contents

Part One

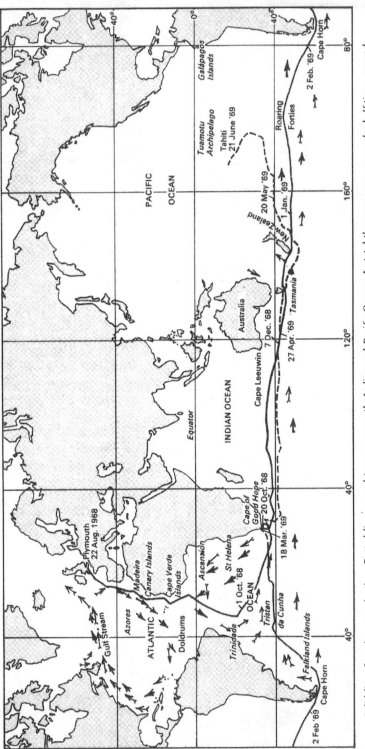

Solid line: first circumnavigation. Dotted line: second passage across the Indian and Pacific Oceans. In total the voyage was one and a half times around the world.

ONE

Full Sail

Thursday August 22, Loïck and I pop our heads out of the hatches at the same time. . .we had just listened to the weather report.

'Did you hear? Shall we clear out?'

'And how! Tomorrow is a Friday!'

Our boats lie at anchor in Plymouth harbour and the BBC forecasts favourable winds today and tomorrow, but also fog. Too bad about the fog: it will have to be today. Sailors do not like to leave on Friday, even if they are not superstitious, and waiting for Saturday is out of the question; the wind would have time to shift back to the west. We may be crazy to want to fell the three capes at a single blow, but we are not stupid enough to deliberately risk getting blackjacked by the approach of another low in the Bay of Biscay. The good Lord had given us the green light, it is not a Friday, let's clear off! Bill King still has a few little things to take care of. He will leave day after tomorrow, on Saturday. Hmm. . .could it be that Bill King doesn't like Friday either? As for Nigel, he cannot leave before the first of September, because of his job in the Royal Navy.

From then on, everything went very fast. I remember Françoise's small face struggling vainly to keep the tears back. Françoise is my wife. I was upset to see her cry. 'Listen, we'll be seeing each other again soon! After all, what is eight or nine months in a lifetime? Don't give me the blues at a time like this!' I felt such a need to rediscover the wind of the high sea, nothing else counted at that moment, neither earth nor men. All *Joshua* and I wanted was to be left alone with ourselves. Any other thing did not exist, had never existed. You do not ask a tame seagull why it needs to disappear from time to time toward the open sea. It goes, that's all, and it is as simple as a ray of sunshine, as normal as the blue of the sky.

All that canvas up in the air! I will heave everything taut when we first come about beyond the corner of the breakwater.

The sheet winches creak, the water murmurs on the bottom as *Joshua* gathers way and begins to come alive. . .People who do not know that a sailboat is a living creature will never understand anything about boats and the sea.

Françoise had stopped crying. She was fascinated by the power and harmony of the long red hull trimmed with black, its great white wings bellied by the wind, full of one man's dreams and the thoughts of many others. She shouted to me, 'You can't imagine how lovely she looks; take care of her, she will pay you back!' But she was crying again when the launch turned back after the breakwater, leaving me alone with my boat and the horizon.

Suddenly, I thought very hard of my children. We had often talked about the voyage. Had I been able to make them understand, in those days when technical preparations called for all my mental and physical resources? I think they felt the essential, and will know enough to obey their own inner voices.

The wake stretches on and on, white and dense with life by day. luminous by night, like long tresses of dreams and stars. Water runs along the hull and rumbles or sings or rustles, depending on the wind, depending on the sky, depending on whether the sun was setting red or grey. For many days it has been red, and the wind hums in the rigging, makes a halyard tap against the mast at times, passes over the sails like a caress and goes on its way to the west, toward Madeira, as *Joshua* rushes to the south in the trade wind at 7 knots.

Wind, sea, boat and sails, a compact, diffuse whole, without beginning or end, a part and all of the universe. . .my own universe, truly mine.

I watch the sun set and inhale the breath of the open sea, I feel my being blossoming and my joy soars so high that nothing can disturb it. The other questions, the ones that used to bother me at times, do not weigh anything before the immensity of a wake so close to the sky and filled with the wind of the sea.

Before leaving Toulon for Plymouth, I had been incensed at the *Sunday Times,* which had decided to organize a solo non-stop race around the world, with two prizes: a golden globe for the first to finish, and £5000 sterling for the fastest voyage. There was no need to be officially entered, and the rules were simple:

all you had to do was to leave from any English port between June 1 and October 31, then return to it after rounding the three capes of Good Hope, Leeuwin and the Horn.

The idea came to the *Sunday Times* after they heard that Bill King and *Joshua* were preparing for the long way. My old pal Loïck Fougeron was also readying for the trip; we had exchanged confidences at Toulon. We talked rigging, equipment, stores, useless weight, encumbering but essential weight, sails light and easy to handle, or heavier and more solid but harder to furl in a real blow, collecting rainwater, foul weather, cold, loneliness, seasons, human endurance. . .only things of the sea. After the *Sunday Times* announcement we decided to sail our boats to Plymouth, hoping to be able to carry off one or even both of the prizes, the good Lord willing, without risking our freedom, since the rules did not specify that we had to say 'Thank you'. From a strictly technical standpoint the run to Plymouth would also be an excellent trial before the main event, to shake out the bugs; once there, to get everything really shipshape to the least detail.

The wind is holding, *Joshua* is moving very fast, I feel passing through my whole being that breath of the high seas that once felt is never forgotten. What peace, here in the open sea! And it seems ages ago that I stopped resenting the staff of the *Sunday Times*. In fact my rancour dissipated at Plymouth during our first meeting with the chaps who work on the paper. Robert, the head of the team, would have liked me to ship a big transmitter with batteries and generator. They offered it gratis, to Loïck as well, so we could send them two weekly messages. The big cumbersome contraptions were not welcome. Our peace of mind, and thereby our safety, was more important, so we preferred not to accept them. Robert understood the meaning of our trip, though, and we were friends. Steve, his fellow from the Press Service, loaded both of us with film, as well as watertight Nikonos cameras. He told us, 'We are giving you all this, we ask nothing in exchange.' And Bob, the *Times* photographer, shared all the tricks of his trade with us. He too was sorry that I preferred my old, quiet friend the slingshot to two or three hundred pounds of noisy radio equipment, but he could feel the 'how' and the 'why' and helped me to find good rubber bands, supplying me with aluminium film cans to contain messages I would shoot onto passing ships. A good slingshot is worth all the transmitters in

the world! And it is so much better to shift for yourself, with
the two hands God gave you and a pair of elastic bands. I will
try to send them messages and film for their rag. It would make
them so happy. . .and me too.

Madeira is already on my right, with an average of nearly
150 miles a day since leaving Plymouth. I wonder which route
Bill King and Loïck will choose—to the right or the left of
Madeira? To the right or left of the Canaries, further on, and
the Cape Verde Islands? Loïck, Nigel and I had often talked
about these problems during our six weeks' preparation at
Plymouth, while our boats[1] were tied up in Millbay Dock. At
that time, we all expected to leave the Cape Verde Islands to
port, since the doldrums are normally narrower to the west.
But we had not yet studied the Pilot Charts on a point that we
would have plenty of time to settle later at sea. There remained
so many important jobs to do before weighing anchor.

I would like to know where Loïck is. And Bill King, where is
he? The BBC has not announced his departure, or at least I
have not heard it mentioned. Pity we do not have tiny battery-
run transmitters, like walkie-talkies but with a range of five or
six hundred miles. That way, Loïck, Bill King and I could have
kept in touch until the distances between our boats became too
great.

The name *Joshua* is in black letters which stand out well
against the white of the cockpit coaming. When I first painted
the foot-high letters on, they were so eye-catching they made
me uncomfortable. I was tempted to paint everything out
again, particularly since my mainsail has a big identification
number that would let Lloyds know that the boat was indeed
Joshua (No. 2). Nigel's good sense persuaded me otherwise:

[1] Loïck Fougeron's *Captain Browne*: 30 ft gaff rigged steel cutter, formerly the Van de
Wieles' *Hierro*, which he had sailed from Morocco to Plymouth. Nigel Tetley's *Victress*:
37 ft plywood trimaran. Bill King's *Galway Blazer II*, a 42 ft moulded ply schooner, with
a rigging drawn from the Chinese junks, unstayed masts, turtle deck and a reverse
sheer.
  All told, there were nine starters for this adventure. I only know Bill, Nigel and
Loïck personally, since we were together at Plymouth. Many had left long before us,
others afterward, the place and date for sailing being up to the individual. Of the nine
starters, only Robin Knox-Johnston brought his boat back to England after rounding
the three capes. Nigel was almost home, with three capes in his wake as well, when
Victress broke up in the Atlantic. I learned of it a few days after *Joshua*'s arrival in Tahiti.
Crowhurst died at sea. All the others had to stop en route because of serious damage,
boats rolled by breaking waves, etc.

'Don't be a fool; if you have MIK up without *Joshua* written in very large letters, some ship is going to run you down trying to get close enough to ask you your name. That would be smart!'

Yesterday the radio forecast a big gale for the North Atlantic and the Mediterranean. I couldn't care less, I'm far away! It is nice to be at a safe distance when things start cutting loose up north. Noon latitude 30°19'. The wind is very light, but there are flying fish just ahead, dorados too...I can tell just by looking at the sky and the sea.

September 1. We meet a ship early in the morning. I get out my mirror, and she answers with an Aldis lamp. She has understood and will radio my position to Lloyds. Françoise will know that all's well; I'm happy—right off, my day is made.

Feeling great, I go below to finish my mug of coffee; glancing out the hatch, what do I see...the ship coming back! She has made a big circle (I can see her wake on the calm water) and is bearing down on me from astern. Wow! I get pretty rattled...She comes by about fifteen yards off, towering like a wall far above my masts. The ship is enormous; she must be well over 300 ft long. When the bridge draws abreast, an officer shouts through a megaphone, 'We will report you to Lloyds. Do you need anything?'

I wave 'No' with my hand, my throat is so tight. The monster takes forever to go by; I pull the helm all the way over to get clear, afraid she would wobble in her course and sweep both my masts away. But the captain of the *Selma Dan* has a good eye and knows what he is doing. I have cold sweats just the same, and my legs feel like rubber. At this range I could pelt the bridge with my slingshot, but there was no time to prepare a message. And I dare not try to get them to understand by signalling: they are so nice they would turn around and come back. I have had enough thrills for one day, and I know someone who is not about to take on any more ships with his mirror for a while.

Flying fish come with the NE trades, which I picked up before the Canary Islands. No squalls, except once between Gran Canaria and Tenerife, which meant a few hours under storm jib instead of genoa. Actually, it was not a squall: the trade wind often reaches force 6 to 7 in the strait between the two islands.

The average speed climbs day after day, on a sea full of sun. I am glad to see that *Joshua* sails definitely faster than before. This improvement is largely due to the fact that she is much lighter. Also, the longitudinal weight distribution is far better; she is less loaded down with useless gear, and I was able to completely clear out the forward and aft compartments. In the old days, we had two dismantled dinghies in the forepeak, one dead and the other useless, not to mention an incredible pile of junk collected over the years. When in Plymouth, I unloaded engine, anchor winch, dinghy, all unnecessary charts, a suitcase full of books and *Sailing Directions* that did not cover my route, four anchors, 55 pounds of spare zinc anodes, 900 pounds of chain, most of the $\frac{1}{4}$ in. diameter line, and all the paint (275 pounds!) after splashing a last coat on deck and topsides.

Incredible, the amount of spare equipment a sailboat outfitted for cruising the trades, with stopovers, can carry. Without speaking of masses of improbable bits of gear which add up to a lot of weight. The whole mess was stored with my friends Jim and Elizabeth, or thrown away, or given to neighbouring boats, greatly relieving mine.

Naturally, I did not completely disinherit myself, in spite of cutting to the bone. Though I kept a strict minimum of charts, they covered all possible landfalls around Good Hope, Australia, Tasmania, the northern and southern islands of New Zealand, the Horn waters with parts of the Patagonia channels, and even a few atolls in the Pacific. In case of trouble, I would not be caught with my pants down.

I therefore left Plymouth with that which I considered necessary, but also that which might become so. My ruthless war on weight spared the 55 pound CQR anchor and the 35 pound Colin Tripgrip, 200 feet of $\frac{3}{8}$ in. chain (in three lengths in the hollow keel), and a coil of $\frac{3}{4}$ in. diameter nylon anchor line.

Though stripped to bare essentials, *Joshua* is ready for an emergency landfall in case of damage, discouragement or illness. Despite all precautions, health always presents a number of unknowns on a trip this long. Above all, there is the great and most beautiful unknown, the sea itself.

Continued fair weather, but very little wind. The speed is still impressive, as *Joshua* can carry more than 1560 sq. ft of canvas.

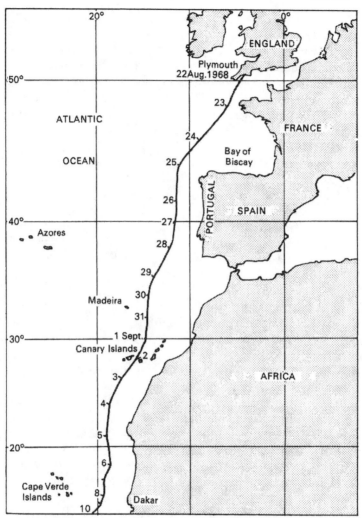

22 August to 10 September 1968

I rigged a 54 sq. ft storm jib as a bonnet under the main boom, in addition to the genoa bonnet, and a lightweight 75 sq. ft storm jib as a second staysail. The sea is calm, my rig picks up the slightest breeze. I watch the boat slipping along at nearly 7 knots on a smooth sea in the setting sun. What peace! Two weeks already, and a daily average of 143 miles since Plymouth.

Compiling figures may seem odd, when the wind and sea range so far beyond them. But to a sailor's eyes, the sight of miles drawn on a chart reflect the long wake furrowed in the waves by his boat's keel, the measure of his offering to the boat and her offering to the sea. If we are indeed racing, I do not feel that it is against other sailors and other boats.

Anyway, Loïck, Bill King, Nigel and I do not have the same boats. Even if we could conceive of the trip as a race, the trump cards are not evenly dealt. Each of us has the boat he likes best, the one that lets him live aboard as he sees fit.

The wake stretches on and on. The Canaries are now astern, the Cape Verde Islands on the right, Africa to the left. Flying fish hunted by the dorados glide in big schools in front of the boat. At times, a beautiful rainbow plays with the foam of the bow wave. I film it, securely wedged on the bowsprit pulpit.

The doldrums are fairly close now. It is a zone of calms and light variable winds, with rain and squalls, caused by the meeting of the two trade wind belts near the Equator. At the latitude of the Cape Verde Islands, the doldrums stretch approximately between the 15th and the 5th parallel north, or about 600 miles.

For the big square-rigged vessels of old, the doldrums meant long, exhausting days handling the heavy yards in the damp heat under a leaden sky, taking advantage of the least shift in the wind, continually coming about. For our small yachts, the doldrums are annoying but nothing more, since coming about is easy; the zone should normally be crossed fairly quickly. Just the same, a sailor will always take on the doldrums with an uneasy conscience. I wonder where my friends will cross? I have not quite settled on a course to the left or right of the Cape Verde Islands.

Joshua has been dragging along for days that feel like weeks. When the breeze drops completely, I have to sheet everything flat and drop the 650 sq. ft genoa-bonnet combination, which would chafe too much, slatting against the staysail stay as the boat rolls. Every time the inconsistent breeze picks up the genoa has to be raised again and the sheets trimmed to the inch to catch the faintest puff, to sail south at all cost.

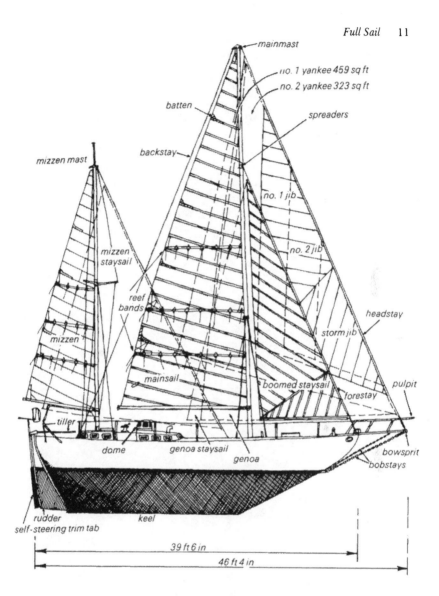

I eat badly, I am losing my punch. Several opportunities to make a few miles south have been passed up, because I was disgusted with the rain, or did not want to get wet, or was just not up to it, not having had the heart to fix a decent meal for days.

When rain falls, it is not even useful. On a trip this long, every drop of fresh water is a gift from the heavens. I left

Plymouth with enough water to reach New Zealand, though, and will have a dozen opportunities to top up my tank between here and Tasmania. Just the same, I collected 15 gallons yesterday and today, with a bucket rigged under the mainmast gooseneck. Strictly as a matter of principle, as if I did not want to leave this rotten place completely emptyhanded.

I feel empty, like this sea without sun, without fish, without birds, dead as a doornail despite the goddamned swell that tosses the boat, wearing the sails out and wearing me down. I have to pull myself together and hang on, trim the sails twenty times an hour, move out of the doldrums at all costs, before I get completely fed up with everything.

TWO
Clear
Light

I slowly stretched for all I was worth this morning, first my left
side, then my right, then in a circle pulling each joint one by
one, yawning till my eyes watered and filling my lungs and all
my body with new air. I felt penetrated by something like a
great peace and a great strength. That is how life begins. I did
not have to get up; my whole body knew that today would be
very different from yesterday.

All last night water rustled along the hull; I even seemed to
hear it in my sleep. Whenever I cocked an eye open I knew even
before I turned the flashlight on that the compass at the foot of
the bunk would read SSW. Each time I went back to sleep with
an immense hope in my heart.

The spare staysail halyard could be heard tapping against
the mast; I had forgotten to replace the shock cord that pulls it
toward the shrouds. The rapping usually bothers me; it in-
terrupts the whispered talk between sea and boat. But last night
it joined the chorus of sounds a sailor needs, tapping out 'the
wind is back, the wind is back, tomorrow's clouds will be the
shape and colour of the trades, pink-lined petals in a sky
becoming bluer with the climbing sun'.

I stretch again, wedge the pillow to leeward, and immediately go back to sleep. A sailor's joys are as simple as a child's.

Joshua is doing 6 knots, closehauled to the light SE trade wind,
which we picked up on September 17 in 4° north latitude.

The doldrums turned out to be wider than expected. I had
figured on 600 miles; where we crossed, it was closer to 900.
Joshua averaged 90 miles a day, never doing less than 50 miles
noon to noon. The rainy squalls were not bad, but it was still a
very long ten days. The overall average fell from 143 miles at
the beginning of the doldrums to 125.4 at the end; it will be
hard to make up.

Also, I have to fill out a little; I did not have much fat to start, and there isn't any left. My inner barometer has been rising rapidly since last night, though. This morning I downed a huge mess of oatmeal and three mugs of Ovaltine with renewed appetite.

Spirits are high again, and except for my lovely torn bonnet, ripped in the doldrums and rotting in the cabin, all's well with crew and boat. The barnacles took advantage of the calms to hitch-hike on the rudder and probably the aft part of the bottom. I will dive down and clean them off at the first chance.

The flying fish returned with the wind. So did the dorados, to chase the little gliders as they burst from the water, fanning out in sheets sometimes so compact they look like big, luminous palm-fronds and glimmering with hundreds of silver wings. Here and there, a brief swirl reveals a life and a death.

Watching the struggle for life, you wonder how there can be any small fish left in the sea. Do the flying fish's wings keep them safe from a dorado? True, they can take to the air instead of zig-zagging like a sardine in front of the hunter's mouth, but a dorado swims fast enough to follow a flying fish under water and snap it up on landing, sometimes in full flight. On a calm sea the worried shoals run the greatest risk, with their whole flight visible to the dorado following just beneath the surface.

I catch my breath at a sight I have only seen twice before in all my years at sea. Caught unawares, a flying fish shoots straight up in a twenty foot leap into the air. A huge barracuda takes off after it and snatches the flying fish at the top of the arc. The really amazing thing was seeing the barracuda contorting its entire body and beating its tail, modifying its trajectory to follow the prey, which had angled off to the left at the top of its leap.

I felt sorry for the little one, but was so struck by the terrible beauty of a master-stroke that I let out a big 'Aaah!'

The air is warm tonight, the wind gentle; there is hardly any swell. From the cockpit, I can clearly hear the rustle of water when a whole school takes off, with *Joshua* or the dorados in pursuit. It sounds like the faint trembling of coconut leaves near a lagoon when a breath of air bestirs the quiet night.

I had gone below to turn in, and was listening to the water flowing along the hull, half asleep, when a noisy flapping broke out on deck. I jump from my bunk yelling 'flying fish!'

and catch it on the first try, still luminous from the water's phosphorescence. But I let it go immediately—the fish is so huge, it must be a young barracuda or some other menace to wayward fingers. I suddenly flashed back to the misadventure of a sailor I had met in Alicante, in Spain, at the end of the trip with Françoise back from Tahiti via the Horn.

He had been trolling, and caught two mackerel towards the end of the afternoon. As night came on, he looked astern and saw that his line was taut again. He hauled it in, and grabbed the fish to break its back. It turned out to be a big weever, a long fish with an extremely painful, sometimes fatal sting. He was sailing singlehanded without an engine, and was almost unconscious when he reached a Spanish port the next day.

Mine was a flying fish though, but an unbelievably big one. Just as I instinctively let him go, his wings brushed my wrist; a second reflex quickly closed my hands again—too late. Now he is flopping around the deck, and it is like chasing a bar of soap in pitch black darkness. He gets away, after caressing me one last time with his enormous wings. I am heartsick. My mouth waters as I curse myself.

I like flying fish better than anything. It tastes like sardine, but much better. I did not see mine too clearly, but he was gigantic, possibly over two feet long. I am not sure that my hands could have met around his body. To think he will probably wind up in some dorado's belly, when I had him a yard from my frying pan! Others land on deck, of course, but they are just babies. I want the big one so badly I can taste him.

The sea is full of life here, nervous then calm again. The Pilot Chart puts us in the middle of the westbound Equatorial Current, whereas the alternating areas of choppy and calm water suggest veins of current setting to the east. That would explain the concentration of marine life.

At dawn, *Joshua* passes near a school of a dozen big puffer fish floating belly up, completely inflated. It is the first time I see any blown up of their own accord; when I catch one I usually have to scratch his belly to make him puff up. Seeing them like that, I wondered what could have happened. Did they all die, for some mysterious reason? Was a branch of the current carrying a plankton that was poisonous to puffers?

My quick deduction was obviously idiotic. If they actually had died of a poisonous plankton, they would not be floating all together in a ten foot square, felled at the same time by a universal tummyache. Just then I see a fin followed by a swirl; in the eddy, one of the white balls disappears, swallowed by the shark. The other white balls don't lose their nerve. They just float there, serenely awaiting the call of destiny, perhaps wishing all the same that someone else would be the next to go, and hoping the shark would die.

I do not see the story end; *Joshua* is doing 7 knots and I was too engrossed to climb quickly up the mizzen mast. Those puffers blew themselves full of air to fool the shark, but he didn't fall for it. I would give a lot to know how the shark is feeling right now, because puffers are usually poisonous. In Mauritius, I saw a litter of kittens die that had eaten one left on the beach by a fisherman.

Oddly enough, the flesh of the puffer is delicious. Yves and Babette Jonville ate plenty of them during their visit to the Galapagos in *Ophélie,* but they knew the trick, and were careful never to eat the head, liver or skin, which are extremely dangerous.

When I was in the Galapagos, the De Roys told me the story of a yachtsman who did not believe the tales. He swallowed the raw liver of a puffer in front of André De Roy, who was struggling to stop him. His tongue swelled up to enormous size, he started to suffocate, and very nearly died.

Probably nothing more serious than after-dinner drowsiness will befall my friend the shark. Now that I think of it, I remember a perfectly healthy dorado speared from the deck of *Marie-Thérèse* in about this latitude, which had ten little puffers in its stomach. How those slow and apparently defenceless fish could have got there, at the mercy of any foe and a thousand miles from shore, I can't imagine.

I wonder why such inequality is so common in nature? Sharks and dorados can eat all the puffers they like, and their victims can't raise a fin to stop them. Whales snuff out half a ton of lives at a single bite, without even looking. What is the reason behind all that? Yet it must serve some purpose.

Why was I thinking about those things, so complicated yet so simple? I forgot to climb the mizzen mast to see how many white balls were left in the wake.

Each morning the sun tinges the little clouds with pink and mauve as they drift along like snowflakes. Then it begins to climb, a clear light in the pale blue sky—the trade wind sky of the South Atlantic, where the weather is constant, without squalls or calms. The wind breathes into my sails the life of the open sea; it runs murmuring through the whole boat, to blend with the rustling of water parted by the bow.

Joshua has been sailing in the trade wind for a week, averaging 159 miles a day. I listen to the sound of water along the side, and the wind in the rigging. By turns, I read *The Roots of Heaven* and *Wind, Sand and Stars,* in little sips. I spend long moments on deck, watching the flecks of foam rising in the wake. There are so many things in the flecks of foam and the water that runs along the side. I could not ask for more; I have it all.

The sun rises, peaks and sets, and one day gracefully makes way for the next. I have only been gone a month; my boat and I could have been sailing forever. Time stopped long ago, I have the feeling nothing will ever change; the sea will stay the same luminous blue, the wind will never die, *Joshua* will always carve her wake for the pleasure of giving life to sheafs of spray, for the simple joy of sailing the sea under the sun and the stars.

THREE

Sunday
at Trinidad

Calms, calms, light breezes from the north, more calms . . . the
sun is shining to raise my spirits after the noon sight: only 45
miles covered in the last 24 hours. The shortest run since the
start.

The overall average dropped from 132.4 to 130 miles since
this time yesterday. That will be hard to make up, as any sailor
knows. What consoles me a little is that as the breeze has
shifted to NE, the 45 miles on the chart run due south, toward
the little island of Trinidad.

Next day, September 28, the breeze returns to the south; I
come about and steer for Good Hope. We are not going fast,
but at least make a few miles in the right direction. Up to now
Joshua has been sailing SW close to the wind, to pick up the
following winds which should be blowing along the 35th
parallel this time of year. Better to head SE along the 35th than
give up ground by continuing westward.

The average again dropped after the noon sight: 129 miles,
down from 130 yesterday and 132.4 the day before. I do not
lose my head, but I meditate on the vanity of things. . .

The breeze shifts to SE force 3; I come about again onto the
other tack. Trinidad is only 90 miles to the south. The sea turns
unpleasantly rough: the presence of a heavy southerly swell in
this latitude (19° south, well in the tropical zone) surprises me a
bit. A distant gale probably, but a very violent one to have sent
a residual swell this big so far north.

Best not head further south than necessary. It is still spring
down there; the gales are more frequent, and their average
path runs further north than during the favourable summer
season.

The breeze really does not know what it wants: now SE, then
east, at times even NE, but always light. I take advantage of

every favourable shift to make for Trinidad, where I want to drop off a package of film for the *Sunday Times*. We have been doing about 4 knots since yesterday. If the little breeze holds, and the sky says it will, *Joshua* should be in sight of land tomorrow morning, under full sail.

Early in the afternoon the wind steadies to force 3 from the east. My spirits start to rise, though I hate landfalls. They upset the normal cadence of things; they alter the very slow inner rhythm a sailor develops after a time away from the dangers of the coast, in the security of the open sea where everything takes its true place, without demanding but also without deception.

For the sailor, the coast is often like a great whore. I should know: two of my boats have been lost. If I do have to sight land, I like it to be from as far off as possible. Moreover, in chasing weight at Plymouth, I simply forgot to take along the *Sailing Directions* for Brazil, which include Trinidad. Not a very smart move.

I had read the description of the island during Tahiti-Alicante, and remember that the east coast is fairly straight-forward, with a small settlement. They probably have a radio transmitter, and can notify Lloyds if I am not able to deliver my package for some reason—like the fact that tomorrow is Sunday.

I hope the radio operator, probably the only person to know what MIK flags mean, will not decide to take a dawn to dusk siesta. Even if the whole town is snoozing, though, the appearance of a red yacht is sure to dispell its tropical torpor.

Early next day, September 29, land ho! The wind is a steady NE force 3 under an absolutely blue sky. No problems—the wind will not drop. I can't say why; it is just one of those things you feel instinctively, from a hundred little signs in the sea and sky. And this time the coast is a friendly one, with a perfect steady breeze to take us there.

Will there be coconut trees on the beach. I wonder? I would like to caress them with my eyes, just in passing.

For once, everything is turning out exactly the way I had hoped yesterday. Trinidad gets bigger by the minute, first its colours, then its features showing through. It is high and jagged, with big cliffs and rock faces shading from light purple to dark blue depending on the angle of the sun. There are patches of pink too, but very little green. The island is beautiful. I would like to sail round it, a stone's throw from the cliffs, perched on the lower spreaders to keep an eye on the bottom. I bet the coastline is absolutely clear of dangers.

The breeze, still NE, has gone to force 4. Through binoculars I can make out the little settlement. It is tiny, like a pretty miniature. The roofs are green. I am intrigued by a long red thing at the breaker line, that looks like some sort of peculiar jetty. What the devil is it?

Joshua closes with the coast at 6 knots. The red thing is not a jetty, but a boat anchored offshore, rusty as a nail. It seems to be a whaler, like the ones I saw at Cape Town fifteen years ago. That means the coast is perfectly clear, as I thought.

The distance narrows pretty fast. Under my feet *Joshua* feels easily manoeuvrable, ready to gybe or come about at a moment's notice. Already the sea is much calmer. The rusty boat still intrigues me; if I were a whaler captain, never would I anchor so close to shore. I keep it in view in my binoculars.

Way out! I was right the first time, it's a jetty! Or rather, the wreck of an old steel whaler, no doubt sunk deliberately and filled with stones to make a breakwater in front of a tiny small boat anchorage.

If there really is an anchorage, it is out of sight behind the wreck. I do not see any rowboats or canoes on the sunswept beach, so there has to be some sort of manmade harbour if the villagers want fish from time to time. But who knows? They may catch all they want just by casting from the beach.

Toward 11 a.m. I heave-to 300 yards from the wreck, staysail and genoa aback, and from the lower spreaders check for shoals on the leeward side. Everything is deep blue, except for a few suspicious yellow-green patches close to shore.

The climbing rungs screwed to my masts are really useful. I first saw the trick on Bardiaux' *Les Quatre Vents* when he came through Mauritius, then on *Didakï* at Cape Town after his visit there, then on five or six other boats. Nigel mounted them on *Victress*. Bill King wanted to do the same, but had a touchy problem: his Chinese junk rig sails are laced to the mast, which has to be perfectly smooth. I hope Bill worked it out, because with rungs you're at the lower spreaders in two shakes.

Bardiaux had carried the idea one step further. The Mauritians still remember him sitting on the spreaders while tacking around the coral heads under club-footed staysail and main, when entering a difficult pass. He had a combined watch and steering position on the spreaders with a control system rigged to the tiller.

Joshua drifts slowly. Everything is clear for a couple of hundred yards at least. There is a questionable patch far to the right of the village, and another to the left, where there is a tell-tale brown discolouration. It is all imprinted on my memory, for a few hours at least.

I climb down and scan the village with my binoculars: not a soul. The windows seem to be closed with green shutters, the same green as the roofs. I give a blast on the foghorn, then shoot a reel of movie film with the Beaulieu. I blow the foghorn again, then gybe to get closer before altering course.

Headsails aback again, I ease the staysail sheet with the helm well alee, beating very slowly along the shore. The Beaulieu is near at hand, and I shoot more film between horn blasts. My signal flags flutter in the wind. They have been up since Plymouth, and are still in good shape; a bit faded, after five weeks at sea, but easy to make out with binoculars. I hope the people on shore have a pair of binoculars, at least. Nothing stirs.

Another horn blast: no greater success. It is past noon and I am hungry in spite of my excitement. I would like to pick up the smell of the earth, but the wind is from the sea. The island probably does not have much aroma, it shows so little green.

The foghorn again: nothing. After all this trouble, I would hate to turn tail and leave. Still, I am tempted to forget the *Sunday Times* and just sail around this beautiful island, slipping by the rock cathedrals that scale the cliffs. I would give myself just enough leeway to gybe, in case the genoa got backwinded by a downdraft so close to the coast.

But that would mean letting Francoise and my friends down, who would be glad to get any good news. Also, if the paper got a radio message from Trinidad, the BBC might announce that *Joshua* had been sighted on such-a-such day, and give positions for Bill King' and Nigel as well. I will stay glued to the radio for three days after Trinidad. I would be so happy to find out how my friends are doing, wherever they are. I do not expect to hear anything of Loïck; like me, he has no transmitter.

The foghorn—nothing. It's unbelievable! They must be noisily filling their bellies with all the windows shut!

At last! One, two, three...nine...I lose count...They pour out of a big house onto the steps. I was right: they were all stuffing themselves at Sunday lunch, probably making enough noise to raise the dead. Maybe some kid sent to stand in the corner raised the hue and cry, shouting *'Bella barca! Bella barca!'*

By now there are at least twenty people jamming the steps, but they just stand there motionless. I wave my arms like mad: no reaction. Wait...one man runs down the stairs and dashes into a little house. He is not wearing any uniform. Nobody else moves; they look petrified. If I were in their shoes, I would have already sprinted down across the beach and been out in the water, without even taking my trousers off.

What the hell is going on? I can't figure them out. In any case, there are no boats in the place; passing south of the rusty whaler I did not see any shelter behind it, so the ship is just a wreck, with no particular use.

Those people are not going to move. The one who ran into the house emerges with something in his hand. Quick—the binoculars: he is peering at me with his, but does not answer my friendly waves. It worries me.

Nothing doing in this bay. I gybe, release the tiller and snap on the windvane set for a beat to get out. Just in case, I dip the MIK flags five or six times.

The one with the binoculars could easily make out the name *Joshua* painted in large black letters on the white cockpit coaming. I hope he read it, and also the big number 2 sewn on the mainsail.

Joshua heads for the sea again, her lee rail nearly awash, steering well clear of the green and brown patches. Squatting in the cockpit, my elbow resting on the coaming and chin in hand, I gaze at the people grouped on shore, who have still not moved, as if afraid. As if they were looking at the Devil. I am almost relieved that they have no boats here: I was beginning to wonder whether an armed party would come out 'requesting' that I show them a visa authorizing me to spy on their island.

I really don't understand. These people are very isolated; at most, a grey naval supply ship from Brazil visits them twice a year. If I were one of them, my heart would really start pounding at the sight of a man coming over the horizon in a little red boat, carrying the world's vastness in his sails. What makes them like this?

I stand up, and make a wide, slow gesture with my right arm, the gesture that men all over the world understand, no matter how savage: the gesture that means goodbye. Suddenly all the arms start waving, and everybody runs down to the beach with a chorus of friendly shouts. Three men run into the water up to their waists. I can feel their warmth coming out to me, and get a lump in my throat.

At first they all thought I was going to anchor there. They were waiting, hoping, afraid to believe. For fear the dream would suddenly vanish, they did not move a muscle.

I did not understand, either. But they have no boat, and I have no dinghy.

Still waving, the arms get further and further away. The shouts from shore begin to blend with the rumble of the sea as *Joshua* rushes towards the horizon. I feel as though I want to cry.

At sunset, Trinidad is in the wake. I can see the island in the distance, magical and unreal, its dark blue profile showing against an orange sky.

A little dorado hits the trolling line I had put out, from habit. But I'm not hungry tonight. I unhook the fish and return him to the sea. It is the first fish I have ever thrown back. I suppose I could have kept him for tomorrow, but I did not feel like it. The dorado is lucky.

I look at Trinidad, tiny now and blurring into the sunset. The entire island comes back to me—its cliffs, its rock cathedrals, its colours, its shadows and warmth: I can see the village with its green roofs and the men running on the beach, shouting and waving.

Were there any coconut trees? I don't even know. That is the one thing I forgot to look for.

FOUR

Muchos Pocos
Hacen Un Mucho

In the three days since Trinidad disappeared astern *Joshua* has crossed a square predicted on the Pilot Chart as having 5 per cent calms. And yet, the average was 148 miles a day. For the horse latitudes that is real luck. She is heading SE, leaving to the north two other squares marked 6 per cent calms, with a strong predominance of contrary winds predicted as well as the damned calms.

By now, the wind has eased a little, but the sails are full and *Joshua* is still moving fast on a broad reach, not tossing at all in the nearly following swell.

The log turns steadily. Before I left, I could not see the point of continually towing a log in the middle of the ocean, wearing out the mechanism for nothing. I find a log most useful when nearing the capes or in coastal sailing, where accurate dead reckoning is essential.[1]

Nonetheless, I promised the Vion company to tow the log during the whole trip, to test out their equipment. I do not regret it, because the log helps me trim the sails to their optimum. A variation of a quarter of a knot is hard to feel; the log picks it up. And a quarter of a knot means six extra miles in 24 hours. The overall average has risen to 129.5.

On October 3 the log turns more slowly; on the 4th, not at all. It recorded barely 93 and 23 miles for those two days. The overall average falls abruptly to 126.2 because of a two day bummer. Actually, it is not so bad. The wind has really treated us very well since Trinidad. *Joshua* is in the horse latitudes, and

---

[1] In working a celestial sight, one can base the calculation on an estimated position that is completely absurd; the position line will bring the boat back to her true location. If the intercept is too long one need only redo the calculation using the new estimated position, which will be more accurate than that shown by the log, especially after a meridian sight. Just for fun, I have sometimes deliberately picked a position 600 miles off. In two calculations (easily done with the HO 249 tables) the boat took her true position on the chart.

it is natural that the normally prevailing conditions return. Flat calm now. A long SW swell moves across the sea, with a shorter one from the south. In addition, the sky was covered with cirrus yesterday, with lots of altocumulus this morning. These signs all point to an early return of the wind.

I pull on my wetsuit. Now is a good time to take care of the gooseneck barnacles, which have probably thrived since the Equator, and must slow us down somewhat in light airs. They are crustaceans with a peduncle long enough to keep their branchiae out of the toxic zone of the best antifouling paints. The few I find are big ones, especially on the zinc anodes which protect the hull from electrolysis, and under those parts of the keel that could not be treated when I hauled out at Toulon in June.

The sea ripples, and the wind rises again. It blows gently from the SW for the first time; force 2 then a nice steady force 4. Fantastic, in only 26° south latitude!

Joshua gets all the right cards: 110 miles covered by the October 5 sight, 147 next day, 143 on the 7th.

The sea has got cooler, and I have two sweaters and a pair of wool trousers on. The 484 sq. ft genoa is back in its bag, replaced by the little 161 sq. ft jib, with the storm jib on the pulpit, all ready to use.

To think we have actually caught the westerlies where there are normally calms and SE winds! The barometer is falling slightly, so it is going to last. I spend a lot of time on deck adjusting the sheets to make the most of this miracle.

Racing? Yes!—racing the seasons. Hitting all three capes at their best times is not possible, so you try to press on to avoid reaching the Horn during the southern autumn. If everything goes according to schedule *Joshua* will round Good Hope a little early in the season (no choice), Leeuwin and New Zealand just right, and the Horn still at a good time. There's no sense in thinking about that for the moment; it's still too far ahead. I just have to get my boat to do her best.

I hoisted the 75 sq. ft storm jib in addition to the big 194 sq. ft staysail, and a second 54 sq. ft storm jib as a bonnet under the main boom. While I watch the log turn, I watch the wake, I heave on the staysail halyard just a bit. . .no, too much. . .I slack it half an inch. . .there, it's perfect now, and the staysail draws all the wind of the sky and turns it into flecks of foam that come to life in the wake. The whole universe meets in the staysail.

A school of porpoises keeps us company for nearly half an hour. I just finished Robert Merle's fine book *The Day of the Dolphin* and am filled with images of porpoises playing with men, teaching them wisdom. I think I would dare swim among them now, in a flat calm. . .

I film them for a long time from the bow, the bowsprit, the mainmast: three reels; they are certainly worth it. Have to start watching my film, though; I have already shot 47 of the 100 reels I started with.

An hour later my porpoises are back. Two of them start spinning in the air like corkscrews. I rush to get the camera, stowed in its locker—too late; they are leaving already. I am as disgusted as if I had dropped an anchor without shackling it to its chain. After missing the terrific shot of the barracuda catching the flying fish in mid-air, I had sworn to leave the Beaulieu in the cockpit during fair weather, all set to go, with a cloth to protect it from the sun. But that is not enough. I am starting to realize that I too need to be protected from the camera.

In the beginning, I thought that you just set the lens and released the shutter. It is not like that at all. You have to give the camera something more. And now it is trying to suck my blood. It would be easy to stuff the camera in a waterproof tank and forget it exists, but it is too late—and in any case I am not sorry.

From a technical point of view, I have no experience at all; I had never shot stills or movies before this trip, but left everything up to Françoise. It was just as well, because I never did try to master the ASA and DIN, aperture and shutter speed business. But I have made real progress since setting out thanks to Quéméré's *Cinema et Photo sur La Mer* (Blondel la Rougery), an excellent little book, clear and simple; the author is able to put himself into the shoes of the rankest or even hostile beginner.

We often regretted not having a movie camera during Tahiti-Alicante, and to compound the oversight we only took three rolls of 20-exposure black and white film along. Yet we never dared take pictures of the sea before the Horn, and least of all after our big gale in the Pacific. Not because of danger or fatigue, but because we felt, in a confused sort of way, that it would have been a kind of desecration.

I think the previous trip was to see and to feel; I would like this one to go further.

The sea is already that of the high latitudes: long, full of restrained power, a little jerky at times. The log turns and turns, and the barometer falls very slowly, without wavering. Don't go too far south. . .

Watch this: we'll try a little finesse, just to keep our hand in — skirting the last square marked 6 per cent calms and 47 per cent SE winds . . . It works! Two days later, the square is astern and can only try to catch up. Go to it *Joshua*, have at them! Great! Beautiful!

There was a little gale yesterday, like a first brush with the high latitudes. Mostly force 7, 8 at times, always from the SW; the low was therefore far to the SE. Very manageable sea, and very beautiful; a little surfing, just to make sure everything is all right. The bow lifts like a feather.

The barometer is a good deal higher today, and the wind eases to force 3. I take the opportunity to bend on the small 280 sq. ft mainsail and the little 150 sq. ft mizzen; they will stay up until after the Horn.

Changing the sails is a big job, especially folding the big trade wind mainsail properly and wrestling it into the cabin. I lay it flat on the floor, with the genoa and mizzen sailbags wedged side by side on top. It clutters the cabin a little, but I prefer to concentrate weight as much as possible, which can be crucial in these seas, and more so every day.

I watch *Joshua* sailing as fast as before under her new heavy weather sails — small, light, easy to handle, with very high reef bands and reinforcements that would take a sailmaker's breath away.

I will have to keep an eye on the South Atlantic spring, if I am not to get stabbed in the back. During yesterday's little gale everything was going well; the waves were heavy and breaking fairly hard, but not dangerous. *Joshua* was on a broad reach, taking them almost astern.

The wind let up a little, then dropped to barely force 5; the sea stopped breaking though it was still fairly heavy. Next the wind shifted to SSW, still force 5. It was the normal swing, and

I set the wind vane for a beam reach. I had not been below for over a minute when a huge breaking wave smashed into the boat, knocking her down more than 60°. *Joshua* was barely heeled when it hit, so the cabin took the blow squarely. At the time I thought all the windward ports had shattered. No damage...but I set the vane to take the waves broad on the quarter. The cockpit was full.

The odd erratic breaking sea was probably due to a cross-current of about a knot that the Pilot Chart shows for this area. Also, we were not far from the line of a subtropical convergence of warm and cool currents. Details that bear watching. First blood in barely 31° south latitude: beware of spring in the southern hemisphere. Remember the safety harness when going on deck, for whatever reason.

Good Hope is 1500 miles away, and the wind is holding. At this rate, ten more days...

October 12 brings another gale. Not too nasty for the moment, but the wind is NW, the barometer falling, and the sky overcast. The low is therefore coming in from the SW. Two reefs each in the main and mizzen at 1 a.m. and the 161 sq. ft jib changed for the 38 sq. ft storm jib. What a joy, watching my boat sailing that fast under so little canvas!

The sea is not really heavy. It never is, during the NW phase of a gale. It is afterwards that things can get nasty, because the wind swings around to west, then SW, and raises cross-seas.

The wind is picking up and gusty now. Since dawn, a reef has reduced the big 194 sq. ft staysail to 97. It is less complicated than changing the sail, but not always easy. The 100 sq. ft of extra material make a big bundle to gather in the wind and tie down with reef points. Best to have close-trimmed fingernails for that kind of job.

Still too much canvas: the log shows 7.8 knots, with probably more than 8 in spurts. The speed is illusory, though, because *Joshua* is moving at her hull speed in the fairly heavy sea, and her yawing just makes the distance longer. I drop what is left of the main and staysail. Perfect: the speed steadies at 7 knots under close-reefed mizzen and the 38 sq. ft storm jib. Much relieved, the rigging seems to say 'thanks'. If this little gale really bares its teeth between now and sunset, I need only drop the remaining 75 sq. ft of the mizzen to keep *Joshua* in good shape (Inch' Allah!). We are in 35° 30′ south.

The sky clears by 9 a.m. The wind shifts to the west, only force 4, as the barometer rises a couple of pegs. At noon the wind drops to force 2–3 and the sails slat in the heavy swell. False alarm! Shake out the reefs.

Yesterday at the noon sight *Joshua* had covered 182 miles in 24 hours. Only 173 today, in spite of the moderate gale. The Cape of Good Hope is less than a thousand miles away. No point in heading further south for the moment. I will make the final decision in a few days, whether to pass close to land to try to give word to a fisherman on the Agulhas Bank, or head for the open sea south of the 40th parallel to avoid the dangerous meeting-ground of warm and cold currents, which can raise a monstrous sea (the word is not too strong) in the vicinity of the Bank in a gale. For the moment, Good Hope is both very far and very close. Although it is a thousand miles away, we will be there in a week if all goes well.

The wind has been fresh for days now, SW to NW. There are often squalls in the sky and reefs in the sails, both dispatched as soon as possible.

Food has picked up in the last two weeks, and I feel great: willing to take a reef, willing to shake one out, depending on the sky and the weather. Night and day, I sleep with one eye open, but I sleep well. Last week we covered 1112 miles, despite two short runs of 128 and 122 miles.

The temperature falls to 55° when the wind is SW and climbs to around 60° when it is from the NW. I don't usually like cold weather, but I feel brisk when the temperature drops, because I am well bundled up and the SW winds blow in a fair weather sky, even when they are strong.

The sea is often heavy, and *Joshua* surfs at times. The bow lifts much better than before. The ton of excess weight taken off at Plymouth has certainly improved safety and performance. Also, *Joshua* is only carrying 90 gallons of water instead of the 200 for Tahiti-Alicante; another half ton to the good, added to all the rest. But a sailor is never fully satisfied with his boat's security or capacity.

For the high latitudes this is vital. The Spanish have a saying: *Muchos pocos hacen un mucho* (a lot of little things make something big). So, yesterday I took advantage of the wind's easing to force 4 to throw overboard a pile of precious little

Joshua's layout

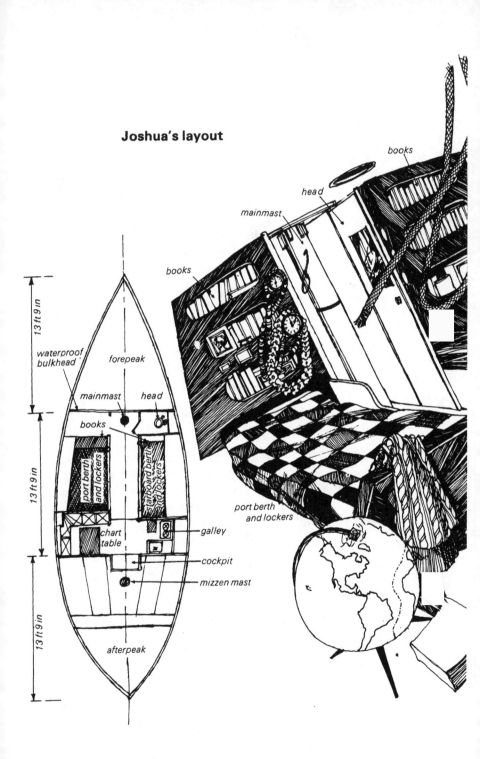

starboard berth and lockers

galley →

chart table

treasures I would have guarded with my life two months
before: a box of army biscuits (35 pounds), a case of condensed milk (40–45 pounds), 25 bottles of wine, 45 pounds of
rice, 10 pounds of sugar, about 30 pounds of a jam I don't like,
and a box of batteries for the tape recorder. I have enough
food to last easily another eight months. For the last two I have
kept careful track of my consumption.

Kerosene gets the same treatment: I took more than I
needed...heave ho! Four jerrycans hit the drink along with a
couple of gallons of denatured alcohol. That much less to haul
around. I also jettisoned a coil of ¾ in. diameter nylon line
weighing some 60 pounds (in case I have to anchor, I still have
some ½ in. line).

Throwing the coil away got me...I remembered the
deprivations and sleepless nights spent working with Henry
Wakelam in the deserted boathouse of the Royal Cape Yacht
Club during our hobo stopover there, making sheets for
Wanda and *Marie-Thérèse II* out of heavy nylon lines the whalers
had thrown away. In those days we would have crawled a mile
on our bellies for that coil of ¾ in. line—it was worth almost as
much as our boats! But the days of garbage cans and miracle
boats are gone; it's a different game now.

Thanks to this extra lightening (food, kerosene and line
weighed 375 pounds) I was able to completely empty the
forward and aft compartments, concentrating all possible
weight amidships. As minor as it may be, the point is scored on
three different levels:

Faster in light airs. It is not obvious, but I prefer that *Joshua*
take as little time as possible for the trip; a week saved could
make all the difference to the health situation.

Less sail up in fresh winds, so less fatigue and effort involved in
handling or shortening sail further. Less fatigue for the rigging
too, for the same distance.

Better prepared for the very foul weather in the south, and foul
weather in general, thanks to the 375 pounds saved, which
allowed maximum weight concentration.

This last point is essential, in spite of starving Indians and
those who can't all afford to treat their boats to a nice coil of
¾ in. nylon line. For beyond any starving Indians and penniless
sailors, one grim scene keeps coming back to me: the big gale I
took with Françoise a few years earlier, during which *Joshua*

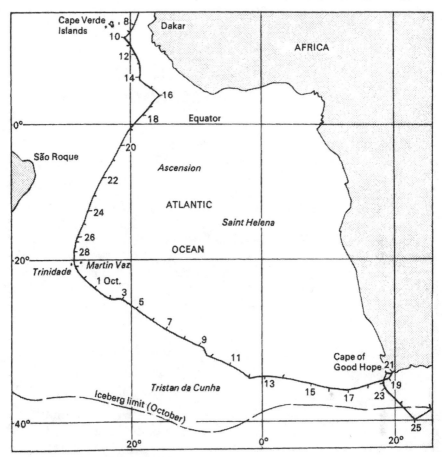

8 September to 25 October 1968

nearly pitchpoled. In the face of that, the wasted line, kerosene and even the food have no importance. 'Destiny deals the cards, but we play them.'

The great game of the high latitudes is just ahead. I am going into it without any troublesome cards. . .except maybe the Beaulieu.

At the noon sight, Good Hope is 310 miles to the ENE. I still do not know which course I am going to take. The barometer is high. I think I know, but not definitely. Things can change too fast in these parts.

FIVE

Played and Lost . . .
Played and Won!

Fifty-nine days into the trip, the October 19 sight places us about 40 miles SW of Cape Agulhas, the extreme tip of South Africa.

The sky was cloudy all yesterday, with a force 5 NW wind, shifting to SW during the night. The barometer, already high, continues to rise. Today it stands at an abnormal 1027 millibars, a sure sign that the permanent South Atlantic high has moved well toward *Joshua*'s waters. For several days I have tried to tune in weather reports on the wavelengths indicated in the Radio Weather Aids manual, but in vain. Even if I picked up the dit-dit-dah of the South African Morse code broadcasts, it would not do any good, as they are transmitted in an international code which is Greek to me.

Greek or not, it is more than likely that with the barometer so high, the wind will shift to the east by tomorrow. Not too strong, I hope!

If I had played by the rules, *Joshua* would have raced south, to get away from the edge of the high pressure system and not risk losing the westerlies. But the die was cast yesterday: I intend to cross the Agulhas Bank close to shore and have a ship report me to Lloyds. With a little luck (lots of luck) *Joshua* may even meet a fishing boat, to whom I could heave a package for the *Sunday Times*.

I have photographed my log twice, page by page, to spread the risks during a flying trans-shipment to the deck of a trawler. I pack the rolls of film in two of the heavy watertight plastic bags Bob and Steve gave me, with the address of the *Sunday Times* and forwarding instructions printed in four languages. I added a few rolls of snap-shots as well: Trinidad with its green roofs, a gannet who could read MIK, the dorado caught as we entered the trades, a burst of flying fish, albatrosses, flocks of little silvery web-footed birds that have kept us company these last days, porpoises playing with

Joshua—life at sea, so simple and so transparent, with its calms and breaking waves,

I imagine Robert, Steve and Bob's joy at receiving one of these marvel-crammed packages. I can see Françoise's joy as she realizes all's well aboard, that I have not lost weight (she will not know that I have—none of her business). I can just see my children's excitement, shouting all through the house, *'Joshua* is rounding Good Hope!'

Yet it is a hard card to play, this need I feel to reassure family and friends, to give them news, pictures, life—to bestow that infinitely precious thing, the little invisible plant called hope. Logic shouts at me to play the game alone, without burdening myself with the others. Logic would have me run SE, far from land, far from ships, back to the realm of the westerlies where everything is simple if not easy, leaving well to the north the dangerous area of the convergence.

But for many days another voice has been insisting 'You are alone, yet not alone. The others need you, and you need them. Without them, you would not get anywhere, and nothing would be true.'

The sun has long since set when my heart starts to pound: the Cape Agulhas lighthouse!

As common as I know it is in this age of modern tables and radio time signals, for me a perfect landfall will always stay wreathed in magic, like an answer from the stars, whom I had earlier asked 'Where am I?' And the stars had answered, 'Don't worry, you'll see Cape Agulhas before midnight.' Warmth fills my chest at the beacon's little flash, showing between the black of the waves, right where I was looking with binoculars two hours after a star sight. Warmth in my chest and a little chill down my back. . .because this cape is a Great Cape.

Shortly after sundown, the wind had veered to the south, then SE. Now *Joshua* is sailing closehauled, the beacon clearly visible a hand's-breadth to the left of the jib.

At two in the morning, all the sails are close reefed to a SE force 7 wind. It was to be expected with the barometer so high. Yet I feel inexplicably happy.

The lighthouse is only eight or ten miles ahead when I decide to heave-to on the other tack and wait for daybreak before making up my mind.

All at once, I am very tired. I have to sleep, if only for an hour or two. Strange, how fatigue can cut a man down without warning. You hang on and on...and suddenly you collapse. But only when it is all clear ahead.

I light the lamp, and go below to take a nap. All clear: there are no ships where *Joshua* is lying hove-to. They pass either close to land or far offshore, making the most of the current.

Nearly four in the morning! I slept like a log, all my fatigue has lifted. I stretch, yawn, light the stove. A small mug of coffee is followed by a big Ovaltine and three army biscuits spread with butter and orange marmalade. I feel great.

I gybe to get underway without having to touch the sheets, already trimmed for a beat. While I was asleep, the wind eased to force 4 or 5 and shifted to ESE. The beacon is now a finger to the right of the jib.

I keep the reefs in; all signs point to a SE gale. No sense trying to tack into it for days on the Agulhas Bank, with the ships and contrary current. Sailing is a compromise between distance covered and mounting fatigue, for both crew and boat; and fatigue can snowball fast.

Heading south would be no better. Sooner or later, *Joshua* would wind up in the area of current convergence on the steep edge of the Aghulhas Bank. That would spell trouble in a gale from any direction.

Best heave-to until the wind returns to the west, a matter of two or three days. Before I do that, though, *Joshua* could easily run before the wind along the coast between Cape Agulhas and the Cape of Good Hope,[1] and drop in at Walker Bay where the chart shows a little port, which means a few yachts. It is Sunday, so I am sure to find one out in the bay, and could pass her my bags of film.

Simple! It could even kill two birds with one stone, as the yacht will certainly have news of Loïck, Bill King and Nigel. Their names have not been mentioned once in the BBC overseas broadcasts. Where are they?

The wind picks up at dawn, force 6 around 7 a.m., nearly force 7 an hour later. The cloudless sky is magnificent, the coast is five or six miles off, the sea a bit heavy, but *Joshua* is running downhill.

[1] Good Hope is in the Atlantic, about 30 miles NW of Cape Agulhas.

Three lines of position a few minutes apart confirm my dead reckoning: the entrance to Walker Bay is about 20 miles ahead.

A good force 7 is blowing now; the gale is almost upon us. Spray flies high against the ships making for Cape Agulhas. For those heading north, it is a piece of cake. For *Joshua* too. . .but I am beginning to wonder if I will find a yacht out in Walker Bay in this weather. I have replaced my old MIK flags with a new set.

More and more, I get the impression no yacht is going to put her nose into Walker Bay. The gale should be here any minute, and one of the ships that have been passing for the last hour may have already reported me to Lloyds. The catch is that they will report me as being on course for Europe.

Walker Bay is about 15 miles ahead now, and I have a sinking feeling that absolutely no yachts will be out; no fishermen either, as it is Sunday. And all the passing freighters can read my MIK flags. . .as I steer North! There is a little one astern, all dingy and black, belching a big plume of smoke that spreads out ahead. She can't be making more than 8 knots, because *Joshua* is doing 7 and she has been trying to catch up for a long time. The freighter will pass close. . .

I quickly go below and write two copies of a message asking the captain to slow down and stay on a straight course, so I can draw level and heave him a package. The message also states that I am continuing toward Australia, regardless of appearances. I roll my two handwritten notes and stuff them in aluminum film cans. Each can is weighted with a bit of lead. If the first message falls in the water, I will still have the carbon copy for a second shot. And the freighter's very low deck will be perfect for eventually transferring the plastic bags, each tightly rolled and tied to make them easy to throw in spite of the wind.

I return to the cockpit with my two projectiles and the slingshot.

The black freighter is 25 yards off to my right. Three men are watching me from the bridge. Snap!. . .the message lands on the ship's foredeck. One of the officers twirls a forefinger at his temple, as if to say I must be a little nuts to be shooting at them.

The bridge draws level. I yell 'Message! Message!' They just stare at me, bug-eyed. At this range, with lead balls, I could knock their three hats off with three shots. When I was a kid, slingshot practice consisted in hitting a tin can thrown into the air by one of my brothers. And using a slingshot is a little like ping-pong—you never lose your touch, even years later. Still, I do not dare shoot the duplicate message right at the bridge, because these film cans are a lot less accurate than lead balls: I might break a window, or hit one of them.

The bridge is almost beyond us: I have to salvage the situation fast. I brandish the package, and make as if to give it to them. An officer acknowledges with a wave, and puts the helm over to kick the stern my way. In a few seconds, the main deck is 10 or 12 yards off. I toss a package. Perfect!

It is time I pulled away, but I am going to make a serious mistake by throwing the second package instead of racing to the tiller to steer clear. I won up and down the line with my first package; I will lose it all with the second. By the time I dash to the tiller, it is already late. The freighter's stern is still slewing my way. To make matters worse, she has blanketed my sails by passing me to starboard while I was on a starboard tack.

Joshua begins to pull clear, but not fast enough. By a hair, the stern's overhang snags the mainmast. There is a horrible noise, and a shower of black paint falls on the deck; the masthead shroud is ripped loose, then the upper spreader shroud. My guts twist into knots. The push on the mast makes *Joshua* heel, she luffs up toward the freighter. . .and wham!—the bowsprit is twisted 20° or 25° to port. I am stunned.

It is all over, the black monster is past. I gybe quickly and heave-to on the port tack, drifting away from the coast. That is the main thing right now, so I can repair the shrouds without hurrying.

No doubt worried, the freighter has changed course. I wave that all's well, because in coming back to help, she would finish me off!

A trifle often irritates me and can send my spirits tumbling. But when things really get rough, I sometimes seem to become a cold, lucid observer from another world. I did not even read the freighter's name, keeping to the strict essential of saving the mast.

Outside of that, nothing has the slightest importance. I feel neither anger nor weariness nor fear. I did not mutter 'The beautiful trip is over, you can never continue non-stop with so much damage; we will have to put in at Cape Town or Saint Helena for repairs.' Saving the mast, without thinking beyond that. Afterwards, I will see what else needs to be done. But above all, do not think of the twisted bowsprit, irreparable with what I have on board.

I have played and lost, that's all; it is not the end of the world. A kind of temporary anaesthesia. Later, perhaps, it will hurt. But later is far away.

I had the same reaction, though a hundred times stronger, when I was swept overboard in a gale off Durban as *Marie-Thérèse II* lay hove-to.

I found myself in water made very light by the millions of bubbles of foam from the enormous breaking sea that had capsized my boat. In a flash, I had glimpsed the cabin hatch cover, ripped off its tracks. With an opening like that, and her keel out of water, *Marie-Thérèse II* could only go to the bottom. Yet I felt no despair, no bitterness. I just whispered to myself 'This time, old man, your number is up.' And I remembered the page on destiny in *Wind, Sand and Stars,* on the absolute need to follow one's fate, whatever its outcome. I, too, was going to end up like Saint-Exupery's gazelle, whose destiny it was to leap in the sunshine and die one day under a lion's claw. Yet I regretted nothing as I floated in the warm, very light water, making ready to peacefully leave on my last journey.

Marie-Thérèse II had righted herself before shipping a fatal wave through the big opening. I climbed aboard easily, with the hatch cover. Then I pumped for five hours straight, glad to start living again.

The two shrouds have been repaired less than two hours after the collision. I did not have to climb the mast; only the lower cable clamps had slipped.

The spreaders did not bulge, thanks to their flexible mountings. For the mast I feel nothing but admiration: at the moment of impact it looked like a fishing rod bent by a big tuna. It confirms the trust I had instinctively felt for the good old telephone pole. All in all, I have had a lot of luck in my misfortune.

The problem of the bowsprit remains; that is more serious. It is 6 ft 10 in. long, made out of a 3 in. steel pipe about $\frac{3}{16}$ in.

thick, reinforced by a second steel pipe inside. The bowsprit bent very slightly when it was hot-dip galvanized, and it took me nearly an hour's work on the quay to straighten it with the help of a friend.

So I will have to run the jibstay to the stem and do without the benefit of the bowsprit; and more than 20,000 miles yet to go, in a mutilated *Joshua* . . . just thinking about it makes me sick. We will see tomorrow; I am too tired now.

October 21. SE gale. I finally caught the Cape Town weather forecast at news time. *Joshua* lies-to peacefully, with the foam of the breaking waves scintillating in the sun.

I did not get much sleep last night, thinking all the time about the bowsprit. I had the impression that Henry Wakelam was there, close to me. From time to time I mumbled, 'Good God, if you were here, you would have already figured a way to straighten it.'

Yesterday, as I worked on the shrouds, the problem of the bowsprit hovered in the background, and I felt my friend's breath and presence next to me. I talked to him from time to time; I would ask him not to drop the crescent wrench we were using to tighten the cable clamps. And he helped quietly, without lecturing me, without a word on the real problem. The shrouds were just tinkering, an odd job tossed off with wrench, cable clamps and $\frac{1}{4}$ in. nuts. It took no particular genius, beyond watching that the wrenches did not fall overboard when the boat would heel lying hove-to. The real hurdle would be the bowsprit, on which I did not want to crystallize my thinking prematurely.

When Henry and I had had to work out a really sticky problem together, neither of us was allowed to mention it. No bursting out with 'Say, I've got an idea! What do you think of this?. . .' It was not allowed, because the thing had not matured enough, and putting forth an idea that was not worked out in detail wasted the other's time and kept him from letting it 'ripen'. Only that evening or the next morning would we talk about possible solutions. By then, the ground had been gone over in detail, and all we had to do was get to work without groping, by the shortest path.

October 22. The sea is still heavy in the morning, but the gale is over. At 2 p.m. the sea is all right again. The wind has dropped considerably, but there is enough filling the sails to keep us from rolling. I have prepared a large four-part block and tackle, with the spare mizzen boom to increase the angle at which the block pulls. I hinge the spar to the foreward bitt with a shackle. No, that won't do, another shackle is needed as a gimbal, so the spar can move both horizontally and vertically.

Good, that should do the trick. The spare staysail halyard serves as a topping lift. The rig is strong, and swings easily off the starboard bow. I run a ⅜ in. chain from the tip of the bowsprit to the outer end of the spar and secure the tackle opposite, with the line running back to the big starboard Goïot winch.

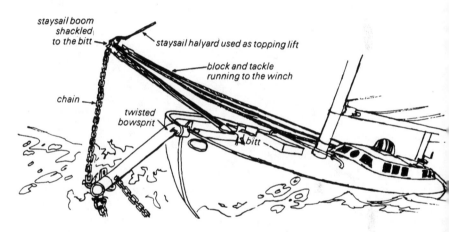

Incredible, the power of a tackle on a winch. . .I feel I am going to start crying, it's so beautiful. . .the bowsprit begins to straighten out, very, very slowly. I am wild with joy!

Henry old pal, you would be proud of your disciple.

By sundown everything is shipshape again; bowsprit straight as before, bobstay and whisker stays tightened. They are ⅜ in. galvanized chain; one stretched several inches in the collision, and I merely cut two links out. With wire rope the damage would have been much harder to repair. The pulpit, which took a real beating, is also back in place, nice and straight, securely bolted and good as new.

Worn out by fatigue and emotion, I fall into bed after swallowing a can of soup for dinner.

The day before yesterday, I had played and lost. Then I saw Henry and all his power. I saw César as well, the foreman during *Joshua*'s construction, when a steel sheet refused to fit. César used to repeat 'Man is always the strongest.' And the sheet wound up in the proper shape.

I am tremendously tired, yet I feel crammed with dynamite, ready to level the whole world and forgive it everything. Today, I played and won. My beautiful boat is there, as beautiful as ever.

Part Two

SIX

Good Hope

On October 24, *Joshua* crossed the longitude of Cape Agulhas, 200 miles from the coast. She will continue SSE until tomorrow, to gain more offing and leave the zone of convergence well to port.

It is my sixty-third day at sea, with 7882 miles covered between noon sights, a quarter of the distance from Plymouth to Plymouth by the three capes. The Atlantic is in the wake; ahead, the Indian Ocean. Yet *Joshua* is not actually in the Indian Ocean, despite the theoretical boundaries, but in a kind of no man's land: the waters of Good Hope. They stretch between the longitude of the Cape and that of Durban, some 600 miles.

This area can be dangerous—often worse than the Horn—because of seas raised by the Agulhas Current. Many 25 to 50 ft yachts remember it. *Atom* was rolled over near the Cape and emerged with her deck flat as a raft. *Awahnee* encountered the most terrible weather of her career in these waters, and she is a veteran of the Horn. Between Durban and Port Elizabeth *Marco Polo, Eve, Adios, Walkabout, Wanda, Marie-Thérèse II* and others were knocked on their beam ends, or hit very hard, by breaking seas kicked up by gales blowing against the Agulhas Current, which reaches 5 knots in places.

According to the *Sailing Directions,* the most dangerous area is off the steep SE edge of the Agulhas Bank, where frequent gales raise an enormous sea, reinforced by the meeting of the warm, salty current from the Indian Ocean and the cold (less salty) Antarctic Current. When you have seen the eddies caused by salinity differences in the Panama locks, one prefers to give a wide berth to similar phenomena when they are on an oceanic scale.

Yesterday there was a gale from the west. Today Radio Cape Town announces that nothing is expected before midnight. I should take advantage of it to get cracking. But I let *Joshua* drag along at 6 knots fully reefed, whereas she would better 7 if I replaced the 54 sq. ft storm jib with the 161 sq. ft jib, and raised the big staysail instead of keeping the 38 sq. ft handkerchief she is carrying now. The fact is, I don't have much resilience left. I got hardly any sleep last night; it was blowing hard, with an occasionally choppy sea that made me suspect a current convergence.

The sky is fairly clear now; the westerly wind varies between force 5 and 6, without any real gusts, and the barometer seems steady at 1013 millibars. Yet the sea is strange: it subsides right away when the wind drops to force 5, only to rise very fast, with big breaking seas as soon as it exceeds force 6 in the moderate fair-weather squalls. I am also reluctant to hoist the large jib because I would have trouble bringing it in, should the weather worsen again. Last night I had difficulty keeping the jib under control and raising the storm jib in its place. My motions were clumsy and inefficient; it took me three times longer than usual to secure gaskets and reef points. And my reflexes were dangerously slow: somehow, I got caught with water up to my knees at the end of the bowsprit, without having seen it coming. The mounting fatigue and undernourishment of these last days may be to blame.

Sure, I would like to get out of this lousy place by crowding on canvas. But if the weather turns mean, as it very quickly can here, I am much better prepared with shortened sail. Wiser in my weakened condition. Nothing to worry about, far from it. . .but I am asking *Joshua* to do her best until I get back into shape.

Outside are the high latitudes and the sea rumbling a little under the force 6 westerly wind; inside, the calm and peace of my little world. I smoke, dreaming before the little globe my friends on the yacht *Damien* gave me. They went north, I went south. And it is all the same, since we are at sea in our boats.

I gaze at the long curve drawn on the globe: *Joshua's* route since England, with porpoises and albatrosses, joys and sometimes sorrows.

During Tahiti-Alicante, Françoise and I would draw the route covered in the same way on the tiny school globe our children had sent us. And we would always wait until *Joshua* had covered ten degrees of longitude or latitude before extending the line. To have done it sooner would have brought bad luck, attracting a contrary gale or an endless calm.

I raise the big staysail at sunset, but keep the storm jib. A reef is shaken out of the mainsail and mizzen a little before midnight. The bow wave glows with phosphorescence, and the wake stretches out far astern, full of sparks.

The old-timers in the great days of sail come to mind: for centuries they furrowed the oceans in trade or discovery. But always for the sea. I reflect on what they bequeathed us in nautical documents, where words stand for the sea and sky, where arrows try to tell of currents and winds, of the anguish and joys of those sailors, as if that could be done, as if experience of the great laws of the sea could be passed along, as if the vibrations of the sea could go through you with only words and arrows.

And yet...I see myself in Mauritius again, fifteen years ago, studying the *Sailing Directions* and the Pilot Charts for the run from Port Louis to Durban. I would underline in red the ominous portents of an approaching SE gale blowing against the Agulhas Current, in blue the signs propitious to a return or holding of fair weather. Closing my eyes, I tried to see and feel what emanated from the rectilinear arrows, the dry phrases, the whole austere, scientific technicalness, full of hidden things trying to emerge in me.

Once under way for Durban, I felt at times that I had covered the same stage before. The sea had shaken itself free of the morass of words, and I was reliving a journey already made, reading in advance the Indian Ocean's tidings.

The next day's sight shows 164 miles covered. *Joshua* is 70 miles inside the iceberg limit, but she has reached the 40th parallel, and can now head NE to leave the ice area by tomorrow, while staying away from the current convergence.

The sky is covered with a lot of flattened cumulus, real fair-weather clouds for these latitudes, with sometimes large sweeps of blue, almost empty of cirrus. The wind, force 6 since dawn, has veered to WNW. This shift worries me a little, especially as I was not able to get the weather report. But the barometer is steady; that is the main thing. The sea is very beautiful, meaning very heavy. On the other hand, breaking seas are few and generally not too large.

I spent most of last night in the cockpit again, because of the broken red line on the Pilot Chart showing the iceberg limit. This second sleepless night has not tired me. Still, it is about time I got out of here, otherwise my supply of tobacco and coffee will not last the trip! *Joshua* is doing 7 knots; at that rate we should soon be over the line.

I wonder if my apparent lack of fatigue could be a kind of hypnotic trance born of contact with this great sea, giving off so many pure forces, rustling with the ghosts of all the beautiful sailing ships that died around here and now escort us. I am full of life, like the sea I contemplate so intensely. I feel it watching me as well, and that we are nonetheless friends.

I made two serious mistakes today; my first since the beginning of the trip. I had just observed the meridian. Instead of stowing the sextant immediately, as I always do in these latitudes, I just boxed it, and wedged the case in a corner of the cockpit: it was very important that I trim the sails a little before going below—a matter of a few seconds. Actually, it could easily have waited.

I was busy taking up slack in the mizzen preventer when a fairly large breaking sea crowned the rudder. I gauge it out of the corner of my eye, and pull myself up by the shrouds, knees tucked under my chin to avoid getting soaked as the wave flows over the aft cabin and fills the cockpit; the sextant is afloat.

Luckily, I had not snapped on my harness, and am barefoot and extra mobile. I dive for the sextant before the next roll carries it overboard along with three-quarters of the water flooding the cockpit. I am already in the cabin, both proud and ashamed of my double stunt.

I take the sextant out of its case, wipe it off, and wedge it with pillows on the port berth. 'You barely pulled through, old pal.' The case has to be rinsed inside to get rid of the salt, which would absorb moisture from the air and soon spoil the silver on the mirrors.

I light the stove to dry the case on an asbestos pad over a low flame, and go on deck to take a second reef in the main and mizzen, and a reef in the staysail. The wind is still WNW, now blowing a steady force 7. For this region it is still a fair-weather sky.

My eyes sting when I go below again. The sextant case, while not exactly burning, is certainly dry now! I turn off the stove, remove boots, harness and oilskins, wipe my hands, face and neck, put on my slippers and roll myself a cigarette. A spot of coffee? Why not! God, it's good to be inside when things are roaring out there.

I am pleased with the way I had shortened sail: quick reflexes, good grip. The staysail came along without any fuss when I reefed it, swallowing 75 sq. ft at a gulp.

I smoke, musing over the chart. *Joshua* is behaving beautifully under so little canvas, with almost no yawing in spite of her speed. Tomorrow we will be far away: 180 miles? 190? The Pilot Chart gives a 1 knot favourable current for the area, so we could well break through the 200 mile ceiling if the wind holds. I am not tired; I have never been tired.

So, *Joshua*, we are taking Good Hope in our stride.

I have not finished my cigarette when an enormous breaking sea hits the port beam and knocks us flat. All the portholes have shattered. . .no, they are intact (at least in my cabin); I can hardly believe it. A muffled torrential roaring and a sound almost like sheet iron under a blacksmith's hammer fill the air.

I open the hatch and stick my head out. The sails are flapping because the boat has luffed. Incredibly enough, the booms are not broken in spite of the preventers.[1] Luckily I had slacked off the one on the mainsail, just in case we were suddenly hove down on a broad reach. The $\frac{3}{8}$ in. nylon preventer on the mizzen had parted. The line was three years old; I should probably have got rid of it long ago. . .but I liked it, and had got used to it during Tahiti-Alicante. Its parting probably saved the boom, but the latter, pushed amidships by the force of the water, neatly snapped off the wind vane shaft. Not serious: half a minute is all it takes to change the vane, thanks to a very simple rig. I have seven spare vanes left, and material to make more if necessary.

[1] Preventer: line running from the boom end forward, and then secured to the boat. In case the boat yaws while sailing downwind, it prevents the boom from swinging to the other side, which could cause damage. Preventers are also useful in light airs to keep the sails from chafing against the shrouds, and also to prevent the mizzen boom hitting the self-steering wind vane on a roll, when the wind is not strong enough to keep the sails constantly filled.

I go on deck to connect the steering wheel, and quickly duck below again, soaked by a blast of spray. The aft cabin portholes are intact, a sight that warms my heart. I fill the sails again, steering with the inside wheel, and go back on deck to replace the wind vane with a much smaller one set for running downwind, since *Joshua* was on a broad reach when the breaking sea hit. The only other thing is to replace the mizzen preventer with a new line. Quickly done. This time I give it plenty of slack, as I did for the mainsail.

Everything is shipshape on deck. I can go below to get warm and straighten up the cabin. I pick the globe out of the sink, on the starboard side, and wedge it back in place, to port. The island of Java is a bit scraped.

The sextant. . .I had forgotten it on the port berth, buried in the pillows. Now it looks out at me from the starboard berth. Poor little pal, if this hasn't done you in, there really is a guardian angel for sextants, and morons too. First I leave it in the cockpit, then on the *windward* berth. . .It took an eight foot free fall through the cabin when *Joshua* went over. One of its legs sheared off at the thread, though it is nearly $\frac{1}{4}$ in. thick. There are three holes in the plywood facing of one of the drawers. The one on the left is at least $\frac{1}{4}$ in. deep, the right one a bit less, the top one barely visible. They are the holes made by the legs of the sextant when it smashed into the drawer.

Joshua has a second sextant, a big Poulin micrometer drum model, very accurate and easy to read; a light in the handle makes it particularly handy for star sights. The other one (now an amputee) is an old vernier model which I very much like for sun shots in the high latitudes because it is small, light, and easy to handle. I will try to glue the leg back with epoxy cement when I find it. I will also have to adjust the mirrors, which must be out of alignment after such a shock.

By and large *Joshua*, the sextant and I came through all right. But two such serious mistakes, one after the other, are inexcusable, and cause for concern.

Barely an hour later, *Joshua* had another knockdown. This time, I saw nearly all the action.

I was squatting on the inside steering seat, watching the sea through the little rectangular ports of the metal turret. The wind had noticeably eased since the first knockdown, to force

6 at most. But the sea had become strange, with peaceful areas where it was very heavy, yet regular, with no dangerous breaking waves. In those areas, I could have walked blindfolded twenty times around the deck. Then, without any transition, it would turn jerky and rough; high cross-seas overlapped to provoke sometimes very powerful breaking waves. It was probably one of these cross-seas that hit us earlier. Then *Joshua* would again find herself in a quiet area for ten minutes or more, followed by another rough one.

From time to time I stood up on the seat to take a few deep breaths and get a better feel of the conditions. During the quiet periods I went out in the cockpit, but without letting go of the hatch cover handle, ready to dive below.

If I were rounding Good Hope in the same direction again, I would probably stay between the 41st and the 42nd parallel (instead of the 40th), to avoid skirting too closely the area of convergence of warm and cold currents. True, this would force me much further beyond the red line on the Pilot Chart, with a longer period of vigilance. Last night's watch for icebergs was enough, but I will hardly need to stand one tonight as we will be practically clear of the red line. So if I had to do it over, I might just do the same as now, if the barometer behaved. Which it is; it has even tended to rise since this morning.

I went below to suck on a can of condensed milk and roll myself a cigarette. Then I regained my perch, again watching the sea through the closed turret. We were crossing another rough stretch.

An exceptional wave rose astern; it looked like a small dune. It was not very steep, but seemed twice as high as the others, if not more. The sea was not breaking yet, and I had the impression that it would not break, that it did not need to.

I jumped to the floor and gripped the chart table with both arms, my chest flat against it and my legs braced. I distinctly felt the surge of acceleration as *Joshua* was thrust forward. Then she heeled a little, seemed to brake, and was slammed down hard. Water spurted through the hatch cover joint, but I am not sure the wave responsible even broke. *Joshua* righted herself in four or five seconds. It took longer than after the first knockdown; a huge force seemed to keep her pressed to the water.

Again, no damage. Mast and spreaders held. The sails did not split. There was plenty of slack in the preventers, fortunately, and nylon can stretch. If things inert to us could do more than grit their teeth, I would have heard some real screaming up there on deck. Even the miraculous little wind vane held, and *Joshua* does not seem to have luffed; she is running downwind again, as if everything were already forgotten. Just the same, I am astonished to see the radar reflector in place on its masthead pivot. It too has already forgotten.

I am almost sorry now that I did not stay glued to the seat to see the whole show, my eyes riveted to the little turret ports . . . but when I saw the dune-like sea I felt *Joshua* could have pitchpoled,[1] in that case I would have broken my neck on the hatch coaming.

Pitchpoling at force 6. . .I know very well it is impossible . . . but I feel anything is possible around here.

The wind drops further towards the end of the afternoon. The sea takes on its grandeur of old, tranquil and powerful. I feel the night will be fine, without treachery. I ought to stretch out for an hour before tonight's watch for possible ice; I have been on the go since dawn. . .for many dawns. But the sun will soon set, and I cannot tear myself from my contemplation of the sea and the boat.

I do have to get more sleep, though; catnapping is easy. I should pay more attention to food. I rely on coffee and tobacco to keep me going, and sustain myself by nibbling here and there. I ought to be able to find time for solid sleep and hearty meals. After all, there is not that much to do on a boat, even rounding Good Hope. Or even the Horn. But there is a lot to *feel* in the waters of a great cape. And that takes all the time in the world.

So one forgets oneself, one forgets everything, seeing only the play of the boat with the sea, the play of the sea around the boat, leaving aside everything not essential to that game in the immediate present. One has to be careful though, not to go further than necessary to the depths of the game. And that is the hard part. . .not going too far.

The weather turns beautiful the very next morning. For two days the wind romps between NW and SW, the barometer is

---

[1] Pitchpole: to capsize forward, turning end over end. This happened to *Tzu-Hang* and *Sandefjord*. When a boat pitchpoles the shock is frightful. *Tzu-Hang*'s doghouse was ripped right off, as if by a giant sledge hammer. *Joshua* nearly pitchpoled once in a gale during Tahiti-Alicante. She was very heavy at the time.

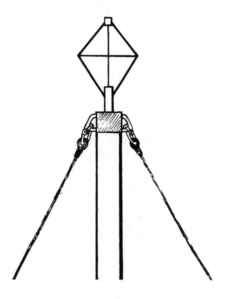

high, and the sun burnishes the curve of the long westerly swell. It looks as if the sea too is happy to rest.

I eat with a terrific appetite; at night, I sleep as soundly as possible, and take little snoozes during the day whenever I feel like it. The October 26 sight shows only 117 miles covered, and the next day just 68, partly thanks to current. But calms and light airs are welcome sometimes; we both need them. I work calmly at the odd jobs that make up my universe, without haste: I glue the sextant leg back on with epoxy, adjust the mirrors, replace five worn slide lashings on the mainsail and three on the mizzen, splice the staysail and mizzen halyards (they are Tergal; the jib and mainsail halyards are steel) to freshen the nip on the sheaves.

Flat calm now. I am busy doing a little extra job near the end of the mizzen boom, using my Swedish marlinspike. There is a jerk, I don't know why, and the marlinspike falls overboard. . .I dive instantly, fully dressed. It did not sink very deep thanks to its wooden handle and light wedge-shaped spike. I am happy and proud, bringing it back aboard, because that way *Joshua* will not have shed the least of her feathers since the start. As for me, I dove into the icy water though it did not seem necessary, since there is a spare marlinspike. Yet it was necessary. . .not one feather missing!

Joshua is in full regalia, the shrouds festooned with all the soaked sweaters and wool trousers now drying in the warm sun. Clothes with salt in them get clammy as soon as the air becomes humid. But if one shakes them vigorously when they are good and dry, the salt crystals are dislodged, and the clothes will stay dry (or nearly).

Jean Gau taught me the trick when *Atom* and *Marie-Thérèse II* were together at Durban. He wore impeccable shirts washed in sea water with Teepol detergent, and hung to dry as high as possible, out of range of spray. The wind snapped the cloth, and knocked the crystals out.

Right now, the breeze is too light to snap my heavy woollens, so I lend a hand, shaking furiously, and brushing them from time to time. It works perfectly; you can see the crystals flying. The big green and blue checked blanket had got a little damp, and is soaking up the sun on the warm deck. It will go back on the berth as soft and fluffy as it was at Plymouth. *Joshua* is just as fit as when we left England, further lightened by two month's sailing and in better trim to face heavy weather. The sails are like new; I did not have to replace a single Goïot sail hank. They do not even show signs of real wear after 65 days of chafe, not counting the 30 day Toulon–Plymouth run.

Judging from the appearance of the rudder, which I can see very well in calm periods, the bottom must be spotless. The barnacles removed after Trinidad have not grown back, and there are no stains on the antifouling. Me? Very well, thanks.

Jean Knocker, *Joshua's* designer, gave me three bottles of champagne when he called at Plymouth on *Casarca*. I was to drink one at each cape.

I wanted to wait until *Joshua* had crossed the 30th meridian (160 miles ahead) before opening the first bottle. If I downed it too soon, Good Hope might see me and get angry before I had time to run. Geographically, it is already 400 miles astern, but the damned cape has a long arm. It could still say 'Come here, little boy, come get your spanking, because you know the two miniature breaking seas the other day were just a joke, so come over here, my pet, and I'll show you breaking seas from Good Hope!'

Tonight, I am almost sure Good Hope has been completely rounded. I slowly warm a big can of fish soup in the pressure cooker. It will stay hot for a long time. To flesh it out, I toss in a handful of cooked rice left over from lunch and a big dab of butter.

The sun sets in a reassuring blaze of red, and the barometer is high, 1022 millibars. What little breeze was left this afternoon has died, and I heave to for a really quiet night; sheets aback, helm down and sails fully reefed, ready for any surprises.

Complete rest, no decisions to make. *Joshua* waits for the wind to come back, as do the gulls and albatrosses resting on the sea all around.

Night. There is not much moon, but it is high, and the whole night is lit up, so clear is the air. No cirrus, still no cirrus[1].

A burning mug between my hands. I drink the fish soup in little swallows, and the soup becomes blood and warmth within me. Radio Cape Town, which I had not been able to get for the last four days, forecasts no gales on the coasts of South Africa. I knew it: the sea, the sky, the albatrosses, the missing cirrus had already told me. But it is nice to hear it confirmed by that friendly voice.

I like the Cape Town announcer. When he warns of a gale, you can feel the worry in his voice; he gives the warning twice, then repeats it at the end of the forecasts. He is not just talking to hear himself talk, lulling himself with the sound of his own voice. He is communicating with people at sea, and one feels he gives us all he has to give. He brings humanity to his work.

As the westerly gales announced by Cape Town are linked with lows moving from west to east observed in the South Atlantic, I know I can count on at least two more days of good weather, even if a gale reached South Africa tomorrow undetected (*Joshua* is already 430 miles east of Cape Agulhas).

I don't like ceremonies. . .but I really feel like having that champagne! I drink it very, very slowly, and finish the whole bottle in little sips. The fish soup practically boils in my veins. I am terrifically happy. I feel so happy, so much at peace with the entire universe, that I am laughing and laughing as I go on deck for a perfectly normal urge after all that liquid. But there, I behold a scene so amazing as not to be believed.

There was this guy standing aft; yes, that's right, a guy. He

[1] Cirrus clouds form in front of weather disturbances and generally indicate their approach.

looked happy as could be, and he laughingly said (I repeat word for word) 'Hey there, Good Hope, since your arm's so long, it must be mighty handy to scratch your ass, eh?'

It was cause for concern, but he vanished without my seeing him go, while I was picking my way aft to shut him up. I threw the empty bottle overboard, and went below. Just then, I saw the Southern Cross to port, *Joshua* having swung around little by little in the flat calm, unnoticed. So the other guy blasphemed with his back to Good Hope. Nothing serious, thank God!

The stars are twinkling very brightly up there in the night. When i was a kid, an old Indochinese fisherman explained to me why the stars twinkle, and why they twinkle very strongly when the wind is going to come back. But I can't tell that story tonight, I'm too sleepy.

Slept well. The wind has come back, just as the stars promised. The October 28 sight shows 188 miles covered noon to noon. We are sailing at top speed; it is terrific, with the heavy sea shining under the sun. I spend nearly an hour sitting on the pulpit, unable to take my eyes off *Joshua*'s bow slamming

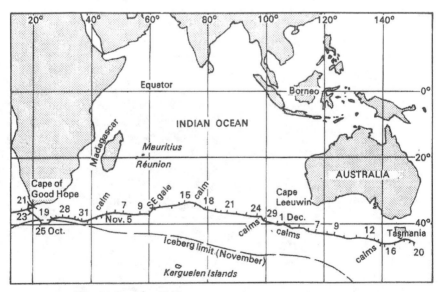

21 October to 20 December 1968

through the sea. To think I almost had no bowsprit at all! She would never have done that well, even helped by the current.

I put the rice on to cook at 2 p.m.; despite my hunger, I was unable to tear away from my nearly hypnotic contemplation of *Joshua* plunging into the foam and sun on the sea. The line on the *Damien* globe has lengthened again. Good Hope is in the wake, Leeuwin and the Horn remain.

No. . .only Leeuwin remains. One thing at a time, as in the days when I was building *Joshua*. If I had wanted to build *all* the boat at once, the enormity of the task would have crushed me. I had to put all I had into the hull alone, without thinking about the rest. It would follow. . .with the help of the gods.

Sailing non-stop around the world is the same. I do not think anyone has the means of pulling it off—*at the start*.

Leeuwin remains. . .and all of my faith.

SEVEN

A Saw-tooth Wake

Joshua is sailing due east along the 39th parallel. Now, the iceberg limit is far enough away, about 150 miles south. The weather is still fair—you can't be too choosy in a place like this. But the wind has dropped a lot, with periods of near calms, and there is a swell from the east I don't like. Moreover, the barometer is too high, a sign that the anti-cyclone has moved south. If I wanted to play it by the book, I would stay closer to the 40th parallel, to make sure of not losing the westerlies. I hesitate though, because that's the mistake I made three years earlier, dropping further than necessary to the south; *Joshua* was nearly wiped out by the gale of her career in the Pacific, about 3000 miles before rounding the Horn.

If the east wind announced by the swell and the barometric rise does not show up in the next two days, I may put a little north in my east, because of the austral spring. Actually, this is conjecture; I don't know what I will do. . .it depends. on too many little things, as always at sea.

The first gale of the Indian Ocean hits on October 30, from the SE. The forecast mentions a NE blow on the coast of Natal, soon swinging to the west when it will diminish. Natal is far behind, but it always helps to know what is happening there.

It would be possible to beat, as the wind only reaches force 8 in the gusts. Just the same, I heave *Joshua* to under double reefed main and mizzen, 54 sq. ft staysail and the storm jib aback, with the helm down. Not only is it much less tiring than diving into the fray on a close reach, but I prefer to renew cautiously my acquaintance with the Indian Ocean, the most savage of the three.

The wind becomes NE during the night, without increasing. I put the tiller almost amidships and trim the staysail sheet for a close reach, leaving the storm jib aback so as to slowly jog along ESE. The dead water from our drift no longer protects us, but the breaking crests remain moderate, as is usual in an easterly gale. *Joshua* takes two of them without any fuss.

The wind then backs to north, and finally to NW in the morning, dropping to force 3. The sea becomes exceedingly choppy. At one point, the boat took seas simultaneously *fore and aft*. It is an odd feeling, but is not dangerous. The seas have become extremely steep, with pyramids of foam at their peaks, which stay on the backs of the main west and SW swells. It is very much like the strange sea *Joshua* met just after the Horn a few years ago, in an almost complete calm. I am glad some wind now remains to press against the sails. Fairly big breaking seas once in a great while.

Gradually the bigger breaking waves become less frequent. The sky turns completely blue to windward, without a cloud on the horizon. The barometer begins to rise again. What is left of the wind is still from the NW. But that will change soon. . .nothing stays the same long in these waters.

I leave the sails close reefed, and do not even change the headsails, because we would not sail any faster in the enormous chop. It comes from everywhere at once, and whips the rigging around. Actually, I still don't quite have my old punch. Before Good Hope I would not have stood the storm jib another minute. Since Good Hope, I tend to save my strength.

At the end of the afternoon the entire sea begins a sound. It reminds me of an angry termite colony, when the soldier-termites who escort the workers start clicking their mandibles together by the thousands. The Indochinese termites have such powerful mandibles that the planters in the bush used them to close wounds when there was no doctor available. Here, the entire surface of the sea shivers with the same rustling like dead leaves. Each crest is covered with foam, none breaking dangerously; one could not even call them whitecaps. and all this in a nearly complete calm. I have never seen anything like it. Add a gale on that, and you would see terrific breakers. Thank God, the barometer looks OK!

A few hours later not a sound—just the long swell cut by many secondary wave trains. Not a breath of wind. The sails slat and chafe, so everything has to be sheeted in.

I put the helm alee, and will get under way when *Joshua* starts heeling. Conor O'Brien, whose Indian Ocean crossing I am re-reading, recommends a solid day's rest from time to time, when it does not pay to wear yourself out trimming the sails. O'Brien adds that he himself is too restless to follow the advice, but it suits me just fine. It is nice to be in my bunk. Hardly any motion. The wind will come back.

I think of the little plank I saw alongside this morning, squared off, planed smooth, and perfectly clean, without a speck of seaweed, as if laid there by a mysterious hand. I had given a long, sweeping look around. Nothing. Just the little board, already disappearing in the wake of the gale...the sign of a human presence, so close, so fugitive, in waters visited only by seabirds.

Where are Bill King, Nigel, Loïck? I had hoped day after day to get news of them from the BBC or Radio Cape Town after my message to the little black freighter. Not a mention. I am playing alone with the entire sea, alone with the past, the present and the future. Maybe it is better this way...but I would like news of my friends.

Loïck is probably a week away from Good Hope, watching the mood of the barometer, wondering whether it would be better to pass close to land, like Vito Dumas and Conor O'Brien, or far off the Agulhas Bank. Is he growing his seeds in the plastic saucers we brought together at Plymouth? Very easy: you take seven saucers, punch a few holes in them, and line them with cloth. Fill with wheat grains, soybeans and watercress seeds. Stack them one on top of the other, and moisten with a little water. After a few days, the sprouts are long enough. Remove the bottom saucer, and boil the sprouts or make a salad. Refill the saucer with fresh seeds, put it on top of the pile and sprinkle; next day, remove the bottom saucer, eat the sprouts, refill with seeds, put it on top, sprinkle, etc. and you have perpetual motion! It is easy, but I find it a bother, and I prefer Ovaltine, which contains barley germ and lots of other good things. I tossed my seed packets overboard after a month at sea, except for a pound bag of soybeans, just in case.

Nigel laughed at our germination experiments: he thought we were going to a lot of trouble for nothing, and he was probably right. Where is Nigel? How far will he get with his trimaran?

And Bill King, where is he? Perhaps far ahead, perhaps behind if he got hung up in the doldrums, perhaps very close if the gods have permitted. It would be a victory for all of us, if Bill King's trip made it possible to perfect a Eurasian rig that is close to ideal, thanks to its extreme simplicity of handling. It is surprising that I did not hear about anyone on the BBC or elsewhere, since Bill and Nigel have weekly radio contact with their sponsoring newspapers.

Maybe they just chucked it...transmitter, batteries, brain-rattling generator, jerrycans of explosive gasoline, heave ho!—the whole bloody lot overboard, for a little peace and quiet.

Nearly midnight. I slept for a few hours, as usual. The rhythm of the sea is not the same as that ashore. At sea I wake up almost automatically around midnight, feeling fresh, and go back to sleep an hour later. This gives me plenty of time for a turn on deck to feel the heart of the night and sense what is around. Then I roll myself a cigarette at the chart table, dreaming before the *Damien* globe.

When I feel really conscientious I fix myself a mug of Ovaltine and munch a biscuit. When I feel less so, I settle for coffee and another cigarette; rolled not too thick, because a package of tobacco has to last three days.

The sea has very quickly become fine again. Barely twelve hours ago it was breaking under a thick overcast. Then it started to boil with cross-seas from the east quadrant when the wind eased. Now the wind is back, force 2 from the west, and the sea is all smiles in the moonlight.

I get under way, shake out the reefs and set the big staysail. I will wait for dawn to replace the storm headsail with the working jib.

The middle of the night is the moment I like best when the weather is nice; it is as if the next food day were beginning then instead of at dawn. But my cigarette and coffee taste a little stale, because I am a bit sick at the thought of *Joshua* doing a knot less than she could in such fine weather. I finally set the working jib and treat myself to an extra spot of coffee before curling up in my bunk.

Ashore, coffee keeps me awake, but not here. And I sleep all I like during the day. People often imagine that sailors are a breed of supermen; that we almost never sleep, spend all our time handling sails, never get a hot meal. If they only knew!

The wind has come back. *Joshua* is sailing east in the belt between the 37th and 38th parallels. In theory, she will stay there until she is 2000 miles from Australia, then put a little south in her easting to round Cape Leeuwin and Tasmania. Conor O'Brien, a model of lucidity and seamanship, adopted that tactic to avoid the area further south, with its high percentage of gales. Vito Dumas, who went far north to the 35th parallel at one point, encountered long periods of calms and light variable winds there.

I hate storms, but calms undermine my spirits. I will have to be careful not to commit any big strategic blunders; I don't feel as tough as I used to. But I know that despite the most painstaking and technical study of the best routes, whether you get wind or not is up to heaven.

A quarter of the Indian Ocean is already astern, and the weather has been fairly nice for the last few days. Huge cloud systems pass overhead from time to time and drop some rain, but the few quarts collected in the buckets under the booms are still brackish. The sails got covered with a thin crust of salt during the days spent lying hove-to west of Good Hope, when the wind was filled with spray and the hot sun dried everything in a few seconds. It will take a hard rain to get rid of the salt.

I am not worried yet—rain is hardly lacking in these latitudes—but I would still like to raise the level of my tank. About 50 gallons are left of the 100; this means a range of about a hundred days, figuring normal consumption at half a gallon a day.

The days go by, never monotonous. Even when they appear exactly alike they are never quite the same. That is what gives life at sea its special dimension, made up of contemplation and very simple contrasts. Sea, winds, calms, sun clouds, porpoises. Peace, and the joy of being alive in harmony.

Albatrosses, malamocks, Cape pigeons, shearwaters and a species I do not know which I dub 'Cape robins' have been keeping *Joshua* company since the 35th parallel in the Atlantic. They seem to feed on spray and fresh air, skimming the waves without ever dipping their beaks.

Albatrosses and malamocks are loners. The others live in communities, with the smaller birds like the Cape robins making up the densest flocks. *Joshua* passes through groups of more than a hundred of these very little birds, about the size of robins, with silvery plumage, whose quick turns and sideslips remind me of swallows before a storm. Their undersides are white, the tails dark grey, and a big W marks the tops of their wings. They zig-zag along the water, often putting a leg down as if to help them turn. No relation to the tiny black and white petrels, who play in the air as lightly as butterflies. They too often turn by pushing a foot against the water.

Vito Dumas described his tame Cape pigeon as a black bird with lovely white markings. Without that description I would worry sometimes; seen head-on, Cape robins fly just like pigeons, and I read somewhere that big flocks of Cape pigeons are a sure sign of icebergs nearby. Two or three Cape pigeons have been keeping us company since Good Hope. They are exactly as Dumas described them, with large white spots blending into the black of their wings.

The shearwaters are the size of a big gull, and look just like crows sitting on the water. Their even plumage, very dark brown, shows reddish highlights in the sun, but looks black in overcast weather. They glide along without beating their wings, a little hunched over, in groups of eight to fifteen, often abreast. They look as if they were raking the sea as a team, making their lithe, harmonious turns nearly in formation. The same group has been with us a long time. I can recognize one by a feather missing from his left wing.

The most beautiful are the malamocks, a kind of albatross only smaller (6 ft wingspan) and infinitely more graceful. All the ones I see have nearly the same wardrobe: white belly, neck and tail, with wings of dark grey on top, pearl grey underneath along the leading edge, and very light grey, sometimes almost white, along the trailing edge. All display an attractive almond shaped pattern around the eye, like a vamp's makeup.

Malamocks have real feathers, whereas the albatrosses (wingspan over 9 ft) seem covered with a woolly down. Each has his personal attire, and it would be impossible to mistake one albatross for another. There is one I always look for when I come on deck: very big, cindery grey underneath and nearly black on top, with a brown spot under his left eye. With malamocks, on the other hand, it would take a sharp eye to pick one out from twenty others, even after a month of daily contact.

The birds here behave in a completely different way from the ones in the tropics. There, everything is gaiety, screaming and diving. I know few sights to compare with forty gannets tumbling from the sky like rockets on a school of sardines. On *Marie-Thérèse II,* between Cape Town and Saint Helena, I danced around the deck echoing their cries, to see them working with such gusto. Often one would leave the group to glide in close to the mizzen for a moment, before going back to his fishing. The wideawakes and tropic birds were friendly too. Even the frigate birds, usually stand-offish, took an interest in my boat.

Here, albatrosses, malamocks, shearwaters, Cape pigeons and the tiny petrels glide along indifferent. *Joshua,* for them, does not exist. Yet she must, because my big cindery albatross is often there, as well as my shearwater with the missing feather. But above all, they seem to be searching for something, something very important in the wind and spray.

Nevertheless, Cape robins are friendly and curious at times, when they show up to pass the time of day. Just for fun, they come over in twos and threes to check on the rigging and play with the eddies in the lee of the sails. They sideslip so nimbly that I can't keep them in the Beaulieu's rangefinder.

I would give a lot to tame a Cape robin. They do not stay long enough, though, and each flock I meet keeps to its own territory.

Though we have almost reached the 37th parallel, the weather keeps changing, sometimes abruptly. It rained or drizzled all last night and finally rinsed the sails, allowing me to collect eight gallons of water. At sunrise a light band far to windward cuts across the low ceiling. An hour later the sky is blue, with little round cumulus and a SW wind announcing fair weather. Towards 11 o'clock I begin to wonder whether the sun will be out for the noon sight and I take an early sight just to be on the safe side, as heavy altocumulus and probably stratus close in very quickly from the west. I still manage to catch the sun at the meridian through the veil of stratus; then it clears. But a little while later the southern horizon is blocked by a very heavy cloudbank showing protuberances and rain. I shook out the reefs this morning; I tie them in again, one each in main and mizzen. No point in reefing the staysail; since I have to stay on deck, it will be simpler to take it down if the wind turns gusty, and raise it again later.

No gusts. Yet the seas build and begin to break without any real increase of wind. Then it starts drizzling and the wind eases to force 4, veering to the SSW. I go below to gulp down a can of camembert with army biscuits and some custard, as I had not eaten and the clock says 2 p.m. When I go back on deck ten minutes later, I find that the two buckets hung under the booms have more than a gallon of water. I pour my precious gallon into the jerrycan, thanking heaven and cursing the unstable weather, as the wind is down to force 3, and the choppy sea is taking its toll of the sails.

I shake out the reefs at 3 p.m., under a sky blanketed from one horizon to the other. Still, the log shows 18 miles covered since noon; that is 6 knots, for the moment. But miles are hard-won around here. SW force 5 wind again at 3.30 p.m. Same sky, same type of weather. A little nap.

By the next day's sight 160 miles have been covered. Beautiful weather from the SW, wind force 5 to 6, very pronounced seas, all blue and lovely. The cumulus are nice and round, instead of flattened as they usually are here. It rained or drizzled again last night, in spite of the usually dry SW wind, and I got up to collect water from the buckets. They are nearly full again this morning. So I now have more than 10 gallons in my jerrycans, which I pour into the tank. The two last months' near-absence of rain had me worried, as did the sails' stubborn saltiness.

I have been feeling tired for a week. Moreover, my back has started acting up, probably due to a weakening of the muscles along the spine, caused by too little exercise and a certain lack of variety in diet. I was already seven pounds underweight when I left Plymouth. A few days ago I managed to weigh myself in a flat calm: another couple of pounds lost in three months. . .

Yes, I feel tired. Occasionally I find myself taking a long look at Mauritius on the chart, not very far north of here. It is the most beautiful place I know, with Saint Helena. But Saint Helena is far, very far away, beyond the Horn and at the other end of the world; I do not even dare think of it. Mauritius, on the other hand, is close, too close, and filled with memories of my Mauritian friends with whom I spent three of the most beautiful years of my life. I feel very weary at times. If I do not get on top of things, *Joshua* will not reach the end of the long ribbon of foam that leads to Plymouth. But now there are moments when I feel a great emptiness inside, when I am no longer sure where to go.

I have started taking Pentavit tablets (vitamin B complex), and will keep at it for a month, because my fatigue may be due to vitamin deficiency. But I will also have to take more interest in cooking: vitamin tablets will never replace a hearty appetite. Above all, start exercising, as I used to do in the old days. And go on deck more often, regardless of weather. Many things are cured by wind and sea, if you stay on deck with them long enough.

Sticking to the 36th parallel may be wise also, to let my feathers grow back in a kinder climate before turning south for Cape Leeuwin and Tasmania. But how far, and how vain, all that seems to me when I really think about it.

Take reefs in, shake them out, take them in, shake them out, live with the sea, live with the birds, live with the present, never looking beyond today, knowing that everything comes with time. . .

Progress is slow, as the weather is very unstable and also because I have decided' not to carry maximum sail between sunset and dawn, so as to spend a week with no worries at night. One day we covered 136 miles at the noon sight, 134 the next, then just 29 because of a great calm full of sunshine, then 88 miles, 159 miles, 131 miles, 119 miles, 160 miles, 167 miles. . .a real sawtooth wake.

SE gale on November 10 and 11. I was forced to heave-to on the starboard tack and drift north for 24 hours, to avoid being pushed south. Next day, 145 miles on the 36th parallel, then 162, and 183 in a SSW gale that raised really big breakers. I have to take them nearly astern, losing still more latitude, to avoid serious damage. Then 146 miles on the 15th in a terrifically choppy sea, 150 miles on the 16th. . .and here I am, becalmed on November 17 in 34° 38′ south latitude, with barely 45 miles to the good since last night. For all my careful planning to avoid Vito Dumas' mistake, I fell right into the same trap.

Nonetheless, the line on the *Damien* globe is longer; we are nearly halfway between Good Hope and Tasmania. The sun is glorious, and I am grateful just to rest for the day, watching the calm while my bedding airs on deck.

I go below to straighten the aft cabin, where grapefruit,

lemons, garlic and onions are stowed. The garlic will last a
century! The lemons have kept perfectly too. Françoise wrapped each of them in a page from the *Reader's Digest,* which is
just the right size. I will eat my last grapefruit today. Of the
hundred taken aboard three months ago, only five or six went
bad.

The little purple Morocco onions that Loïck gave me at
Plymouth are still in very good shape; at most, a few sprouts,
which are not wasted since I usually put them in my rice. On
the other hand, picking through the big white onions again is
pointless. They are completely rotten, and I heave the bag
overboard.

Seven malamocks and a flock of shearwaters are gliding
nearby at that moment. Many of them fly right over the bag of
onions without seeing it. I suppose their eyes are focused at the
distance that allows them to make out whatever it is they are
looking for (just what that is, I wish I knew). Finally, one of
them notices the bag and makes a sharp turn to land by it.
Only then do the others realize that something interesting
might be happening, and they come and land next to the first,
one after the other. What the devil are they looking for, among
the wave tops? It must be awfully hard to find, for them to fly
right past that enormous thing ten times without so much as
noticing it. And how about you, old man. . .what are you
looking for?

Absolutely flat calm; sunshine everywhere, above and below.
Filling a bucket with water for the dishes, I notice that the sea is
covered with plankton. It is made up of tiny animals smaller
than pinheads, zig-zagging along the calm water. Scooped
along the surface, the bucket harvests a good hundred of the
living mites; a foot or so deeper it only brings up three or four.

There is also a carpet of pretty, flat jellyfish the size of a
penny, that I do not recognize, and a few Portuguese men-
o'-war, lovely in the sunlight. They look like blue-tinted oval
balloons, capped by a translucent crest for sailing into the
wind, when there is any.

The calm becomes a breath of air, nearly transparent, but
steady. The wake appears on the smooth sea. Today I would
like to see some of the water spiders that fled from *Joshua*'s bow
as we were leaving the doldrums in the Atlantic. I wasted two

reels trying to film the long-legged insects, whose bodies are no bigger than flies'. They were too quick, impossible to catch in the lens. The boat frightened them moving at 4 knots. It would be easy today; they would keep still in the glitter of the sun.

They were the same water spiders as those in the streams of Europe and Asia. On *Marie-Thérèse* I encountered lots of them in mid-Indian Ocean, very far west of Sumatra. At first I could not believe it, yet there they were, skittering over the sea on their long, curved legs. They do not dive, and are carnivorous, so there must be invisible lives on the surface of the sea. How could they survive, so fragile in appearance, when the waves turn ugly? Yet they managed very well; there were thousands around *Marie-Thérèse*. It was a day of calms. The night before, we had been hove-to.

Two tiny things are swimming alongside. One chases the other, catches it, lets it go, catches it again. They fight, I trap them in the bucket for a closer look. They resemble two miniature cicadas. They do not fight, they procreate. Marvellous, to see life going on, so far from everything and against all odds.

I look for others, while *Joshua* drifts in the light airs, but there are just two of them, no bigger than a baby's fingernail, for the entire sea. Yet they managed to find each other despite the dangers of this great open sea.

When I was a child, my mother told me God had painted the sky blue because blue is the colour of hope. He must have painted the sea blue for the same reason. I feel myself going far back to my childhood in Indochina to the period when I hunted barefoot with my slingshot. It was not so much to kill birds as to listen to the murmurs, the reflections, the imperceptible crackings and the abrupt silences of the forest, full of clues and secret things.

I wipe off my Beaulieu slowly, with affection. Little by little, it has become more than a mere tool. There are only 27 reels left, to finish a trip that has just begun. Will it be possible to bring pictures that say everything, where nothing needs to be explained?

The wind picks up after the noon sight, northerly, force 3 to 4. The barometer has not thrown any fits in the last three days and *Joshua* sails very fast on a sea that is still flat, steering SE so as not to lose the wind. I have added a bonnet under the mainsail boom, an extra staysail and storm jib forward, and a mizzen staysail: 1075 sq. ft in all.

I gaze at my boat from the top of the mainmast. Her strength, her beauty, her white sails well set on a well found boat. The foam, the wake, the eleven porpoises on either side of the bowsprit. They are black and white porpoises, the most beautiful I know. They breathe on the fly, almost without breaking the surface, without wavering from the course, towing *Joshua* at nearly 8 knots by invisible bonds. Climbing down to fetch the Beaulieu is out of the question. I would lose everything, and what they give me is too precious; a lens would spoil it all. They leave without my touching them, but the bonds remain.

My big cindery albatross, the malamocks and the shearwaters have resumed their endless quests, level with the waves. They almost all landed during the calm, showing no interest in *Joshua*. I threw them a few pieces of the dorado caught in the trades, which has been drying in the mizzen shrouds for two months at the mercy of the weather, without rotting or smelling bad. It did not interest them either. Just the same, two shearwaters ducked their heads under to watch the little cubes sinking toward the depths.

They are all gliding now, happy as I that the wind has come back. Their slender, motionless wings flutter at the tips as if feeling the air, sensitive as a blind man's touch. The Cape robins have not been around for a good week; perhaps I went too far north for them. My shearwater with the missing feather is not there either. It is not the first time he has disappeared though, and I know he always comes back.

EIGHT

The Days
and the Nights

The wind's strength is unsteady, but sailing has become restful, with the barometer at its best for days. Drizzle alternates with blazing sun. I spend my time reading, sleeping, eating. The good, quiet life, with nothing to do. And little by little the water tank fills up.

Since I left Plymouth, I've been listening to as many English and French speaking radio stations as I can, hoping to get news of Nigel, Bill King and Loïck. I haven't heard anything about them, but I have been listening to a lot of political talk from many different countries. What a laugh! Now I really understand why so many people just turn their backs and go away when political leaders open their mouths.

The Vietnamese radio programmes come in more and more clearly. But after twenty years away from my native land I hardly understand the language I used to speak fluently. At most, I can make out a word or simple sentence from time to time. Just the same, I leave the radio tuned to Saigon by the hour; it stirs old memories of Indochina. The announcer was talking about Rach-Gia today. I was all ears, but couldn't pick up the keys to my mother tongue. I could see my beautiful junk though, and the rice shipments I made in the Gulf of Siam. My rice was loaded at Rach-Gia, in Cochin-China, and taken from there to Kampot or Ream in Cambodia, sometimes as far as Koh-Rong, near the Siamese border. Then I headed back to Rach-Gia with a load of wood or earthenware jars of palm sugar. . .but most of all with my lovely junk, beating through the Hong-Ray archipelago, its islands full of memories of my childhood spent with the Vietnamese fishermen.

The police suspected me of gun-running to the Viet Minh, by way of Siam. I may well have smuggled dried prawns from the Camau area for the Chinese merchants, but never weapons. The police really bothered me at times, because they could not understand, in that troubled period, that I loved only the Gulf of Siam; that I loved my junk as one can love at that age, that my junk was not only all my present life, but would give birth to all the rest.

I recall the Rach-Gia harbour. . .its big-bellied Phu-Quoc junks unloading their *nuoc-man*; the ones from Camau, slim and elegant, lug sails furled right to the yard; the flat-bottomed Koh-Rong junks crammed with pottery, their lateral rudders rigged to leeward with a system of bamboo bark hoops, and having to change sides at every tack.

Life in the port of Rach-Gia was the richest on the coast, the most colourful along with Kampot in Cambodia. But for some obscure reason dried prawns from Rach-Gia could not be unloaded in Cambodia. So we all toed the line and shipped rice, and the competition was fierce.

My junk normally carried 20 tons of rice, 25 in very fine weather, but only 15 to 17 during the SW monsoon, as the waves were higher with the wind from the sea. The bags of dried prawns were the little extra, taken on without shouting it from the rooftops. They didn't weigh much, but let me take better care of my junk. She was lug rigged with stayed masts, like almost all the junks of the Gulf of Siam. The little bowmast carried a small fully-battened sail that one man could raise without a tackle. Six people, on the other hand, were needed to hoist the mainsail; each of its battens was made of a double male bamboo. Yet nothing is simpler to handle in bad weather than a Chinese sail; one man is all it takes to reduce that enormous area, no matter what the wind strength or direction. He has only to slack the halyard and the first batten comes to rest along the boom of its own accord; it is like a fan folding up. Another reef? The fan closes a little more, as the system of multiple sheets running through blocks at the end of each batten adjusts itself automatically.

But that huge, lovely Chinese sail, which looked like a giant batwing, had its drawbacks. I can see it now, thrashing from side to side with the boat's rolling when the wind died. Chafe made it a glutton for lines, and it needed a new set of sheets (150 to 200 ft) every 3 weeks, and a set of topping lifts every month. It also went through a set of sails every 5 months during the dry season, and every 3 months in the rainy season. Sails, there, were made of woven latania palm fronds. The Chinese merchants sold this material very cheap, in 2 ft widths. They were sewn together with heavy coconut string, using the curved needles normally used on burlap bags in the

West. With a full crew, one day was enough to sew, rope and rig the mainsail, with its 5 double battens, boom, yard and topping lifts. We would then soak it alongside overnight so that the salt would protect it from rot. And twice a day, at dawn and sunset, the sails were wetted with a bamboo cup on a long, flexible pole, that sent seawater splashing up to the top of the yard. Just the same, a new set of sails would be needed 3 months later in the rainy season.

Everything hovering in the air of Asia at that time, the richest, most formative period of my life comes back to me with incredible clarity. I smell the aroma of wood oil that permeated it, the smell of the sugar jars during the sail back to Rach-Gia, the slight noise of the sheet blocks, the creaking of the heavy battens. All that gave birth to *Snark*, my two *Marie-Thérèses*, and then *Joshua* and her search for a truth which I had perhaps lost, but which is gradually being reborn in the wake of the present trip.

The wind strength is still irregular: 175 miles, 180, then 105 and 121 because the breeze fell again. Another 180 miles, 152, 151, with 16 gallons of rainwater collected amid the simple sounds of the sea.

Joshua moves surprisingly fast for such light airs. Her paint was put on with a roller, as I could not find a spray gun, and using a brush was out of the question because of the thickness of the paint. I had fretted over the 'orange-peel' look of a roller-painted surface: the thousands of irregularities would surely slow us down. But the chemical engineer in charge of painting at the Toulon navy yard assured me that the laminar effect of the water would make the bottom perfectly smooth in a few weeks, and he was right. Also, *Joshua* has become much lighter in the 3 months since the start.

Cape Leeuwin is now 900 miles ENE. The birds are more and more numerous, seemingly as aloof as ever. The shearwaters sometimes hang around the wake to pick up my leftovers though.

I have a thoughtful look at the masthead radar reflector, bent 45° to starboard, and straighten it. Yesterday, when I made my weekly climb to oil the steel halyard and blocks the reflector was straight, as it has been for years. Even the two knockdowns off Good Hope had not budged it. Only a real wallop could have bent the shaft 45°. Some unsuspecting albatross or malamock must have run into it. It was certainly no shooting star! But I find no feathers on the reflector.

I wonder how I would react if I saw a big hole in a sail after breakfast one day, just like that, for no apparent reason. Yet a hole in the sails would only half surprise me, after seeing an albatross narrowly avoid the bowsprit, which he was about to slam into at full speed. I have finished *Avant que Nature Meure* by Jean Dorst. All our earth's beauty. . .all the havoc we wreak on it. God, how good it is to be here, in no rush to get home.

The wind slackens, the barometer is still high. We are protected by the western edge of the Australian high. It drives possible lows to the south, but in exchange could give us calms, maybe even contrary winds. Radio Australia often mentions light to moderate easterly winds on the whole southern coast of the continent, with numerous bush fires due to the drought. We are still far away, and in a much more southerly latitude than Cape Leeuwin. It could be the right time to swing below the 40th parallel.

What tactic did Bill King select for the Indian Ocean? Did he take the half-quiet route, or tear along south of the 40th parallel? At Plymouth, we both anticipated taking the half-quiet way. I think Nigel will do the same with his trimaran, from the upshot of our discussions. I do not regret my route, despite a rather low speed. It is full of sunshine right now, and the shearwaters are getting tamer. I call them each time I do the dishes on deck, and they come to look in the wake. Albatrosses and malamocks remain completely indifferent. The big one, cinder grey underneath, is still there.

The wind eases further, then dies. Flat calm. There are many birds now, all resting in the water around the boat, the shearwaters fairly close, almost friendly, the albatrosses and malamocks further off, disdainful.

I suppose my birds would not find much to eat if they stayed on the wing, and probably prefer to save their strength for better days. Many of the shearwaters go to sleep in broad daylight, heads under wings. I had never seen that before, and suppose the calm period will be fairly long. My birds seem to know that the calm is going to last.

Calm. . .the shearwaters are closer than yesterday. I toss them some big biscuit crumbs. They come to look, unhurried, but are not tempted. The pieces of dried dorado, on the other hand, spark a few arguments. They have a taste, enjoy it, start to squabble.

Little by little, they come closer. I yell 'Kew-kew!' each time I throw them a piece. My voice does not frighten them. Soon they recognize the rallying call, come still closer, and I film them at point-blank range as they duck their heads or disappear underwater to retrieve a piece of dried fish. A few malamocks join in, but they are much less nimble than the shearwaters, and perhaps less trusting.

Calm. . .calm. . .At dawn, a good 60 shearwaters are bobbing in the area. They do not react while I clean the porridge pot on deck, but stop preening their feathers, raise their heads, and swim closer as soon as they hear my rallying call. The dorado was finished yesterday. I offer them my cheese and friendship. They like it a lot better than dried fish. Then, with time and patience, one comes to eat out of my hand.

The shearwater decided to try it a little before sundown, with incredible gentleness, without haste, almost without fear. He slowly stretched out his beak, took the white piece from my fingers, dipped it in the water as if to dilute it, and swallowed, without watching me. Then he fluffed himself up, and stretched his beak out for the next piece.

The others crowd around in a half-circle, almost within reach, but they do not dare. I toss them pieces of cheese which they fight over noisily. Mine waits to get his from my hand. I would like to be that shearwater, just for a minute, to know his very simple joy in the face of such a miracle. It might be the very simple joy that I feel myself.

I get up very early to await the dawn as the flat calm continues. As soon as the shearwaters spot me, the ones I take to be the more intelligent paddle over, periodically ducking their heads to see if I have thrown any cheese! At my calls, the whole flock closes in, and when I toss out the pieces of cheese, the daily festivities begin.

The shearwater I was feeding yesterday is alongside, beak outstretched. The others jabber, whereas he really expresses himself, with a modulated chirping different from the shouts of the gang. He may be twitting me for also feeding the others. . .but at any rate he expresses himself.

From his size and behaviour, I think he must be the oldest of the flock. He refuses to dive, even a short way. The others go down more than twelve feet to catch a nearly full box of cheese dropped in the scuffle. As they are right under the boat, I can see that they fly under water—actually fly, sculling with their wings.

I am not quite sure any more how long the calm has lasted. I listen to the Australian weather forecast with half an ear. One look at the still high barometer is enough to know what the announcer will say: high pressure centre, fair weather, light winds or calms. I am in no hurry. I hope I will never be in a hurry, ever again.

Splashes reach all the way to the Beaulieu, and real free-for-alls break out. Only 19 reels left. I shoot another one at close range. I have never seen birds so unrestrained and so trusting. Moreover, these shearwaters have a sense of fair play, and do not double-cross each other; the quickest one wins, and when he has won the others leave him alone, which is only fair. In other waters frigate birds, for example, bully the gulls and gannets into spitting up their fish so they can grab it, only to be forced to cough it up by their own kind. I have seen a fish go into four different bellies, before winding up in the right one. Here, though, there are no dirty tricks.

My shearwater returns to eat out of my hand. I recognize him now from tiny details of his behaviour: his way of taking the cheese by cocking his head slightly to the left, the way he always puts himself a bit sideways, dips the cheese in the water before swallowing it, fluffs himself up afterward. And always, the little modulated chirps that I could recognize with my eyes closed. What surprises me somewhat is that the others still do not dare. This one is surely a respected chief! He still refuses to dive, leaving that to the noisy, likeable mob.

Calm. . .calm. . .calm. . .There must be a hundred shearwaters around *Joshua* in the early morning. My cheese supply can still withstand the onslaught, but in rummaging through the hold I come across a big plastic jar of butter. Françoise had prepared it by melting sweet butter mixed with salt. 'This butter is certainly rancid,' I tell myself, 'I'll give it to the birds, they may like it.' (In fact, this butter is perfectly preserved.)

The shearwaters love cheese, but I never expected them to be so crazy about butter. At one point, two shearwaters throw themselves on a big piece together. The one on the left gulps it right down, instead of sharing a little. The other one shoves him so hard and so angrily that the first shearwater is flipped on his back, beating his wings in the water and screaming with rage or terror. The aggressor stands on his stomach to prevent his escape. Suddenly, taking advantage of the wide open beak, he sticks almost his entire head down the other's gullet, and recovers some of the butter.

Malamocks and albatrosses still keep a little way off. They are getting intrigued, but do not dare come close yet.

How long has this calm lasted? I have lost track, and it doesn't matter. The birds are there, right at dawn; they seem to be waiting for me. All the birds of the Indian Ocean seem to be waiting for me.

I shoot two more reels with the Beaulieu, scenes of completely frenzied shearwaters. The giant albatross gets filmed too, at close range. He has trouble taking off in this calm, and does so reluctantly, when the cries of the shearwaters fighting over the butter tickle his palate just a little too much. So he takes off heavily, running on the water, and lands with his webbed feet sticking out like two little surfboards. In his fury at arriving too late he lashes out with his beak in the thick of the noisy shearwaters, who swipe the butter right out from under the big lout's nose. He sometimes manages to grab a few crumbs, and it makes him all the madder. He knows it is good and is beginning to recognize the rallying call, but he is always a good step behind the others.

The wind will never come back. Yet I feel lighter with each dawn, happy to be alive, happy to feel all that life around the boat. The weather is fine, the sun is out, the birds are there.

Each offering is accompanied by the rallying call shouted at the top of my lungs. The shearwaters can hear it many hundreds of yards away. It provokes instant stampedes and splashing all over the sea as they come running. Even when they are alongside, I do not lower my voice. Odd, that such a loud sound never frightens them, though my voice can't compare with the gentleness of the sounds of the sea, even when it breaks in big rollers on its worst days.

Three shearwaters swim behind the boat moving at half a knot. Being out of butter, I throw them a few pieces of Swiss cheese. Without hesitation, they use their old technique: duck their heads, spot the piece of cheese, and try to grab it before the others. They have memories, since I have been feeding them butter, which floats, for the last two days. Yet they immediately reverted to the earlier method for cheese, which sinks.

I try something else just as tasty, and open a can of liver paté. As soon as I give the rallying call, all the shearwaters following in the wake (who let themselves fall behind while I was in the cabin opening the can) come running across the ater and flop down in rafts alongside.

I cut a piece of paté and throw it a few yards ahead of the group. The whole gang, about ten now, rushes to where the piece fell. All the heads duck underwater, peering right and left towards the level at which the little piece of what they assume is white cheese ought to be: nothing. Paté is pink, and floats. One of them spots the piece at last and swallows it. Seems good.

Second piece: all the heads look about underwater, unable to pierce the mystery, except for the first shearwater, who grabs it on the surface without hesitating. He has already got the point.

Third piece: all heads duck except for that of the shearwater who happened on the first piece, seized the second without hesitation, and now grabs the third the same way, *while pretending to look underwater to throw the others off.* He isn't about to explain the invisible cheese mystery! Of course the others catch on before the can is finished.

My tame shearwater is back. He has eaten six ounces of paté in two sessions of less than an hour, and I think he could down another three-ounce can without any trouble.

How does this bird, who has swallowed six ounces of rich food in a short time, manage to find his usual daily food ration (probably over eight ounces) in waters where I see absolutely nothing? And if a shearwater, weighing at most three pounds, locates that much food, what about the albatrosses, who probably weigh more than twenty? Yet I have never seen these birds dipping their beaks in the sea. I would like to know what they feed on, and how. Is there some kind of flying plankton? After all, there are flying fish in the tropics.

A fairly simple way to answer the question would be to catch one (with a hook in a piece of cheese) and open its stomach to have a look inside! I am joking, of course, because unless one is starving, I now consider killing a seabird to be a crime against nature. But I have not always been of that opinion, having eaten a good number of gulls and cormorants in my life, and even a pelican, and penguins. Never on the high seas, though.

The days come, and then the nights, then again the days and the nights. The sea is flat to the horizon. Even the long SW swell has gone to sleep.

Sometimes a light air takes over for an hour or so. Then everything around seems to yawn and stretch. *Joshua* takes off again, the birds again take wing.

Then the calm settles in again, and I need not even lower the jib; there is no roll, it does not chafe against the forestay. Usually calms are deadly for the sailor and for the boat. Not here, though, as the sea is flat and the sun shines the day long. Everything breathes, everything soaks up sun, everything lives.

It's marvellous to have wind. It's also marvellous to have a calm that seems always to have been. I have the feeling of having known my birds forever, of being here forever without time passing. It is like a book of images that one can leaf through endlessly.

The wind will come back. My birds have somehow sensed it from something floating in the air. I think I sensed it too, yesterday night, looking at the stars. They were twinkling a little more than these last days. The barometer is also slightly down. But a page will remain unfinished. No matter; the wind will come back and give me other pages for the one my birds did not complete. It happened one evening some time ago, during the great calm.

I was in my bunk, and went on deck to sheet the mainsail and mizzen flat; they were making a little noise in the very slight roll. The moon, in her first quarter, was at mid-sky. Three shearwaters were sleeping a few yards from the stern. They did not move while I worked, though I had awakened them. Two fluffed themselves up, the third preened his feathers.

I was about to go back to bed, but seeing them there, busy doing their little toilet, I went to the stern and spoke to them, very softly, just like that. And they came right alongside. Yet I had not spoken the magic words.

I kept on talking the same way. They raised their heads toward me, cocking them to one side, right and left, from time to time giving a barely audible little cry in answer, as if they were trying to say that they liked me too. They may have added they liked cheese, but I could feel in an almost physical way that there was something more than food to that whispered conversation, something very moving: the friendship they were returning to me. I went below to get a piece of cheese and cut it into little squares. When I came up again, they had gone back to their former places a few yards from the stern. They did not approach as I silently went to the tiller. But as soon as I spoke to them, softly, without any 'kew-kew', they swam toward me, leaving a faint wake gleaming in the moonlight. I stretched out on deck so they could eat the cheese out of my hand.

They took it without squabbling. And I had the feeling, again almost physically, that my hand drew them more than the cheese. I wanted to caress them, at least to try. But I did not dare; maybe it was too soon. With a clumsy and premature gesture I risked breaking something very fragile. Wait a while longer, don't rush things, don't force things. Wait until the waves of friendship, made of invisible vibrations, reach their full maturity. You can spoil everything, trying to go faster than nature.

The wind has come back. The birds are on the wing again, gliding between the blue of the sky and the blue of the sea, as they used to do before the great sweet calm.

The shearwaters are no longer interested in the food I offer them, but they answer with a little flutter. I like that faint sign they give me with their wings to say they recognize my call. . .-'you're a friend. . .you're a friend. . .but we are searching day and night, always. . .let us do our shearwater work. . .you're a friend. . .you're a friend. . .day and night, always.'

NINE

The
Long Way

The wind has held for a week. Malamocks and albatrosses still glide around, aloof yet friendly. The big cindery one has never left me for more than a day or two since we first met near Good Hope. He likes me too.

All the shearwaters are gone though, all but one, who will stay a few days longer, then disappear in turn. Shearwater country must be further west: it can't be helped.

Cape Leeuwin is now 450 miles to the north, and *Joshua* has just crossed the 42nd parallel. There should be no more lack of wind.

I have taken out the general chart of southern Australia, from Cape Leeuwin to Tasmania. It marks the last leg of a long stretch. I look at the whole of Australia spread out before my eyes, with its beaches, its hundreds of little islands in the great southern bight, Bass Strait still far ahead, the small land-locked salt lakes.

I also pulled out the large scale charts. Wisdom, real wisdom, would be to throw them all overboard, to avoid the temptation of closing with the coast to give word via a ship or a fisherman in the dangerous Bass Strait between Australia and Tasmania. There I would be sure of meeting someone, but it would mean the fatigue of coastal sailing in currents and rocks, not to mention that nervewracking possibility, fog. I would like to let my family and friends know that all's well, talk to them of birds and porpoises, winds and calms. But I also remember the little black freighter. So the eternal conflict goes on, between caution and the great wave that joins us to others.

As before Good Hope, I have photographed my log page by page. But I am afraid. I do not even know if the chance I took with the freighter paid off: maybe she did not send the plastic bags on to the *Sunday Times*, for fear of getting involved.

One hundred and forty miles, 110, 123 and a bit of sun today. I put the final touches on two little sailboats built during the long calm with the birds. The bigger one is a 4 ft catamaran, made out of two pieces of purau, a very light wood, that had been kicking around the forepeak since Tahiti. She is square rigged, with a black sail visible from a distance, and a white jib with 'message' written on it. The other is a 2 ft ketch cut from a piece of styrofoam sandwiched between two sheets of plywood. Her hull lines are not bad at all; she has a masthead jib and a lead keel, so that she cannot capsize. Fastened to each boat's deck is a plastic bottle with excerpts from my log and a letter, wishing the finder a happy New Year, and asking him to forward the mail. Life would be pretty sad if one did not believe in Santa Claus from time to time.[1]

Ideally, Loïck and I would have left Plymouth with shipments of little plastic boats. We could have launched a whole flotilla when rounding Good Hope, Australia and New Zealand, with films of the log. Loosed every half day on a port tack with lashed tiller, many would have got through, without our taking the risk of flirting with land.

One hundred and sixty-nine miles and a halo around the sun,[2] 180 miles and a big rainbow, 154 miles with lots of cirrus. The wind, the sea, the barometer, the halo, the rainbow, the cirrus, but still no gale.

For nearly a week the barograph line has been full of little jerks and tremors, as if the gods of the Indian Ocean were restraining their anger. Some say 'Let's clobber him.' Others try to hold them back: 'Come on, leave the little red and white boat alone. Can't you see he's not about to eat your precious icebergs!' And the gods argue back and forth up there, throwing cirrus, halos and rainbows around.

I listen to the sounds of water running along the hull, I feel the main SW swell, regular despite the tremors of the barograph, and all my senses strain to detect a secondary

---

[1] These two models were found more than a year after being launched, one on a Tasmanian beach, the other in New Zealand. The mail carried by the boats reached its destination, and was perfectly readable.

[2] A halo around the sun or moon indicates the presence of cirro-stratus, which announces a weather disturbance. The halo is always 22° in diameter, and should not be confused with the much smaller corona, which does not mean anything bad. Cirrus also announce the proximity of a disturbance.

swell from the NW, which would explain why the sky is so
nervous.

When I was sailing with the fishermen of the Gulf of Siam
during my childhood in Indochina, the taïcong would tell me,
for example, 'Keep the swell two fingers off the quarter, and
you should always feel the wind behind your left ear, looking
forward. When the moon is one big hand plus a small hand
from the horizon, or when that star is one arm from the other
side (in case the moon is hidden by a cloud) then the sea will
become a little more phosphorescent, and we will almost be in
the lee of the island to set the first lines.'

There were no compasses on the Gulf of Siam junks, and I
did not want it used during my sailing school cruises in the
Mediterranean. Instead of bearing 110° from France to Corsica
my crew had to steer with the *mistral* swell very slightly off the
port quarter. At night, it was the Pole Star one small hand
abaft the port beam. And if there was neither distinct swell nor
star, we made do with whatever we had. I wanted it that way,
because concentrating on a magnetized needle prevents one
from participating in the real universe, seen and unseen, where
a sailboat moves.

In the beginning they could not understand my insistence on
getting away from the compass, that god of the West. But in
exchange, they began to hear the sky and sea talking with the
boat. And when blue-tinted land appeared on the horizon,
looking as it did to the mariners of old, all nimbed with
mystery, a few of them felt that our rigorous techniques should
leave a door open to those gods which the modern world tries
so hard to exclude.

The wind, the sea, the halo, the rainbow, the mares' tails amid
the lapping, murmuring of the water, full of worried things
and hopes. And I try to sense the secondary NW swell as
the wake stretches ever eastward.

In a little Indonesian port, I followed the preparation of a
Chinese junk that was to carry a shipment to Djakarta by way
of the Thousand Island archipelago, strewn with reefs and
rocks. The taïcong waited for three days after the loading,
squatting without a word, without a gesture, contemplating the
sky and the sea, in communion with the immaterial things that
float all over the East. Then the junk weighed anchor in a nice
beam breeze, with neither chart nor compass. I had the feeling

she was protected by the gods of the Far East, and by the big eye carved on either side of her bow.

Nearly four months after we left Plymouth I knew my voyage would go far, but I had no idea it might go farther still, among the intangible wayposts of sea and time. Already four months of sky and stars, with fresh winds, calms, gales followed by calms, calms followed by light airs, then more calms and more fresh winds. And now I listen for the threat of a gale in the cirrus and the sounds of the sea.

In the days when I had my junk I was much too young to be my own taïcong, and had hired one known from Ream to Camao.

The crew never spoke to him, because the taïcong needs all his peace to communicate with the gods and read on their faces. At mealtime, the crew would gather round the steaming rice kettle, forward if it was fine, amidships in a seaway. But always far from the taïcong, keeping their voices down so as not to disturb him in his communion. The young deckhand served him aft, respectfully giving him the rice bowl with both hands, without a word. Then he joined the others, slipping like a shadow on his bare feet.

The average has improved, the wake is much longer; Cape Leeuwin is far astern, Tasmania not too far ahead. If we continue at the rate we have for these last few days, we should be there in less than a week. And there may not be any gale, because the cirrus is beginning to lower and the stars are not twinkling much this evening, which tells me the wind is no longer angry up there.

Strong winds in the upper atmosphere cause large density gradients between layers of air at different temperatures. The stars then twinkle more than usual, because of the increased refraction bending the light. And when the high altitude winds blow very hard, this almost always tells of an approaching disturbance, or at least unsettled weather.

One very fine night, a taïcong fisherman told me why the stars announce the wind when they twinkle strongly. It is because there is wind up there, and it blows on the little flames of the stars, just as one would on a candle. So the stars flicker. The wind then blows with all its might, but can't blow them out, so it gets angry and comes down to the sea in revenge for being unable to blow out a single star, even the lowest ones close to the horizon. There, the stars could not resist the wind, which can blow very hard when it really gets angry. But there is a god close to the horizon to protect the low stars.

If it were not for the god of the horizon the wind would make them disappear one after the other. Then it would wait for the high stars to sink close to earth, to blow them out in turn. And men could not go on living, because there would be no more stars.

Years later, I learned that low stars always twinkle more than high ones because their light penetrates a thicker layer of air than at the zenith, making for greater light refraction.

I believe that science may someday permit men to reach the stars with their spaceships. I believe above all in the old East, which lets me go there any time I like with a candle and some wind. And I will paint a big black and white eye on *Joshua*'s bow when she finishes her journey, having found her way among the gods of my native Asia.

Tasmania is barely 200 miles to the ENE. Low clouds, the kind that so etimes bring drizzle without much wind, cover the sky. I launch my two bottle-carrying boats and they head south, where there is no one. But I know they will steer north, towards land, when the right time comes.

The sea is fairly calm. I keep them in view a long time. I imagine the surprise of whoever sights one of them far down an Australian beach. His amazement on drawing closer and seeing that it might be something out of a fairy tale. Then the emotion that catches at his throat as he senses that the little boat may have come from beyond the horizon.

Some rain falls in a light squall. The air is warm, coming from the sands of Australia. If visibility does not improve by to-morrow 1 will have to drop my plan of giving word at Hobart. Southern Tasmania is really full of pitfalls, with rocks reaching far offshore. Bass Strait, to the north, is even more dangerous in bad visibility, with rocks everywhere. The new moon makes things worse: tidal currents are strong, the nights very dark. How long have my family and friends been without news? Did the little black freighter forward the Good Hope package? I have no idea, and I have no word on my mates. Still, I am joyous, four months all alone on my boat.

Alone with the clouds and the waves, the sun and the stars, the wayposts of the sea, which are everywhere and nowhere, a little like the solitary gull I was feeding a can of paté to this morning.

Was it really this morning, or yesterday morning? I do not remember very well, and listen to the sound of water on the hull. It was morning as she landed abaft the beam, her feathers picked up ochre highlights in the rising sun. Like the three shearwaters I almost caressed one night. When was it? Two weeks ago? Two months? I don't know anymore and it does not matter. I only know they keep me warm, and the warmth will continue.

Four months gone in the wake, it could as well be a week as a year, it would seem the same; time has changed its shape. Outside it is drizzling on a sea very calm for this area, with a steady force 3 pulling *Joshua* at 6 knots. Inside, the cabin is warm and cozy, filled with my cigarette smoke, as the rain spatters very gently on deck, with a clearer note sounding on the thin steering dome. It is like being at anchor in a quiet atoll. The rolling can hardly be felt, everything around is so calm. All the things the Indian Ocean has given me, the initial fatigue, the not too nasty gales, the calms, the tiny sea-cicadas who found each other in the sea, the searching birds, the black and white porpoises, the birds again, and many joys now that my fatigue is overcome.

I am not sleepy tonight, I breathe the peace around me; water runs along the sails that join it to the sky and fills the buckets, and I can hear the boom shrug a little, freeing the water caught in the bunt of the first reef, that I did not shake out. The jerrycan is nearly full, I will soon pour it into the tank. I have enough water to last until the Atlantic doldrums, but I pour it in and will only stop when the tank is full.

I recall the little deserted island of Barrington in the Galapagos that we nearly left because the rain did not come. Many bonds then joined us to the seals and birds of Barrington, but there was only half a jerrycan left, and we were to leave the next day, Françoise and I. Then huge cumulus covered the sky, and the first storm of the rainy season came during the night. We watched the water as we would a miracle, running off the tarp and filling the tank, keeping the bond with the island.

The oil lamp glows softly in the cabin, like a star both distant and close. It gives my water its exact weight, gives each thing its true value. And it is far more than the miracle of my freedom, it is something else; something I have felt several times deep down.

I listen to the sea, I listen to the wind, I listen to the sails talking with the rain and the stars amid the sounds of the sea and I am not sleepy. I think of William Willis, alone on his balsa raft in the Pacific for months and months, with the sea all to himself in the middle of the universe. At times, he heard the 'call' with every fibre of his being. For some time, I have been hearing it too. And that, perhaps, is the long way. But I must not speak of it or let it be felt when rounding Tasmania; land is so far away compared to the questions the stars are asking me. I can only give them my first log, with birds, sea, daily sights and little everyday problems. My real log is written in the sea and sky; it can't be photographed and given to others. It has gradually come to life out of all that has surrounded us for months: the sounds of water on the hull, the sounds of wind gliding on the sails, the silences full of secret things between my boat and me, like the times I spent as a child listening to the forest talk.

TEN

The Rule
of the Game

One week before Christmas, *Joshua* reaches the mouth of Entrecasteaux Channel in Tasmania, sailing close to the Cape Bruny light, which is in touch with Lloyds. The MIK flags stand out clearly on their halyard.

It is not as dark as it was. It is not dawn yet, either. The sky is full of squalls. I have not had a wink of sleep since yesterday; it was a hard night. I heave-to, helm down and staysail aback, in the hope some fisherman will pass nearby. But I do not really believe it. At the moment I am too tired to believe anything.

My eyes blur as I study the large scale chart for the tenth time. I am looking for a little cove, neither too shallow nor too deep. The ideal cove on the chart has been located ten times in a row. And ten times I have forgotten where it was exactly. I am not heading there to rest, but to anchor a plastic container with 'message' on it. It is ready, with a long nylon line, a length of chain and a weight for an anchor until it is found.

Inside I put a letter, asking the finder to bring the whole thing to the commodore of the Hobart yacht club. A second letter requests the commodore to kindly mail the envelopes and parcel of films in the container.

Coffee. . .coffee. . .Dawn now. *Joshua* is drifting slowly. My eyes are not as red as before, my brain starts functioning more clearly.

Things almost always pick up at dawn. If you can hold out until dawn, you will probably hold out until the end. I gybe onto the other tack, and wait a while longer. I have already heard two fishermen put-putting by, but the boats passed too far away. I have already put in 99 per cent of the effort getting this far; it would be a real waste to turn around and leave, dropping the container off in the cove just like that. It might not be found before Christmas. Perhaps never if the line is cut by a rock, or a fisherman's propeller at night. I go below to fix a mug of Ovaltine and some biscuits spread with canned butter and orange marmalade, then I stretch out on the berth. The alarm clock is set for a quarter of an hour. I feel much better. There are no more squalls. *Joshua* is hardly heeling.

The sun has come out between the clouds, three fingers above the horizon. Fair weather cumulus have replaced the stratus. A fisherman passes half a mile off, between *Joshua* and the sun. I line him up in my survival signalling mirror, and in less than ten seconds, the miracle occurs. The fisherman has changed course. He is heading toward me. Now it is up to him. I gybe again onto the other tack, so as not to have to manoeuvre until it is over. All my fatigue has lifted, and my brain is racing. The 99 per cent effort is already far behind.

Last night I was searching with my binoculars for a big tower-shaped rock the good Lord put 20 miles offshore. Unable to locate it in the rain squalls and murk, faced with so much risk and fatigue, I came very close to abandoning my plan of giving word. But there was a disturbing glow, like the loom of a town, right out to sea, where there could be nothing but water as far as Adelaide Land. No moon; squalls, rain, a black sky. The glow out to sea worried me terribly. It was no boat, nor a city risen from the sea. I could not believe it was phosphorescence caused by the long westerly swell breaking on the reef I was trying to find on my left, as the glow was on the other side. Only the fact that it was in my way kept me from heading back out to sea. Between squalls I hove-to many times, to try to hear the sound of danger amid darkness.

To me, night is not usually black. I have always liked it, full of things speaking, singing or listening. But here I was afraid. A dull fear that can't be defined, that came because the night no longer spoke. I smelled a trap, somewhere in the darkness, but no vibration of the night told me whether it was really on my left, as I thought. . .or to my right, or on the bow.

At last, I picked up the big rock in my binoculars. And the whole night began to sing in spite of the overcast, squalls and fatigue. Because the fear was gone. The big rock that I had clearly glimpsed a mile or two off (150 ft high) told me that the awash reef, the really deadly one, was cleared well to port. And the night announced that everything was clear as far as the Cape Bruny lighthouse, whose beacon occasionally showed between the rain squalls. By then, I had sworn I would never again try to reassure my family, even at half the price. Yet I had not taken any real chances, and my navigation had been perfect, taking me three or four miles from the reef.

All that is far away—darkness, fatigue, vows. . .The fisherman is 30 yards off. He shifts into reverse to cut his headway at a safe distance. Then he bobs there a moment, comparing his drift to *Joshua*'s. A seaman, he knows what he is doing.

The little white boat pulls up on the correct side, I throw the container, one of the three men catches it, we chat for a few minutes. . .and it's all settled, and time to get under way. The skipper promised to give everything to the club commodore in person when he returns from fishing three days hence. No one could give me news of my friends. One had heard something about an English yachtsman who rounded New Zealand without having stopped. When? The fishermen did not exactly know. They seemed to remember the radio mentioning it last month. I do not think it is Bill King; perhaps Knox-Johnston. Of the three who set out around June, only he had a real sea boat. The two others sailed in little plastic things, really fragile for such a long trip in the high latitudes. Shortly before starting I learned that one of them had to give up, well before Good Hope.

I will listen more caredully to the Australian radio broadcasts for a few days. They might mention *Joshua*'s passing through their waters and take the opportunity to give the whole picture, saying where the others are. But I am not kidding myself. . .we are alone facing infinity.

Beautiful sky, warm breeze passing over the sails like a caress from the West, with all the promise of West and East together. Sea green under the sun, a green I have never known, except around the Horn. The wake is green, the foam is green, everything is green, as green as grass.

Tasmania is barely 10 miles in the green wake, and it is as if it never existed. It gave me a lift though, meeting those nice fishermen who took time out to do me a favour. But to speak of a wonderful meeting with humanity, hardly. We had a friendly chat, with genuine pleasure, and then parted just as simply, each back to the job at hand, with no regrets. They did their part by accepting the package. I did mine in bringing it to them.

I go back to my bunk with a boundless joy. I seem to hear the

cricket I had listened to this morning as *Joshua* sailed very close
to the lighthouse before heading for the open sea. The cricket's
note was high and clear, and the smell of trees mingled with
that of damp earth.

I stretch under the covers, humming a song whose tune and
lyrics I have forgotten, except for a scrap: '. . .and vanishes in
the sunshine without paying for his drink. . .'. I have paid for
mine, and at the same time I haven't, and it is wonderful to be
that free. I feel happy, light, at once detached from everything
and in control of everything, as when all debts are wiped away,
and you can live your own life.

Next day's sight puts Tasmania 73 miles astern, and the wake is
blue, for the sea has turned blue again. The wind is not very
steady, but I have made up all my fatigue. It was only a surface
fatigue, not the deep weariness I felt after Good Hope, that
made me consider Mauritius. Now it is New Zealand I look at
on the little *Damien* globe, and my glance sometimes wanders
toward the Horn. And I feel I am all right, that everything is all
right. I believe everything will be fine as far as *Joshua* and I are
concerned. The rest depends on the gods.

Another 105 miles with irregular winds, then 164, 147, 153.
There are squalls in the sky and reefs in the sails now. *Joshua*
tears along at 8 knots in the gusts, 7.3 knots the rest of the time.

I spend hours watching the water race by the lee ports,
hypnotized by the speed in the surges. I can understand the
multihull fans; it must be terrific to zip along at 15 or 18 knots,
with spurts of more than 20. But five multihulls were lost in
Australian waters last year, with all their crews. Fifteen men
never came back. Even Piver, father of the multihull, was lost
with his trimaran this summer.

Where is Nigel? If everything went well, he may be in the
Indian Ocean. And then what? It would really get to me if I
were to learn someday that Nigel was never coming back.
Where is he? Where are Bill King and Loïck?

The Hobart fisherman must have given my letter and parcel
to the yacht club commodore by now, and I listen to Australia
and the BBC religiously. The *Sunday Times* should have been
notified, top priority, the BBC too. Yet nothing, not a word,
not a mention.

Perhaps the BBC is against the idea of such a voyage being
run as a race. Maybe that is why I have not heard them

mention it once. Yet when we left Plymouth, the BBC was there with microphones, cameras and the whole bit. So how about it? Four friends leave about the same time to sail non-stop around the world, and nobody lets them know about each other.

It will be Christmas soon; I feel that I will not get any news of my friends, that I never will. I feel a bit low. And bitter toward the press. Perhaps that is unfair, since I agreed to the rule of the game: around the world singlehanded.

I do not need anything. I would just like to have a little news of them from time to time.

I am studying the large scale charts of New Zealand. The south coast, which is on my route, is not at all inviting, with dangerous reefs sometimes stretching far offshore. The Admiralty chart for the general area shows caches of food and clothing on a number of the deserted islands, and even whale-boats on some. The chart also states that these islands are visited once a year by a government ship. I suppose it must be for eventual castaways.

My search for the *Sailing Directions* for the area is vain, and I soon have to face facts: in chasing weight at Plymouth, I put the volume ashore, mistaking it for another! Good thing I have the large scale charts. . .

I am very pleased at being able to send word from Tasmania, because it would be a mistake not to give the south coast a wide berth. I will wait until rounding New Zealand before drinking Knocker's second bottle. At that point, we will really have rounded the last cape before the Horn. If *Joshua* keeps up her pace, I'll score a double hit and have my champagne on Christmas!

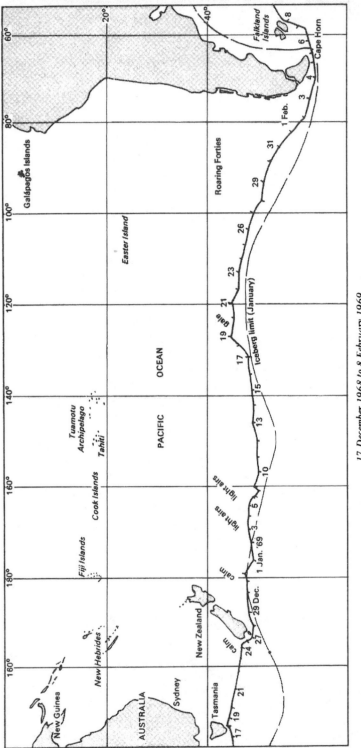

17 December 1968 to 8 February 1969

ELEVEN

Christmas and the Rat

I was too optimistic. . .a moderate SE gale, right on the nose, makes us heave-to under a blue sky. I was so counting on spending Christmas beyond New Zealand. . .

The wind slackens before nightfall and I get under way beating into a big swell. I am mad at myself for steering a direct course from Tasmania, instead of angling south right away, in view of an eventual period of easterly winds.

The wind eases further. *Joshua* pokes along in the night. I listen to the BBC; still no news.

At dawn the wind has nearly died. The sea begins to subside. A black ball with wide eyes looks at me, dives, reappears. It is a little seal, my first since the Galapagos. He swims around the boat, goes off, then comes bounding back across the water, with infinite grace. I do not think there is anything in the oceans as lithe as a seal. This one must be a youngster, he is not the least shy.

And now it is Christmas. Flat calm. The sea is almost flat as well, under the bright sun. The little seal (or his brother) is back, playing near the boat but not jumping like yesterday. From time to time he sticks his hind flippers out of the water and slowly waves them, as if to say 'hello-hello'. If the water were not so cold, I would go say hello too. In the Galapagos, the baby seals would practically rub up against us, they were so friendly and inquisitive. Their parents did not like it, and occasionally chased us out of the water. I can't tell whether this one is very young, or belongs to a small species. He can't be over four feet long.

Complete sunbath on the 46th parallel south! The sails flap a little, the air is warm, almost hot, with a light breeze from the north. All things considered, I am all right here. Still, I hoped to spend Christmas east of New Zealand. I had even planned, if the weather were really nice, to spend it close to Dunedin or

Molineux, with a New Zealand yacht that would just happen to be around. I would have hailed him with my loudspeaker:

> *'Ahoy, there! Want to have a bite with me? I have champagne for Christmas, and wine by the barrel!'*
> *'Champagne? French champagne? French wine?'*
> *'Heave-to a hundred yards off and come over in your dinghy!'*
> *'OK! I'll bring my gin along too, just in case your champagne and French wine don't do the trick!'*

That's the way it is—you make up little stories, alone at sea. Sometimes they come true.

The air is amazingly transparent, the wake barely discernible on the smooth sea. Several times *Joshua* passes through strange large clumps of seaweed.

It's not really seaweed, but the crossed fore-flippers of seals sleeping on their backs. Once awakened, the big ones dive, reappearing much further off. The little ones come over to play every time, but worried mothers round them up and lead them away.

These seal families sleeping in the sun will be my Christmas present; especially the little ones—they're so much nicer than electric trains. If their parents let them, I wouldn't be surprised if they tried to climb aboard. . .we could all have Christmas dinner together.

Taking advantage of the fine sun, and also of Christmas, I unwrap the smoked York ham specially prepared for Loïck and me by Marsh & Baxter, at the request of our friends Jim and Elizabeth Cooper. I had kept it in the hold under its original wrapping, saving it for these cooler latitudes, where it would be safe from heat waves.

The ham is perfect, without a trace of mould after four months in a humid atmosphere. Hey! What's happening to me? I suddenly start drooling like a dog with a choice bone under his nose. I must have had a long-standing ham deficiency. . .on the spot, I snap up a piece of fat the size of my wrist; it melts in my mouth.

For lunch, I fix a sumptuous meal. I pour a two-pound can of hearts of lettuce, well rinsed in seawater, into a pot where a piece of ham has been simmering with three sliced onions, three cloves of garlic, a little can of tomato sauce and two pieces of sugar. Jean Gau was the one who explained that you should always add a little sugar, to neutralize the tomatoes' acidity. Then I take a quarter of a canned camembert, cut it into little cubes and sprinkle it over the hearts of lettuce, along with a big piece of butter.

The aroma wafts all through the cabin as the pot simmers very gently on the asbestos plate. Cook it very, very slowly, because of the cheese. That is another secret. I learned it aboard *Ophélie* with Yves Jonville. One evening, he asked me to stay for dinner, and Babette simmered some cheese in a pot for a long, long time. It turned out to be hors d'oeuvre, main course and dessert. We stuck pieces of bread on a fork and dunked them right into the pot, drinking wine the while. It was so good that if there had been a Mauritian present he would have called it a Manilla duck's climax, because when a Manilla duck has finished, he flops on his back and just lies there, unable to move.

Land in sight!. . .I can't believe it. The mountains of New Zealand, a good 50 miles away, stand out very clearly on the horizon. Such visibility is amazing, but there is no mistake, the sextant confirms our position.

Joshua ghosts along at less than a knot on the flat sea, and passes 20 yards from a family of sleeping seals without waking them. They are already astern when one of them gives the alarm. I could see him tossing in his sleep, moving his flippers instead of keeping them across his chest. It looked as if he were dreaming. I wonder why the seals around here are so fearful, whereas the ones in the Galapagos treated us as equals. It may be because Galapagos seals are sea lions. . .their fur has no commercial value.

The sun sets. What little breeze there was today drops completely. Great peace all around, I will spend a nice quiet Christmas with the stars.

Calm. . .calm. . .I have the blues tonight. I think of my friends. I think of my family. I have everything I need here, all the calm, all the stars, all the peace. But I lack the warmth of men and I feel blue. For dinner, I added a can of corned beef to the remains of my noon concoction to make it edible. And I uncorked the bottle of champagne. I was not supposed to touch it before leaving the last dangers of New Zealand astern. I am not quite beyond the second cape, but tonight is Christmas, the calm is almost flat, the rocks are 50 miles off and not on my way. And above all, I feel blue, and that's why I opened Knocker's second bottle, the Cape Leeuwin one.

Champagne is a good thing; it makes you belch a little, but it chases the blues. Memories come up as the bottle's level goes down. I'm really out of it, dreaming of a little green spot with a huge leafy tree, where I could spend a few moments with my family and friends, tonight.

I would also invite all the neighbourhood cats and dogs to come share Christmas dinner. And even the rats. Because for me, Christmas is the big truce with the whole world.

The shadow of the rat passes before my eyes. He looks at me gravely. I have seen him a few times since that old story. But those stories never grow old. They only change their shape.

It was the night before our Tahiti-Alicante sailing. The rat came in through the open porthole and dropped onto a plate in the galley. I jammed him against the floor with a book before he could hide in the hold.

We did not have a stick handy, so Françoise passed me the slingshot. I held the rat pinned with my foot on the book. But I aimed a little high to avoid hurting myself, and missed. When I pulled the slingshot again for another shot, the rat looked at me. He knew I was going to kill him. But his eyes said I still had the choice.

He was a big good-looking rat, probably fairly young, his brown fur glossy with health. A beautiful animal, healthy and alive, full of hope, full of life.

I felt like grabbing him by the tail and slinging him back to his coconut trees, saying 'It's all right for this once, but don't let me ever catch you here again.' And he would have never returned, because he was a coconut rat, not a sewer rat. But I think man carries hatred for rats in his heart. I shot at point-blank range, and killed him with a stone in the head.

If there had not been that look, before, one rat more or less would not have made any difference. But the look was there, and it put me face to face with myself.

Midnight soon. The Cape Leeuwin bottle is almost empty. I think I've had it. The rat's shadow has become friendly, its look no longer carries the immense question to which I had failed to give the only answer.

I shut the radio up yesterday. They were really getting on my nerves with their infant Jesus. We use Him as a shield, quietly going about our sleazy huckstering, making the sign of the cross all over the place to pretend we are facing up to ourselves. How could we so lose our sense of the divine and the meaning of life? I have been rereading Steinbeck, *Wind, Sand and Stars, Avant Que Nature Meure, The Roots of Heaven* these last months. At times I would close my eyes after reading a line, a paragraph, a page, when it stirred a special response in me. I feel now that the people who wrote those books were expressing themselves not only with words and ideas, but with

vibrations. And those vibrations go far beyond our puny little man-made words.

In the beginning was the *Word*. I have not read the Bible, the print is too small. And it seems 'God' was translated wrong, the Hebrew text actually reads 'gods'. But that does not matter, because there is the *Word*. The *Word* goes well beyond everything, no translation could touch it. Could the *Word* be a vibration, I wonder? A vibration so powerful that out of it the universe was born. I do not know whether I read that somewhere, a long time ago, at a period of my life when those things found no answer in me, or whether I felt it all by myself on this Christmas night. I think it is rather a very distant echo, because I also feel that the books I have been reading since setting out were not written by Jean Dorst alone, or Romain Gary, Saint-Exupéry or Steinbeck alone, that is to say not by *some* men, but by *all* men. And those works are everyone's, and our heritage together.

The Cape Leeuwin bottle is empty. This time I've really had it especially as I drank two extra mugs of wine on top of the champagne. I would have liked to share all that with the guy on the New Zealand yacht. Maybe he needed some warmth too, on Christmas. Every day should be Christmas. That way people would wind up getting together to carry their heritage. Come on. . .time to hit the sack. . .you can't even tell time, the hands are all mixed up.

TWELVE

The Time of the Very Beginnings

I feel a bit washed out this morning. Not too much, though. Calms are all right. The sky has turned overcast. In any case, nothing can take my Christmas night away. The wind is back, barely perceptible. More seals. 'Hello-hello.' *Joshua* glides on the flat sea at 4 knots due south, to give Stewart Island, 100 miles SE, as much leeway as possible. The SW tip of New Zealand is 40 miles to the east; the noon sight put it in place on the chart despite the overcast weather. You know how it is: the whole sky is covered with low clouds and you are really sure that no sight will be possible. Yet you stay on deck with the sextant ready, you follow the spots of dull light between the clouds, where the sun should be. Then you lose hope, and all of a sudden boom!...here is the sun, you grab it fast and throw it on the horizon. And you get so high for the rest of the day. Got it!

The wind dies. Then it comes back a little later, westerly this time, right at nightfall; very gentle, but from the west. The even rustle of water cut by the bow can be heard, on a single note as there is no pitching. I sleep, I watch, I go back to sleep, back on deck to listen to the night. All night long, I will hear the rustling of clean water cut by the bow, in the great peace of the sea and the night.

By the next noon sight, 100 miles have been covered. Stewart Island, south of New Zealand, is now 32 miles to the ENE, and the dangerous outlying reef of South Trap lies barely 44 miles due east.

After that the way will be clear, with the Pacific all to myself, with only the sea and the wind as far as the Horn. For the moment, though, there is no Horn. There is only Stewart Island ringed with reefs far offshore, and South Trap awash, both in the murk.

From time to time, the pale disc of the sun shows through the clouds, and I was able to shoot a perfect sight at noon. The air was dry last night, there was no dew on deck, the clouds were stratus with no hidden tricks. Just some poor visibility, nothing serious.

The cloud cover thins, and what do I see but Stewart Island, right where it should be, little blue-tinted hillocks floating on the horizon to port. I am stirred to feel the Pacific so close. But the wind slackens to force 1 or 2. I continue SE to swing wide, because of the tidal currents which could carry me onto South Trap reef, just under the surface, 20 miles from Stewart. I give the island a long look. The last landmark to be seen before the Pacific. It disappears into the murk again, reappears a few minutes, hides behind a stratus. Hand-bearing compass. I feel happy.

Suddenly I notice I am starving. Landfalls are always like that. I brown four large onions in the pressure cooker, add a big piece of pork with a quart of rice and close it.

The wind shifts to SW force 4, barometer steady at 1012 millibars, speed nearly 7 knots. The mizzen staysail (108 sq. ft) has been up since dawn, as well as another 86 sq. ft staysail, making an extra 194 sq. ft. Come on *Joshua*, shake a leg! Try to leave South Trap in the wake before nightfall. Speed 7.2 knots. The bow purrs with pleasure. A delicious aroma of risotto keeps me company right to the forestay. Long live life, with a good bundle of wind in the sails when the coast is near!

The sky clears as the wind freshens to force 5 from the west. Really nice weather coming back! *Joshua* tears along at 7.7 knots. Coffee, cigarette. I go on deck to watch, then below again to roll myself another cigarette and dream, listening to the water rumbling on the hull; I go up again to listen on deck, forward, aft, everywhere; I trim a sheet that is already trimmed, heave taut the staysail that is just as taut as a moment ago, but I have to heave on it again; it's like that. And the pressure cooker is getting cold; I don't give a damn, I don't have time for it. When *Joshua* has crossed the longitude of South Trap I will be able to eat and sleep, with thousands of miles of open water before the bow. But South Trap is still 23 miles to the NE.

I had a bite, all the same, and muse, sitting crosslegged in front of the chart table, sipping coffee, or smoking, or glancing at the chart, or putting my head out the hatch to look forward, then at the log. No, not nervous. Just doing my job, leading *Joshua* as fast as possible along the shortest and safest path around the last pile of rock in her way at the entrance to the Pacific.

In a very short time the sky has become overcast again, from one horizon to the other. But the wind is holding, the sea is still nearly calm. Its waves have not had time to build after the long rest of the last two days. One rather curious fact, for such a high latitude (nearly 48° south): the very long, very high swell that usually comes from the SW or west is absent today. You would almost think it was the Mediterranean, with the *mistral* rising, but with an overcast sky.

I hear familiar whistlings and hurry out, as always when porpoises are around. I don't think I've ever seen so many at once. The water is white with their splashing, furrowed in all directions by the knives of their dorsal fins. There must be close to a hundred.

I would like to shoot some film, but it is too dark; the shots would not turn out, and I have no film to waste. An hour ago they would have given me the most beautiful pictures of the trip, with the sun all around.

A tight line of 25 porpoises swimming abreast goes from stern to stem on the starboard side, in three breaths, then the whole group veers right and rushes off at right angles, all the fins cutting the water together and in the same breath taken on the fly.

I watch, wonderstruck. More than ten times they repeat the same thing. Even if the sun were to return, I could not tear myself away from all this joy, all this life, to get out the Beaulieu. I have never seen such a perfect ballet. And each time, it is to the right that they rush off, whipping the sea white for thirty yards. They are obeying a precise command, that is for sure. I can't tell if it is always the same group of 20 or 25, there are too many porpoises to keep track. They seem nervous; I do not understand. The others seem nervous too, splashing along in zig-zags, beating the water with their tails, instead of playing with the bow, the way they usually do. The entire sea rings with their whistling.

Another pass from stern to stem, with the same abrupt,

graceful turn to the right. What are they playing at today? I have never seen this. . .Why are they nervous? Because they are nervous, I am sure of it. And I have never seen that, either.

Something pulls me, something pushes me. I look at the compass. *Joshua* is running downwind at 7 knots straight for Stewart Island, hidden in the stratus. The steady west wind had shifted around to the south without my realizing it. The course change was not apparent because of the quiet sea, without any swell, on which *Joshua* neither rolled nor tossed. Usually, *Joshua* always lets me know of course changes without my having to look at the compass if the sky is overcast. This time, she couldn't.

I drop the mizzen staysail, then trim the sheets and set the wind vane for a beat. We are certainly more than 15 miles from the Stewart Island rocks. But since when has *Joshua* been heading for the stratus-hidden coast? Was it before the porpoises' last pass, with their right-angle turn?. . .Or before they showed up, even before their first demonstrations?

I go below to put on my foul weather gear, as it is drizzling and there is spray now that we are closehauled. The wind has eased but not dropped, in spite of the drizzle. I wipe off my hands carefully and roll myself a cigarette, nice and dry in the cabin. I wonder about the porpoises, whose whistles I can still hear. I try, to detect a difference in the loudness of the whistling.

I am not sure there is any difference. It would be extraordinary if there were. But my ear is not keen enough, my auditory memory for sounds may be tricking me. If I were blind I could say for sure; the blind remember all sounds exactly. I do not know any more. It is so easy to make a mistake, and then believe anything. And to say anything at all.

I go back on deck after just a few drags on my cigarette. There are as many porpoises as before. But now they play with *Joshua*, fanned out ahead, in single file alongside, with the very lithe, very gay movements I have always known.

And then something wonderful happens: a big black and white porpoise jumps ten or twelve feet in the air in a fantastic somersault, with two complete rolls. And he lands flat, tail forward. Three times he does his double roll, bursting with a tremendous joy, as if he were shouting to me and all the other porpoises: 'The man understood that we were trying to tell him to sail to the right...you understood...you understood...keep on like that, it's all clear ahead!'

Standing in my foul weather gear, boots and leather gloves, I hold one of the windward mainmast shrouds. Nearly all my porpoises are now swimming on the windward side as well. That surprises me some more.

Now and then they roll onto their sides, their left eyes clearly showing. I think they are looking at me. They must see me very well, thanks to the yellow foul weather gear, which stands out against the white of the sails above the red hull.

My porpoises have been swimming around *Joshua* for over two hours. The ones I have met in the past rarely stayed more than a quarter of an hour before going on their way.

When they leave, all at once, two of them remain behind until twilight, a total of five full hours. They swim as if a little bored, one on the right, the other on the left.

For three hours longer they swim like that, each isolated on his own side, without playing, setting their speed by *Joshua*'s, two or three yards from the boat. I have never seen anything like it. Porpoises have never kept me company this long. I am sure they were given the order to stay with me until *Joshua* was absolutely out of danger.

I do not watch them all the time, because I am a little worn out by the day, by the terrific tension you do not feel at the moment, when you have to give everything you've got to pass into a new ocean.

I stretch out on the bunk for a little while, come up on deck, read the log, have a look around. My two porpoises are still there in the same place. I go below to mark the latest run on the chart, and lie down for a moment again. When I go on deck and climb the mast for the tenth time, to see further, my porpoises are still there, like two fairies in the waning light. I go below and close my eyes for a rest.

This is the first time that I feel such peace, a peace that has become a certainty, something that cannot be explained, like faith. I know I will succeed, and it strikes me as perfectly normal: that is the marvellous thing, that absolute certainty where there is neither pride nor fear nor surprise. The entire sea is simply singing in a way I had never known before, and it fills me with what is at once question and answer.

At one point, though, I am tempted to steer for the reefs, to see what my porpoises would say. Something holds me back. When I was a little boy, my mother told me fairy tales. Once upon a time a very poor fisherman caught a big fish that had all the colours of the rainbow. And the beautiful fish begged him to spare his life. So the fisherman let him go, and the magic fish told him to make a wish any time he needed something. The fisherman asked the fish to make his thatched roof stop leaking, and could he possibly have something to eat a little less seldom. And when he went back to his hut, the roof was new, the table was set, and the soup bowl was full of lentil soup with croutons. And the poor fisherman had never been so happy, as he ate his nice hot lentil soup with croutons floating on top, in his hut with the roof that didn't leak any more. Not only that, but the bed was made, with a nice dry pallet and a brand new blanket as thick as that. But the fisherman kept asking for things, and more things, and still more things. And the more he had, the more he wanted. Yet even when he owned a palace with lots of servants and a whole bunch of carriages in the courtyard, he was much less happy than when he used to eat his lentil soup with plenty of croutons on top, in his hut with the roof that didn't leak any more, and then used to go to sleep on his nice dry pallet, in the very first days of his friendship with the magic fish that had all the colours of the rainbow. So he asked to be the King. And at that the magic fish really got angry: he took away his friendship, and gave him back his hut with the leaky roof and the damp pallet and nothing in the soup bowl.

Marvellous things stir in my head and in my heart, as if they were about to overflow. It would be easy to slack the sheets a bit and run downwind for a few minutes toward the hidden reefs, to see what my porpoises would do.

It would be easy. . .but the sea is still full of their friendly whistling: I can't risk spoiling what they have already given me. And I feel I am right, as one should never treat fairy tales lightly. They have taught me to understand many things, and to respect them. Thanks to Kipling's stories, I know how Pau Amma the King Crab invented the tides in the Time of the Very

Beginnings, and why all crabs have pincers today, thanks to the little girl's golden scissors, and how the Elephant got his trunk from asking so many questions, and how the Leopard got those nice spots on his fur, and how maybe I will round the Horn thanks to porpoises and fairy tales, which helped me rediscover the Time of the Very Beginnings, where each thing is simple.

And after I plotted the last dead reckoning position on the chart, which finally put me beyond the reef, I quickly went on deck. My two porpoises were gone.

It is night. The sky has cleared, the wind is westerly again. The moon, in her first quarter, seems to hang behind the mizzen, making the sea glisten in the wake. The reef is cleared, my porpoises are gone, the way is free until the Horn.

Free on the right, free on the left, free everywhere.

Part Three

THIRTEEN

My Eldest Brother

The Indian Ocean turned out to be mild, with lots of calms and hot sun; the Tasman Sea the same. And now the Pacific seems to be following the same lead, with daily runs of 120 to 150 miles.

No reefs have been tied in, for a long time. No gales have hit in an eternity. Yesterday the wind was blowing force 5, then it eased to 4, then 3. . .and now it is barely force 2, but from the right direction, which is the main thing.

Eighty miles, 20 miles. . .63 miles, 55 miles, then 130 and 140 miles. At one point, the wind over to the east, weakly. It came back to the west, thank God. Sunshine, sunshine!

With such a fine summer and all the warmth in the air, which may reach very far south, I hope there will be no icebergs in my path.

That unknown had worried me a bit, so I wrote to some fifteen Cape Horners, asking them to let me have the benefit of their personal experience with drifting ice: 'Aside from detection by eye, what signs showed the proximity of an iceberg in your ship's lee?' The *Sailing Directions* are a bit vague on the subject in these days of radar, and I had no time to rummage through the old Naval archives in Paris.

I also asked which areas were reputed to be the most dangerous for a west to east route, in view of the fact that any icebergs encountered would be to leeward (ahead) of the boat, and the appearance of the swell therefore unchanged; also whether they had often encountered ice around the Falklands, after rounding the Horn. Icebergs are most to be feared there, as the current sometimes carries them well to the north. I mailed my letters at random, picking names and addresses from the membership list of the Cape Horner's association.

Captain François Le Bourdais, whom I knew personally, reassured me right away. He had just attended a reunion of Cape Horners and none of his fellows there had ever come across icebergs in their careers. Icebergs exist, and can be fatal...but they are not often encountered on that route, even in the very high latitudes where the clipper ships used to sail.

I got similar answers from the fifteen other veterans I had written to: only three of them had ever come across icebergs, including Georges Aubin, the author of *L'empriente de la Voile,* my favourite sea book with Slocum's. He had seen icebergs east of the Falklands, but none further north.

The two other affirmative answers came from Captains Francisque Le Goff (seven Horn passages) and Pierre Stéphan (eleven passages), each of whom had encountered icebergs in the south only once in their long careers.

Describing one of his voyages to Chile, Francisque Le Goff wrote:

> ...*Having spent twenty days in rounding the Horn and making enough westing to steer north, we encountered numerous floes and ice fields. Whereas ice on the Grand Banks cannot be seen at night, the ice around the Horn was clearly visible. Why the difference in visibility? I suppose this ice was composed of high-salinity seawater, whereas that of the Grand Banks comes from the glaciers of Greenland, and is built up with fresh water.*
>
> ...*After knocking about for a good while to make westing, we were sailing under topgallants when we entered a fog bank. Immediately, we found the ship surrounded by a swarm of little floes. The watch was doubled right away, and a few minutes later the fo'c'sle lookout warned of icebergs dead ahead. The captain ordered the necessary manoeuvres and we passed about a mile away from two veritable floating islands of ice, connected by a sea of loose ice...*
>
> ...*One cannot but conclude that large numbers of little floes are to be found in the vicinity of ice packs. Floes which are not necessarily forerunners of their proximity, since the pack drifts faster, often leaving fields of ice floes behind...*

I reread my fifteen letters slowly. I have plenty of time, here. Many are beautiful. All are encouraging.

> ...*Having nearly lost my sight, and barely able to see what I am writing, I beg your indulgence if what you read is a little uneven,*

because I am going to answer your letter to the best of my memory, still sharp despite my eighty-eight years, but I cannot reread what I am writing...

And the old Cape Horner's memory is full of seas and winds. There are eight pages of those in the letter from Captain Pierre Stéphan, with all the southern routes and eleven Horn passages in his wake.

...A little east of the Horn, many ships have been surrounded by floating ice that broke away from the shelf further south. That is how the fine three-masted Hantot, 3500 tons, which left New Caledonia fifteen days before me – then Captain of the four-masted Président Félix Faure, *3800 tons – must have become icebound after rounding the Horn. In any case, she was never seen again...*

...The only iceberg I have seen in the South Atlantic was stranded on the Falkland Bank, south of those islands. We caught sight of it at daybreak. The weather was very moderate, and I set a course bringing us within two or three miles of the enormous iceberg, which allowed us to ascertain its dimensions with the sextant: 240 ft high, 2500 to 2700 ft long. It was magnificent, an enormous mass, and we could just as well have smashed into it had there been any fog. We did not feel any temperature change passing in the iceberg's lee. True, we were two miles away...

I put my letters back in the same big padded envelope. They do not give me too much from a practical standpoint, yet they give me a lot. And I did not even answer them, in that nervous, frantic period of my preparations! I did not thank them, yet their letters are here, with their good wishes and very simple encouragement from old sailors who know that some boats always get through, and others don't. Where are Bill King, Nigel, Loïck? I have quit listening to the BBC, it is pointless. Knox-Johnston could be beyond the Horn, if he is the one the Hobart fishermen were talking about. Good luck to all. . .if it is true, we are not quite alone in this game.

The Southern Cross is high in the sky, much higher than I'd anticipated, because the fair weather is holding and I am keeping *Joshua* well down in latitude, around the 48th parallel, almost on the broken red line of the iceberg limit on the chart.

During an average year I would have worked NE right after New Zealand, to make the 40th parallel and stay far from the spells of heavy weather that are usual in the more southerly latitudes even in summer. Then I would have hugged the 40th as long as I could before shaping my course for the Horn. But I think this is an exceptional year. True, we are right in the middle of the austral summer, but the weather is still surprising for these waters, with generally all blue skies and relatively calm seas, except for the usual long SW swell that has come to look like the peaceful breathing of the universe.

Almost all of the stars are visible at one time or another in the night, right down very low on the horizon in spite of the full moon. There are often clouds but they are nice and round, not too big, with very few cirrus. And there has not been a single halo around the sun since the approaches to Cape Leeuwin, weeks and weeks ago.

The moon rises later, each night changing her shape, becoming smaller and smaller. I can understand why people in the east prefer to tell time by the moon, who changes, disappears, and then returns. I cannot say exactly what it is she helps one feel, but I think all those of who go to sea prefer the moon to the sun.

One hundred and thirty miles, 146 miles, 148 miles, 143 miles, 149 miles, 148 miles. Nothing earth-shaking, but there are still no reefs in the sails, the nights are still guileless, allowing a few turns on deck without foul weather seas, still no frowns or mares' tails in the sky, and the line drawn on the *Damien* globe steadily lengthens. It is almost to the middle of the Pacific, yet the sea is still not rumbling, the cabin hatch is almost always open, everything is nice and dry below, and spray on deck is rare.

Three years earlier, on the same route, yet much further north, the hatch was always closed from the 40th parallel on, with a thick gasket cut out of a towel to prevent icy water from squirting in. And it was exceptional for Francoise or me to go on deck without securing ourselves even for a breath of air. As for taking a sunbath, we did not even dream of it.

During the present trip, I have not yet felt the need to secure myself since Good Hope, except from time to time when reefing the staysail at night, early in the Indian Ocean. And my body is drenched with sun, as tanned as in the trades.

The background to Tahiti-Alicante had been the constant rumbling of the sea, all the way across the Pacific. A rumbling powerful or faint, depending on the weather, but always with us until beyond the Horn, where the great westerly swell is stopped by Tierra Del Fuego. We were surprised then, not to hear the noise in the background, like beach pebbles rolled by the sea.

It really is a fine year, such as must be rare on this southern route. I remember the little plastic bags we used to fasten at our ankles with rubber bands to protect our precious double-thick wool socks from the always wet cabin floor. Woolen gloves inside, mittens and leather gloves for handling sail, chapped fingers, the essential boots, the few clothes we would dry every day above the stove. Even the blankets were more or less damp and covered with salt.

Now. . .the temperature in the unheated cabin is 55° at dawn, 75° at noon. My supply of plastic bags is untouched. I am almost always barefoot on deck, and my clothes are as dry as when I left.

On the other hand, these two months of fair weather must have surely caused an early break-up of the ice in the far south, and I would not be surprised to learn that the icebergs went beyond their normal limit this year. In any case. I have absolutely no idea. I am wool-gathering as usual, as I often do when everything is for the best, and all you have to do is breathe peacefully and thank heaven for its gifts. Anyway, it is likely that the break-up of the pack that sets the icebergs adrift is more closely linked to seismic shocks and heavy gales than to the sun . . . There I go again, my thoughts wandering off in every direction. Not out of anxiety though; far from it. I feel joyful, surrounded by something very imminent in the air around me. I call it 'my eldest brother', the way you call your friends in the Far East. I talk to him a lot: I feel that we agree, but he does not answer. He must have his hands full keeping lows away. Or maybe he thinks I should figure things out for myself, alone with my solitude, so vast and so full.

My hair has grown a lot; it is almost down to my shoulders. My beard is so long I have to trim it around my lips every week, so as to eat my morning porridge without smearing it all over. My last complete soaping dates back to a rain squall in the doldrums, months ago. . .yet I do not have a single pimple on my skin.

It seems a warrior people of some period or other executed any man of their army found washing, because it would make him lose his virility. And one fine day the general himself was caught soaking in the River Ganges. At the court-martial, he just barely saved himself by explaining that he had lost his mistress' ring, and that a Brahmin told him it fell in the water, where he was looking. Well, the Marshal let him off for that once, perhaps because he really valued the commander, or possibly because the next big battle was not scheduled for a while, and the general would have enough time to get his virility back.

I would like to take a dip in the Ganges. . .not to wash, I don't need to; no, just for fun.

Joshua is half way to the Horn. For five days in a row I have done my yoga exercises completely naked in the cockpit, before the meridian sight. I feel the sun entering into me, giving me its power. When there is no sun, or toward the end of the afternoon, I keep a sweater and wool trousers on, and the power comes from the air I breathe.

Physical and mental balance after five months at sea still comes as a surprise, when I look at the long, long curve on the little globe. Certainly I knew it was possible when I left. Anything is possible. . .it's a matter of attitude and instinctive adaptation. But I never thought it possible to attain such fullness of body and mind after five months in a closed system, with a stomach ulcer I have been dragging around for the last ten years.

I am not able to check my weight, because the westerly swell, in evidence despite the fair weather, throws the scales' readings off. Still, I have probably gained a couple of pounds since Tasmania. I have seldom felt so healthy. My ulcer has not bothered me since the middle of the Indian Ocean, and my appetite is excellent.

While many crews were decimated by sickness and scurvy during the long exploration voyages of past centuries, others (Captain Cook's in particular) used to come back in fairly good shape despite months and months at sea, often under extremely hard conditions. Cook avoided vitamin deficiency by making his men drink a kind of 'beer' every day, made on board out of crushed pine needles.

Before leaving, I paid a long visit to Jean Rivolier, chief physician for the French Polar Expeditions (Paul-Emile Victor Missions). His practical experience is genuine, drawn from his trips to the Arctic and Antarctic, as well as mountaineering. He told me (see Appendix) just to be sensible enough to cook varied and appetizing meals, without ever letting myself start down the dangerous slope of alimentary anarchy, which would consist, for example, of eating the same thing too often, fixed the same way or not fixed at all.

I have plenty of all kinds of canned food, enough for a year if necessary. That way I would be self sufficient in case of dismasting, or if I had had to land on a lost atoll, with nothing to eat but the good Lord's coconuts and the sea urchins of the reef (fish is too often poisonous in the atolls). I really have everything I need on board except talent as a chef. There is always something missing, or something extra in my cooking, but I never know just what is it. You're either gifted or you're not—and I'm not. Cooking reminds me of beautiful music: I can appreciate it, delight in it, but not produce it.

I have been at sea for barely five months. The 28 men of the *Endurance* had already been sailing for eleven months when the ship was crushed by ice in the Weddel Sea and had to be abandoned. For another ten months those men continued across the shelf on foot, towing two whaleboats around the blocks of ice. All returned intact, except for one frozen foot, 21 months after weighing anchor[1].

Aside from a few exceptional men, the rest of the team were probably fairly average. But the limits of human endurance are much greater than one would think. In the Far East I have seen what coolies can take, working from dawn to dusk on just a little rice, dried fish and bouillon with a few greens floating in it.

The barometer begins to fall. Mackerel sky stretches across the horizon. There is a lot of wind up there, and the barograph track is full of jerks. After two months of fair weather it had to happen sooner or later, in spite of the gods' protection. The sea is not rumbling yet, but it looks like the graph already, full of nervous tremors.

All steps are taken on deck: 54 sq. ft storm jib, a reef in the staysail, two in the main, mizzen close-reefed. I replaced the

[1] *Endurance: Shackleton's Incredible Voyage* by Alfred Lausing.

usual wind vane by another half the size, and altered course to ENE (almost NE) to get away from both the path of the low and the iceberg limit.

There could be many days and nights at the inside helm if the gale really hits. On two occasions I have stayed at the wheel for 72 hours, the first on *Marie-Thérèse* watching the coast and reefs in the straits of Malacca, the second on *Marie-Thérèse II,* rounding the Cape of Good Hope. There, I steered falling *deeply* asleep in the troughs, and waking up just before each wave, in order to take it on the stern. The extended Tahiti-Alicante gale proved very tiring, because I did not pick up the rhythm right away, and too soon reached the brink of exhaustion.

Now I am probably much better prepared to face prolonged fatigue thanks to yoga, which I have been practising daily since the dangerous rock-bottom period at the beginning of the Indian Ocean. I was on the point of giving up then, and steering for Mauritius. My ulcer was causing me pain. I was really low, mentally and physically.

A year before sailing, a pal had sent me *Yoga for Everyone* by Desmond Dunne, with a letter in which he tried to explain that the rhythm of Europe was making me nervous and tired. Yoga, which he had practised for two years, had enabled him and his wife to regain their balance. Everything he said was true, and I knew it. I had even known it for a long time. . .

When I first leafed through the book in the Indian Ocean, I felt it emanating all the values of my native Asia, all the wisdom of the old East, and I found a few little exercises I had always done instinctively when I was tired. My ulcer stopped bothering me, and I no longer suffered from lumbago. But above all, I found something more. A kind of undefinable state of grace. Some people may possess it by birth or instinct. Others can find it someday in the course of their lives; no one will ever know and it does not matter. The main point is that it exists, and with it things take their natural place, their proper balance in the whole within.

The moon is gone. She will be back in a few days, like a smile, very shy at first, then bigger and bigger. The barometer is falling now, but life goes on at its normal pace, even with the threat of a gale. How long will it last, this peace I have found at sea? It is all of life that I contemplate—sun, clouds, time that passes and abides. Occasionally it is also that other world, foreign now, that I left centuries ago. The modern, artificial world where man has been turned into a money-making machine to satisfy false needs, false joys.

The gale turns the sea white with foam. I drop the mainsail, then the mizzen. *Joshua* tears along through the night under single-reefed staysail and the storm jib, surfing once in a great while on the front of the waves. The little wind vane takes care of everything, correcting the yawing, taking advantage of the peace in the troughs to get back on the right course.

Sitting on the inside steering seat, I watch the phosphorescent water through the portholes of the dome that protects me from the breaking seas as it brings me closer to them. I have almost reached a turning point along my way. I know, I have known since the Indian Ocean, that I no longer want to go back.

From inside, the rumble of the sea sounds muted, as it tells me lots of things. Present things, past things, future things. It is all there, in the sea, and I think joy is the highest expression of life. But the real turning will be after the Horn.

If I hold on, if *Joshua* holds on, then we will try to go further. Round Good Hope again, round Tasmania again, across the whole Pacific again. . .and reach the Galapagos to quietly add things up. Now, too, I could steer for the Galapagos: just a push to the right on the tiller, and continue north; they are so close, I could be there in a few weeks. . .But it would be too soon. I have not really found my Ganges yet, and would blame myself for the rest of my life; it would be as if I had not even tried. I remember a little temple I once found in the forest . . . no, I don't remember anything; I must not remember anything.

Until the Horn, don't look beyond *Joshua*, my little red and white planet made of space, pure air, stars, clouds and freedom in its deepest, most natural sense. And completely forget the world, its merciless rhythm of life. Back there, if a businessman could put out the stars to make his billboards look better at night, he just might do it.

Live only with the sea and my boat, for the sea and for my boat.

FOURTEEN

Joshua
against Joshua

The gale passes over. Not too serious. Twenty hours of force 8 gusting to 9, and the wind vane snapped at night by a breaking wave. Quickly replaced by another, all set to go.

As a rule, a westerly gale in the high austral latitudes is linked to a low; the wind first blows hard from the NW, then shifts to west, then SW. At that point the heavy chop raised by the gale's initial NW phase crosses and overlaps the constant westerly swell, made very heavy by the stress of the wind from the west. This causes sometimes dangerous breaking seas that strike on the quarter, and dictate a course change to south of east when the sea really gets angry.

The sea gets angry, but not too much. I don't even have to steer, sitting in the steering seat, just looking, listening, feeling. The sea has quickly become very heavy and *Joshua* surfs willingly. She has got still lighter over the months. The bow lifts nicely; she can surf without any danger of pitchpoling. . .at least in this sea.

The weather is dull. The wind eases, becoming SW. Then the sky clears in less than half an hour. Sun. . .blazing sun.

I take advantage of a bucket of fresh water collected by the mainsail to rinse four pairs of socks. I hang them up to dry high in the mizzen stays after threading them one after the other on a little line, like fish strung by their gills. A few stitches may break, but it is more secure than clothespins, and I prefer socks full of loose stitches more than socks gone in the wind. I am using a lot of them these days. Although I do my best to seal the foul weather trousers against my boots with a ring of inner tube to keep the water out, it often seeps through. For all my promising to put the wet socks back on when I have to go handle sails . . .I wear the dry pair I put on in the cabin, and they get soaked when I stay on deck longer than necessary, which often happens.

It is getting cold. The sea is icy. It surely was before, but since there was little water on deck, I did not realize just how cold it was. When it gets into my boots, my hair stands on end for a few seconds.

This first gale of the Pacific seems to mark a kind of 'before' and 'after' boundary. It really feels like the high latitudes now, where the sea is always a bit angry, even when everything seems all right.

Overcast again. Mackerel sky, mares' tails. Invisible cirrostratus, shown only by the halo around the sun. Barograph line full of shivers. Four albatrosses and three malamocks. And the log turns and turns: 152 miles, 166, 158, 147, 162, 169.

The bow rumbles day and night. Worried rumbling, quiet rumbling, joyous rumbling, all depending on little things, on a ray of sunshine showing through the clouds at times, on the barograph line, on the NW swell, on the long strong swell coming from the west after rounding the world millions of times.

Joshua regularly knocks off her 10° of longitude every three days, over a thousand miles a week. And two boats that are the same race each other across the chart where three years earlier I had pencilled in the noon positions of Tahiti-Alicante. The present track is nearly straight, fast, standing out boldly on the chart and the *Damien* globe, on which I bear down hard with my ballpoint, well to the south on the shortest reasonable route. It is far from the timid pencil line of Tahiti-Alicante, distinctly further north, slower, a bit irregular, as if gnawed by a kind of fear. I also know fear a little, now, but it is not the same.

It seems the cabin hatch has been shut for days, under a sky that is nearly always grey. It sometimes takes more than an hour's watch on deck before I can trap a pale sun in the sextant between two layers of stratus. It often rains, and the sea rumbles continuously. Frequent cross-seas slap the boat hard, without warning. Torrents of solid water then sweep across the lee deck, and would carry anything away. Only a diving suit could keep my socks from getting wet. Three pairs dangle permanently above the stove.

Handling sail without a safety harness is out of the question; it could be fatal. I am still not quite used to it though; with the harness on I feel tangled up, unable to move freely. To be sure of not forgetting, I stuff it into the chest pocket of my foul weather gear as soon as I get undressed in the cabin after working on deck. That way it is always handy, since I no longer go on deck without foul weather gear.

When I step into the cockpit to fill my lungs and talk with the sea, I leave the harness in the pocket, because I keep hold of the cabin hatch cover then, eyes and ears everywhere at once for erratic breaking seas, ready to open the hatch and jump inside to safety. A second and a half is all I need to open the cover, step through the hatch, quickly flop down on the inside steering seat and slam the hatch over my head, pulling down hard so that the neoprene seal fits tight all around. With the harness I would feel less mobile. And there is something else. . .the intimate participation with things around me. The harness would only link me to some steel cleat, not to the rest.

My harness is marked 'Annie' with India ink. It was part of *Captain Browne's* gear when Loïck got his boat from the Van de Wieles. He kept Louis' harness, and gave me Annie's. I removed the shoulder straps, which were too short and would have hampered me. It is less efficient without shoulder straps but easier to put on and take off. Also, I feel less trapped without them.

The descent towards the Horn has been under way for a week; a little hesitantly at first, to let a second gale pass by.

Rain, hail, heavy breaking seas, occasionally impressive surfing. No damage done, no violent thrills except for the beauty of *Joshua* scudding along close-reefed in the light of the sky and sea as the wind swings around to SW.

No damage done. . .but I suspect my Beaulieu has died this time. It took a big blast of spray as I was filming breaking waves, and water entered the cable release opening on the side. I should have covered the hole with tape.

Without much faith, I stick a match wrapped with cotton in the hole to absorb the salt water. I do it five or six times, until the cotton comes out dry. Then I use cotton moistened with fresh water to dissolve any remaining salt, then more cotton warmed over a flame to dry everything out.

I press the shutter. It works! Sputtering a little, the camera comes back to life. I gingerly rewind the film. Now the film is safe: I'm lucky. Hope it will show the last breaking sea that I was filming. I take the reel out and gently warm the camera above the Primus stove, then stuff it with hot, dry newspapers.

In a saucepan, I heat the packets of moisture-absorbing silica gel. I warm some more newspapers on the stove, screw back the lenses, and wrap the Beaulieu in warm newspaper with the silica gel, after checking to see that it still works. A bad blow, if the camera had let me down. It has become a real friend. I believe it helped me to see things that I may not have seen as clearly on my own, during the voyage.

The wind has dropped and shifted to the NW, force 4 with drizzle. I don't like NW winds; they almost always bring some sort of trouble.

There is another bucket of rainwater under the mainsail boom. So far in the Pacific, I have collected 19 gallons of water, three-quarters of what I used in the last 35 days (at $2\frac{1}{2}$ quarts a day). During *Joshua*'s 56 day Indian Ocean crossing, she collected slightly more than my needs: 40 gallons, of which I used about 35.

All in all I am all right as far as the fresh water supply is concerned; the tank level is nearly the same as at the start. I think that a boat big enough to carry lots of food and spares could circle the globe several times, relying only on rain.

I used this morning's bucketfull to wash the dish towel. A mistake, as it turns out. Last washed in the Atlantic doldrums, the dish towel helped me anticipate weather changes, now that I no longer have lumbago when the humidity increases.

When the dish towel could stand up it meant dry air and I could expect regular SW winds for a while, with relatively nice weather and a generally blue sky aside from the normal cirrus and round cumulus. When it stood a little less stiffly, it was almost always the sign of a swing to the west, as the wind was already not so dry. And when my towel looked all droopy and clammy, as if it had wiped away all the sins of the world, I could expect northerly winds loaded with wet clouds.

The towel is drying now, snapping gaily under six clothes-pins, as high up as possible in the mizzen shrouds. No matter though; my quilted suit with the little songbird and the bubble-blowing fish warns me in much the same way. Still, it can't hold a candle to the dish towel in its day.

Four peaceful days, with 130, 111, 147 and 142 miles, and almost no spray on deck. The sky clears completely towards 10 o'clock and I treat myself to the luxury of a total sunbath during the noon sight on the 49th parallel, a thousand miles from the Horn.

The air being dry again, I hang two blankets in the mizzen shrouds, and vigorously shake the pillowcases on deck; the hatch is wide open for the first time in a long while. Everything goes back as dry as it was the day we left!

Yet, lots of cirrus and cirrocumulus blanket the sky, and the sun warms timidly. The sea is beautiful though, with neither spray nor whitecaps, the wind down to a mere force 3. All the high clouds are moving at right angles to the surface wind, coming from the left as you face the wind. That is the sign of a low approaching from the west or SW, particularly with the 22° halo I have seen around the sun at noon. The barograph line is steady though, without a quiver. It is even 3 millibars higher than usual, and I can't detect the characteristic NW swell.

Overcast, drizzle, WSW wind fresh to strong in spite of the drizzle. With real luck I catch the sun through the veil of low stratus, after spending two hours on deck freezing my feet while it played hide-and-seek.

Tahiti-Alicante continues to take a daily beating of 20 to 40 miles; its daily runs have only surpassed ours now twice in three weeks. But Tahiti-Alicante still holds one enormous edge: having already rounded the Horn without getting knocked out.

I spend long periods on deck, day and night. In the cabin I often gaze at the little globe. The Galapagos are 3,000 miles north. A stone's throw. There is a long way to go yet. I must not look eastward too much. . .the way is so long still, I must not think about it.

I am neither happy nor sad, neither really tense nor really relaxed. Perhaps that is the way it is when a man gazes at the stars, asking himself questions he is not mature enough to answer. So one day he is happy, the next a bit sad without knowing why. It is a little like the horizon: for all your distinctly seeing sky and sea come together on the same line, for all your constantly making for it, the horizon stays at the same distance, right at hand and out of reach. Yet deep down you know that the way covered is all that counts.

Tasmania is more than 5,000 miles astern, the Horn 900 ahead. *Joshua* is now just to the south of the route she took three years ago. We had the same kind of weather. Worried, like Chuchundra the muskrat, who grazes the walls and never dares to run across the room, we had kept to the north of the route as long as possible, to travel in a zone where gales were less frequent. Less violent too, than further south: we had just taken a terrible beating on the 43rd parallel, the kind of beating you remember to the end of your days. And after that, you know that experience does not carry much weight in the face of a *real* gale in these waters, where the sea can become monstrous, with breaking waves that are hardly believable. For a long time, I had thought they could hit at speeds up to 15–25 knots. In fact, the breaking seas of the biggest gale *Joshua* ever encountered in the South Pacific did not exceed a maximum of 15 knots, and their impact was only around 10 to 11 knots as the boat was running with them. I was able to check their speed fairly accurately by timing the passage from stern to bow. And a breaking sea striking at a relative speed of 10 or 11 knots is very manageable for a decent boat if taken astern, provided she is not in danger of pitchpoling.

During the same gale, I saw a pyramidal sea, probably caused by the overlapping of several large waves crossing together at different angles. It collapsed like an avalanche, and the sound it gave made me think of a distant thunderstorm. Eyes wide, I watched and listened, every hair on my skin standing straight up. It was breaking two or three hundred yards off, and the sea was angry all around, Yet neither the sea nor the boat could be heard anymore, only the roaring of that wave, cascading for long seconds and covering all the other sounds.

The sea has been rumbling for two weeks and I handle sails with the help of a $\frac{3}{16}$ in. steel wire stretched flat on the deck from stem to stern on either side. Bill King gave me the idea. He has to use this safety system, his boat having neither guardrails nor shrouds for handholds. I then saw it on Jean-Michel Barrault's *Corsen* a few weeks before leaving and Loïck and I hurried to outfit our boats the same way. It is so handy I would now find it hard to do without: you simply clip a harness snap onto it, and then move about freely; the snap need not be transferred as it slides along the wire. The second snap is held in your hand ready to be clipped to a shroud or anywhere else. It is almost 100 per cent safe; only a terrible breaking sea could sweep you from the deck, especially with both hands free to grab anything along the way. But it does not insure one against floundering around with boots full of icy water at times, not to speak of what comes in at the collar and sleeves of foul weather gear.

The wind shifts to WNW with a heavy swell from the NW. The barometer is still falling. It is blowing force 6, at times 7. Not a sign is missing, so I will drop the mizzen staysail and probably put an extra reef in the mizzen and main before dusk. Then I will spend the night half awake, half asleep, like a cat waiting to pounce but not moving a muscle until the right moment.

The wind, the calms, the fog, the sun are all the same, a single huge presence in which everything mingles and blends into a great light that is life.

At times there is anxiety as well. But in the very depths of that anxiety is the inner joy of the sea, and that sweeps everything else away.

The gale will hit soon, I am almost sure. Yet it does not worry me. . .well, not too much.

One hundred and sixty-six miles. . .and no gale! I feel light. I am almost sorry, though, not to be equipped to talk with ham radio operators; they would have given me news of my friends, helped us to communicate.

We crossed the 50th parallel yesterday and are really in high latitudes, where weather changes very fast, for better as for worse.

Yesterday before sunset the wind had risen to a good force 7, and I dropped the mizzen staysail and took another reef in the mizzen and main. Two hours later, the sky partly cleared, the heavy NW swell eased, and I knew there would be no gale. A little rain fell toward 11 p.m. when a big cumulo-nimbus went, and I poured a quart and a half of water collected by the mainsail into my kettle. It gave me an odd feeling, transferring the rainwater from the sails directly into the pot, ready for breakfast. I made some coffee right away, rolled myself a cigarette, to savour it with the coffee. The barometer stopped falling, the wind did not exceed force 6, the nearly full moon lit up the entire sea astern when it came out between the masses of cumulus, and there was no more cirrus. I shook a reef out of the main and mizzen. The wind was on the point of swinging to the west, then SW. It should increase a little as the barometer rose, but it might increase a lot at the moment of the swing. I preferred to double reef the mainsail and mizzen, so as to sleep quietly until dawn. Then I warmed myself another mug of coffee, which I drank in little swallows, sitting on the inside steering seat and watching a broad clear streak coming from the west. More and more stars came out, filling the sky on the quarter. The swing to the west. Not too strong. I went on deck to harden in the sheets a little, and *Joshua* started surfing on the face of the NW swell, which had become friendly, rounded and regular.

I then curled up in my bunk, nice and warm, nice and dry, after a last look at the curve on the globe. It is getting very close to the Horn; another five to six days if all goes well. But I refuse to see beyond the Horn. I only think my padded suit will not be as clammy at the knees tomorrow, and the thought fills me with tranquility.

I am up before dawn, as usual. In the high latitudes dawn tells what the day will be like. When the sun rises red, it is a bad sign. Dawn here should be a little milky. It is the opposite in the trades, where a red sun rising heralds a beautiful day, nicer than usual.

Today, the dawn is just middling. That is already a lot, and I shake out all the reefs, including the one in the staysail. The bow rumbles louder than the sea—wonderful.

One hundred and sixty-nine miles at the noon sight, and I am staying well within the limits of my strength. Tahiti-Alicante takes another 40 miles in the ear! The difference in efficiency is largely due to the boat's now having a set of small, easily handled sails with lots of reef bands, a present to my boat for this trip. Also to the winches, which were not there before.

Three years ago *Joshua* would not have covered more than 120 to 130 miles noon to noon in these unstable weather conditions. We would have dropped the storm jib before nightfall, as the old one measured 86 sq. ft, far too much in case of a real gale. We would probably have also dropped the mainsail last night; close-reefed, the old main covered 194 sq. ft, and could have made for real problems in lowering and furling it if the weather took an abrupt turn for the worse. So *Joshua* would have lost speed during the night.

Sail trimming used to be hard too. I often hesitated to shake a reef out of the mainsail, knowing that I might have to take it in again a little later. And that meant fewer miles again. Tightening the halyards after reefing or shaking reefs out was irksome as well. Everything had to be done by hand, and finished off with block and tackle—without forgetting the gloves, so my chapped hands would not get worse. Nowadays, two turns on the winch, and presto!...the sail is up taut without any fuss.

Force 8 squalls and hail. I help the tiller to minimize yawing, and bring the wind astern at times to relieve the sails. Only force 5 between the squalls.

Everything settles down at nightfall, the cumulus shrink, the squalls stay under force 6, the horizon clears to the west. The stars come out as the night begins.

I set the mizzen staysail again by the light of the moon. She is full tonight, and will be full for rounding the Horn, in less than 48 hours at this rate.

I am not sleepy; I spend a long time in the cockpit watching the sea. The Horn is so close, the sea so beautiful it really breathes. A moonbeam bounces off a cloud far to the south, becoming a slender spire of softly glowing light rising straight up in the sky. I am wonderstruck. How did the moon pull off such a lovely trick?

The spire widens, glows very brightly. It looks like a huge spotlight searching among the stars. Three times in my life I have seen the green flash above the setting sun like an emerald tongue that suddenly flares up, but I would never have believed this other miracle of the moon playing with a cloud.

A chill comes over me. It isn't the moon playing with a cloud, but something uncanny I don't know about. Could it be the white arch of Cape Horn, that terrifying thing Slocum mentions, the sign of a big gale? The stars shine with a hard glint and the sea looks menacing beneath the icy moon.

A second spire rises next to the first. Then a third. Soon there are a dozen, like a huge bouquet of super-natural light. And now I understand...it is an aurora australia, the first I have ever seen, perhaps this voyage's most precious gift to me.

It adorns itself with new branches, spreads out, soaring like a sheaf. One of the spires, now almost a hand's breadth across, rises over more than half the sky to the Southern Cross. Other glowing rays shrink and hesitate on the point of vanishing, then soar again towards the sky with very slow, sweeping motions, like the long spines of certain bluish sea urchins. Now all the spires are tipped with pink and blue; the whole sheaf is alive like fire, with the strength and gentleness of fire, above the reflected white of the ice fields away to the south.

The stratus drift across the night, hiding first the moon, then the stars above the boat, then my aurora. For nearly an hour I watched it, the most beautiful thing I have ever seen.

Dawn is overcast, with drizzle and fog. Just the same, my eldest brother has really been on the job, pushing the anticyclone far to the south: the barometer is higher than normal. I hope it will stay at the same figure for two more days. The barometer. . .a little genie both evil and kindly according to its mood. I always have an urge to beat it when it falls, and kiss it when it rises.

The average is 120 miles a day for the Pacific, against 115 three years ago. . .but for the moment Tahiti-Alicante is still ahead. And Chuchundra runs as fast as he can.

FIFTEEN

One
Night . . .

The night looks wrapped in milky cotton. The full moon shines through from time to time when the fogbanks turn wispy under the stratus. The entire sea glows with greenish, phosphorescent sheets. It is hardly rumbling, because the fog muffles all sounds. Perhaps also because the Horn is so close now, and the secondary wave trains are no longer those of the open sea.

On one side lies Tierra del Fuego, a safe distance away, but already close enough for no major swell to come from there. Graham Land with its ice fields is on the other, 500 miles SSE: very near on the globe's scale, very far on mine. And ahead is Cabo de Hornos with its associated islands nearby, blocking any swell from the east.

That must be why the sea rumbles so little despite the wind and the surprising height of the seas around the Horn. Also, the wind is NW, almost NNW, coming more or less from the land.

It is not a gale in the real sense of the word, since the barometer is almost quiet, though falling very slowly. Yet the wind is blowing a good force 7, and *Joshua* drives along under close-reefed mizzen, double-reefed main, single-reefed staysail and the 54 sq. ft storm jib. She is moving very fast, yawing a little too much in the heavy sea. But deciding to shorten sail is hard as long as there is no real threat and you want to get to the other side as quickly as possible.

I barely managed a perfect sight this morning. The sun kept under wraps for hours, but had a moment's inattention as some thinner stratus went by, and I threw his pale, ugly mug down to the horizon. Same bit of luck for the second sight just two hours later. Such a short time between lines is far from ideal, but I was happy enough; it rained for the noon sight and the sun has not appeared since.

I hope to see it for a moment tomorrow morning, so as not

to have to grope my way between Diego Ramirez and the Horn. Too far north there is Tierra del Fuego, too far south the risk of icebergs.

The bow rumbles in the milky night. You have to get close to hear it well. In the cabin, on the other hand, the sound is everywhere. We are driving hard.

According to the almanac, the sun set at 8 o'clock. I did not see it because of the cloudy weather. But the moon is out above the stratus clouds, so the night is softly luminous. If the sky were not overcast I would see the entire starboard horizon white with sunlight reflected by the ice. Sailing the free channels of the pack . . . Still, I would be afraid to go that far to the land of white. Just after New Zealand, when the weather was so fine, I often glanced that way. Just a detour to see and feel, then quickly leave again before it was too late, a vision of white stippled with blue-tinted icebergs within me forever.

I have been at the foot of the mast for hours now, ready to drop the main, my harness clipped on at two different points. *Joshua* scuds along the fine edges between the limits of 'too much' and 'not enough', on the very high sea carpeted with long, pale sheets of foam. And always, the milky night muffling everything.

The wind increases to force 8. I am really glad I set the storm jib instead of the working jib this morning. Changing the sail now would annoy me for lots of reasons. I want to be left in peace, and I am.

Very little water on deck, except for spray. My feet are warm and comfortable in their wool socks deep in their boots. They are the same ones I used during Tahiti-Alicante: peasant boots, with heavy, thick soles I had scored with a knife to make skidproof. They became excellent after that drawn-out day-long job, and since they are rubber, without any canvas, they can dry inside and my feet stay warm. I much prefer them to my real seaboots, which always stay damp because of their canvas lining.

I pull off a glove from time to time, and put it back when my fingers begin to stiffen with cold. Then I take off my woollen hood, and put it back again when my ears start to burn. This evening, more than ever, I feel a visceral need to leave some part of my body in direct contact with that which is around, to feel the things that live in the very depths of the night. Eyes,

ears, hands; even the nape of my neck. If I could be barefoot. . .but that is not possible.

I am seeking a smell, that of the glaciers and seaweed of
Tierra del Fuego. I breathe in the night to the bottom of my
being, and feel something like friendly presences seeking the
smell with me. But the seaweed and glaciers are much too far,
more than a hundred miles to the left.

A bit cool, for a NW wind in this season. Must be blowing from
the north across the channels of Patagonia, turning cold in
contact with the frozen earth. Over the open sea the wind is
probably deflected eastward by the belt of the westerlies,
ending up as a NW wind, cold for no apparent reason. It
would explain this gale that is not a real one, since the
barometer is not too low. It would also explain the fairly
regular sea, despite the exceptional height of the waves. They
break in huge sheets, not in heavy cascades as they would in a
real gale. That is why there is so little water on deck, apart from
the freezing spray that jolts me out of my torpor.

A swell this high may portend a westerly gale for tomorrow
or the day after, so we must run very fast, try to stay balanced at
the limit. If it hits tomorrow, the Horn will protect us by
breaking the swell, as *Joshua* will already be making for the
Falklands in the Atlantic.

But if it hits tomorrow, on the 50 fathom shoal where the
enormous swell can rear up as it does off a beach, then I hope
there will at least be some sun and visibility before Diego
Ramirez to aim true, not too far and not too close. Meanwhile. . .full speed ahead.

The lower part of the staysail is full of living pearls. They reach
almost a third of the way up, then run off along the bunt of the
reef. They come from the phosphorescent foam picked up by
the bow and shattered by the whisker stay. If it were daylight,
with the sun on the right side, there would be a big rainbow
spread over fifteen yards in the lee of the bow. It would be no
more beautiful than these thousands of little green stars glittering in the semi-dark of the austral night. The bowsprit is full of
them too, brighter than those of the staysail because the black
of the bowsprit stands out sharply against the clear background of the night.

Here and there, large flashes the size of a soccer ball appear in the sea, shining like giant glow warms. I have often seen them in the trades, and kept them in sight for sometimes thirty seconds before they went out. At first, I took them for the eyes of strange animals risen from the depths. I had even harpooned them, from the deck of my second *Marie-Thérèse,* both disappointed and relieved not to haul up a giant squid gnashing its beak at the end of my harpoon.

Nearly midnight. I am not sleepy. I wait at the foot of the mainmast. I can feel it quiver under my hand during the gusts. Things are still all right. . .

I am almost positive the wind will ease; it has gone to NNW, which proves conclusively that a low is not involved. Yet I know there is no such thing as conclusive proof here. Proof comes later, when you have gone through. And it is still not proof.

I nevertheless decide to take the last reef in the mainsail. It is tiny now, with its big number '2' right next to the boom. I feel better; my feet are warmer than a while ago.

The mast has stopped quivering, except when the staysail pulls too hard in a gust. Taking in its second reef is out of the question. The second staysail reef is only for when it blows to death.

The clearing I was waiting for, without really daring to believe, for fear of the evil eye. The high latitude clearing! It appears like a great light. The sky clears to windward, and its brightness envelops the boat, driving SE the last banks of stratus and the fog beneath. In a few minutes the stars have reclaimed the sky. There is a lot of wind up there, they are twinkling very strongly. But there is little cirrus across the round moon. I hope she will be up when we pass the Horn, early tomorrow night if all goes well. The moon is low, even though she just crossed her meridian, because her declination is north, whereas we are in 56° south latitude. I have never seen the Southern Cross so high, nor so brilliant. The two little nebulae located in the extension of its long axis, straight above the Pole, remind me of two phosphorescent islands. Yet the sky looks like dawn. To the left the full moon, to the right the reflection of the ice fields in the southern sky, and all around the silvery carpet of the sea breaking in long lengths.

The globes of fire that I saw in the waves earlier can be seen

more than a hundred yards away now that the fog has lifted.
They are plankton colonies, not the eyes of monster squids; I
read the explanation somewhere. But I will probably never
know why they shine so brightly, only to suddenly go out for
no apparent reason. I would like *Joshua* to surf into one: at
that speed, it would make fabulous fireworks in the staysail.

Past midnight. The wind is not easing. The seas are high, very
high. The moon probably adds to the impression of height, by
leaving the advancing wave faces in shadow, darker than all
the white around. I ought to drop the main entirely, and
perhaps the staysail. With only the storm jib and close-reefed
mizzen, *Joshua* would still do very well, and stay this side of
going too fast. But we are surfing; it is breathtaking at times,
the log has already registered 48 miles in six hours. The hull
speed has been exceeded. And. . .I don't know, shortening sail
right now, no. . .Some sort of a rhythm would be lost. The
Horn is too close for shortening sail as long as things are all
right, even if they are not quite what they should be.

During the last third of the advancing slope of each sea, the
wind increases to force 9 for a few seconds. Then everything
turns white, the boat luffs about 10° in the gust, and I grip the
mainsail halyard tighter. The last third of the advancing face
always provokes that little gust which draws forward 10° or so,
fills the sails to the limit, and starts us surfing.

I feel a dangerous urge to go out on the bowsprit pulpit. . .I
don't dare go beyond the staysail: it marks the farthest limit
of good sense. In surfing, water is no longer water, but rock.

The swirls of foam raised by the bow fly in the lee of the
hull for a few seconds, a light mist eddying behind the bellied
staysail. The swirl goes on ahead and the boat tries to catch
up. She sometimes makes it when surfing down a sea. A
dangerous game, tremendously elating in this somewhat
unreal world.

My ears are burning. I put my inner hood back on, pull the
hood of my foul weather gear over it, and the sound of the ocean
becomes a distant rumble, as in a seashell.

I listen, I feel, I sift the invisible. A delicious warmth runs
down my leg. I am vaguely surprised; it is already past. It saved
me the complexities of zippers and trouser buttons, which
might have prevented my perceiving something essential.

I try to sense the ice and seaweed that lie in the haze of distance. I know it is impossible, so far away, but I need to search to know what is beyond it.

A swirl of spray skims above the water along the windward side. Conical at first, it takes the shape of a little wave as an eddy from the bow sends it off to the right. The night is so clear I can see the little wave changing shape again. *Joshua* surfs after it, yawing far to starboard in pursuit of the phantom. Falling off. . .not luffing, as she should have.

A gust. This time *Joshua* luffs with more heel. The bowsprit buries itself and solid water roars across the deck. I grip the stay hard. The little wind vane is still there. It must have dunked in the sea when we heeled, but did not break. I blow it a kiss.

A sea approaches, fairly high, all light at the summit, black below. . .and vroouuum. . .the keel hardly wavers in the 20 or 25 yards. A great plume shoots up on either side of the bow, climbs high, filled with swirls which the wind throws down into the staysail, and some into the storm jib.

I listen. One surfing run taken the wrong way in the clear night. . .and my beautiful bird of the capes would go on her way with the ghosts in the foam, guided by a seagull or a porpoise. I am not sure which I would prefer, a gull or a porpoise.

Joshua drives toward the Horn under the light of the stars and the somewhat distant tenderness of the moon. Pearls run off the staysail; you want to hold them in your hand, they are real precious stones, that live only in the eyes. The wake spins out very far behind up the slopes of the seas like a tongue of fire and the close-reefed sails stand out against the clear sky, with the moon making the sea on the quarter glisten. White reflection of the southern ice. Broad greenish patches of foam on the water. Pointed tooth-like seas masking the horizon, dull rumbling of the bow struggling and playing with the sea.

The entire sea is white and the sky as well. I no longer quite know how far I have got, except that we long ago left the borders of too much behind. But never have I felt my boat like that; never has she given me so much.

I have not had my foul weather gear off since yesterday morning, my sweater is wet at the collar and sleeves, my trousers soaked inside, and two cans of sardines were all I ate for dinner. Yet I feel no fatigue, no weariness, the way after a long, strenuous effort of swimming the mind begins to float above the body. One thousand metres, one thousand five hundred, two thousand, two thousand five hundred. . .then you lose track of the laps, moving at the edge of something diaphanous where flesh and what is inside join to brush another dimension together. And then air, water, effort, fatigue, all of that just disappears. Memories of my childhood rise up in warm waves. I gently shoo them away. Now is not the time. They come back, go away easily when I ask them to leave me alone with the Horn tonight, come back again to caress me with infinite tenderness. . .the long barefoot walks with my brothers through the Indochinese forest for wild honey. . .the bee-stings. . .the slingshot hunts. . .the Gulf of Siam with our slender canoes. . .strange, the sky of Indochina and that of the Horn, so close that they almost touch.

The whole pulpit vanishes in the spray of a fantastic surfing run, and the moon managed a ghostly rainbow to the left of the stern. *Joshua* bounced like a sailing skiff and you would have thought the hull hit something hard, from the sound it made. I push back the hood, pull the cowl off and stuff it in the chest pocket.

The air is icy cold. I listen. I feel with all my might that I must shorten the sail area, slow down, stop surfing. And at the same time I feel the thing I want to hear further, still further, the great luminous wave where one could swim forever. I am too high this time, *Joshua* is too high. Come back to the foot of the mast. . .stop playing with the ghosts in the foam, and the gulls and dolphins. . .come back quickly and drop the mainsail fast and hold tight to your boat and your sanity. . .

SIXTEEN

One Day . . .
and a Night

The wind drops a bit, so does the speed. I feel I am waking from a dream. Pity I took the mainsail off. You forget quickly. . .

The seas may soon start breaking dangerously, as often happens when a strong wind slackens after raising a heavy sea. At Good Hope the seas became nice and rounded as soon as the wind dropped a notch. Here, I do not know yet. Perhaps it will be the same, perhaps not. Three years ago, the sea here subsided as soon as the wind eased. But one would have to round the Horn a dozen times to know for sure, and even then. . .

I go below to tap on the barometer, and am surprised to see that it has fallen markedly during the gale, which was not a true one, since the wind did not shift after the clearing: it's still between NW and NNW. Odd, that 13 millibars drop.

I go on deck again to sniff the night after lighting the stove for coffee. The wind is down to force 6. No more teeth standing out against the sky, but beautiful silvery dunes instead. The mainsail looks at me, furled nice and tight. Raise it, or not? I wind up shaking a reef out of the mizzen. The simple, wise thing to do.

A glance at the log, with the flashlight between my teeth to keep my hands free. Thanks to the reef shaken out of the mizzen, the speed has gone from 6 to 6.6 knots. Just right; not too slow, not too fast either, and in case a big breaking sea hit for some reason, the mainsail will be safe and won't cause any damage to the rigging. I will set it again in two hours if no dirty trick occurs in the meantime.

No more porpoises, no more gulls, no more ghosts. The situation is well in hand. Moving around the deck without a harness is out of the question; just one bad one, and wham! . . . nobody on deck.

I go below to fix my coffee and drink it slowly, both hands gripping the hot mug. God, that's good. I did not realize my hands were that cold. They are all swollen from soaking such a long time in wet gloves.

I just can't keep still. I go back on deck to have a look. Moving around the deck without a harness is possible, only a complete moron would be caught unawares. . .Don't be a fool keep the harness! . . . I'll keep it on, but with just one snap, and only when I sit still in the cockpit, not when I walk on deck between the bowsprit and the mizzen. You can start dreaming and then loose attention when sitting still, but not if you keep on moving around with eyes and ears wide.

One more look at the log before I plot our dead reckoning position on the chart and take a little nap. We have made very good time since yesterday noon, nearly 8 knots on average without counting the current which ought to give us another good knot. Nearly 2 a.m. and Cabo de Hornos is 130 miles away at the most. We will have to raise the mainsail again before long, to keep that nice average from dropping. If everything works out, the Horn should be right on the bow at sunset. I go below to sleep for a while.

The clear night is gone. Day is breaking. I didn't see the dawn, I slept through it. I hurry to raise the main and shake out the reefs, except the staysail's, which is a bit hard to take in when things get rough. The whole sky is full of joy and sunshine. I missed the dawn, but I know the day is going to be a beauty.

The entire sea is blue. It should be green, according to the *Sailing Directions,* because of a certain plankton which turns the Horn waters bottle green.

The sun climbs in the sky. The wind rises, and the mainsail is up close-reefed again. The wind rises further, backing gradually from NW to WSW. The mainsail has to be dropped, and the mizzen close-reefed.

The barometer has not fallen any more since last night's gale, and is not too low for the area. There is a terrific sun out. The noon sight is disappointing though, with only 171 miles covered in the last 24 hours. I had expected 20 miles more.

Diego Ramirez is still 47 miles away, so the Horn will not be rounded before night, which will come at 10 o'clock.

The sea becomes very heavy, very long, very high under a force 9 wind that has been blowing since the meridian sight. From the lower spreaders the scene is striking, with the tiny mizzen facing seas that look as if they are about to sweep over everything. Masses must have a hypnotic effect. You stare on and on. . .I am vaguely worried, but also feel there is no real danger thanks to the fairly strong current, 1.5 knots according to the chart, setting in the same direction as the wind, making the seas regular. Also, at 40 miles to port, the coast is too close for any secondary swell to come from here. Yet the sea is heavy, really heavy. It sweeps along in long, high, nearly horizontal crests, dotted with knolls and dips, but nothing like the sharp teeth and rough dunes of last night.

Occasionally a crest higher than the others becomes a wall of water, the sun slanting through its translucent peak giving it blue-green highlights. The sea then seems ready to change dress. But the rest remains deep blue, with hues melting every second into other shades of blue, like a great musical wave of endless vibrations. And the white streams down, iridescent with countless blues, green sparkling now and then. Once in a while part of the wall splits off, topples forward, and comes cascading down with a thunderous roar.

The wind is blowing as hard as before, still from the WSW. The sun slowly moves astern. The green highlights disappear, the blues turn almost violet. Heavy pink-lined clouds to the north tell me where land is, but I feel glad not to see it just now.

The sea continues to build. I drop the mizzen to keep the surfing within safe limits. One can never tell exactly what is going to happen while surfing in the high latitudes. The boat seems so happy, you're afraid she will try something new. I wonder how I dared go so far last night.

Standing on the pulpit, I search for Diego Ramirez, a bluish spot among the white patches sparkling on the horizon. I cannot see it yet. The storm jib boltrope caresses my gloved fist gripping the stay. It gives me a warm feeling. I so badgered the sailmaker about reinforcements that he gave me his competitor's address to get me off his back. I felt then that it was like something sacred; I took my storm jib back and reinforced the clew myself so that the thimble would never rip out, whatever wind it met. And here it is, gathering all the passing wind, and caressing my fist as it pulls with all its tiny might.

I ate nothing this morning, nothing at noon. Not from laziness or nerves; I just didn't feel like it. Penguins and seals go for long periods without food in the mating season, other animals do the same in the great migrations. And deep within himself man may carry the same instinct to leave food aside, as animals do in the solemn moments of their lives.

I watch this fantastic sea, breathe in its spray, and feel blossoming here in the wind and space something that needs the immensity of the universe to come to fruition.

At last Diego Ramirez comes out of the sea, a little dark blue speck of life on the blurred horizon. Each time *Joshua* rises on a crest, the little bit of life shows more clearly. And each time, it is like the flash of a beacon in my heart.

The sun is near the horizon and Diego Ramirez a tiny speck again, its neatly etched profile far astern. The wind has eased a lot, force 6 to 7. The sea became rounded and its rumbling gradually diminished. Only the sounds of the boat in the sea can be heard.

The Horn is very close, barely 30 miles off, out of sight under the mantle of big cumulus hiding the mountains of Tierra del Fuego. At times I seem to vaguely make something out a hand's breadth to the left of the bow. And Diego Ramirez, my whole life when I saw it appear a few hours ago, is now a memory of the southern route.

The sun has set. The sky readies itself for night. The first planets appear. The moon will be up within the hour; she will actually rise, because the horizon in that direction is clear as well. Clear ahead, clear astern, clear to the right and clear above. The stars out, still almost invisible; later they will be bright. The clearness of the sky is exceptional; it has lasted all day long. And the barometer is as clear as the sky, with hardly a tremor.

It is night, a night full of stars. My exhausted body is resting in the berth, but I am in the rigging and sails, listening to the sea, feeling the air grow cooler with the stars, feeling the wind as it eases further, telling me the night will be truly fine.

Everything stretches and blends, the great wave is rocking me. A last lucid glance: alarm set for 1 a.m.. . .the course will take us within 20 miles of the Horn. . .I will be on deck well ahead just in case. . .but the wind will not increase, will not shift to SSW or even SW. . .*Sleep little brother, you've done all there is to do, now it's my turn to watch over you.* . .lightly, the great wave rolls over me, and I see the little islet my brothers and I found in the Gulf of Siam, with a tiny pebble beach facing the SW monsoon, its other beach facing the monsoon from the NW. There were neither water nor fruits, only crabs and periwinkles, so we brought water with us in our canoes and we ate the crabs and the periwinkles and it was the end of the earth, our little island, so pure, so green, with its Indochina trees, its black rocks, its pebbles on one side and white sand on the other, and everywhere the sun of the sea and the forest, the sunshine of discovery. Many monsoons later, on a trip from Kampot to Rach Gia in my big junk loaded with sugar and a little contraband, I planted three sprouted coconuts and a mango pit, so the island of our childhood would also have water and fruits. A coconut tree for each of my brothers and the mango for me. They are 25 years old now, if nothing has happened to them. . .*Sleep quietly little brother, I just went to look. . .there is a junk from Kampot anchored close to the pebble beach, its lug sail well furled, and three fishermen under the coconut trees. There is also a young boy with a slingshot, shooting at the nests the yellow ants have woven with the leaves of your mango tree.* . .the wave envelopes and caresses me; I sleep without knowing.

I see a beacon in the night, it blinks between the waves, and I slowly awaken. The moon comes in through the porthole, brushes my lids, wanders down to my chin, comes back to my eyes for a second, goes over to see what is on the stove, returns to touch my eyes, lightly, insistently, goes away, comes back again.

I lie outstretched, not moving. I listen. The wind has dropped further. Before, it was whispering on the edge of the partly open hatch, talking in an undertone. Now too, but lower. The water sounds have also changed, and there is a slight rolling to starboard that was not there when I went to sleep. I try to guess whether the rolling is due to less pressure of wind against the sails, or to a change of the course. But I don't understand, since the moon is to port, at the right place in the sky. She could not be coming through the porthole if the course had changed toward the coast. Rolling says it has changed, and Moon says no. I try to figure who is right, feeling with my senses. There is no danger, and plenty of time. If danger threatened, the fight of the swell with the coast would fill the cabin with its roaring. And I hear only the murmur of water on the hull, a sound from *Joshua* that says all is well despite the quarrel between the rolling and the moon. I do not want to shine a light on the compass to find out; it has to come by itself.

Yes, that's it, Moon is right, and rolling is right, and *Joshua's* right. No need to look at my watch to understand that I did not hear the alarm at 1 a.m., or to need not to light the compass to know that the wind changed to SW and the boat has angled some 15° toward the Horn. And I know just where the Horn is: 15 miles away right under the moon, I can see it without getting out of my bunk. Not actually see it, because 15 miles is too far in this area, even on a clear night, and there are almost always clouds on the heights of this coast, no matter how good the weather. I also know that *Joshua* has been in the Atlantic for about an hour, as the moon has travelled some 10° or 15° to the west of her meridian and the Horn is right under the moon.

I stretch and get up, and glance forward out the porthole. I know it can't be there, but it is one of those things that are always possible at sea. . .Nothing, of course. And I feel that colossal thing 15 miles to port. Pity I didn't hear the alarm when it called me an hour ago: I would have altered course to pass close. Now the die is cast, the Horn is rounded, we are in the Atlantic and there is no time to waste. At the moment everything is perfect. In twelve hours it could become very bad; best to be far away then. I feel happy, joyful, moved; I want to laugh and joke and pray all at once.

Another long look ahead out the porthole, for possible icebergs. I had not really worried about them up to now. There are not supposed to be any so close to the Horn. I stick my head out the hatch to see better. I would sort of like an iceberg to be there, glowing in the moonlight. . .but then I wouldn't sleep for a week.

The air is cold, the wind only force 5. I look to port, toward the Horn. Nothing. In any case, it is too far away to be seen. A little cloud under the moon, and some big ones to the left. Pity. . .we might have glimpsed it, even at this distance, the air is so clear.

My ears start tingling. I close the hatch again, light the stove and put on the kettle. My motions are slow, as if nothing had happened. As if *Joshua* had not reached the Atlantic again with three capes in her wake. No. . .not quite three capes; the sea is still the sea, one must never forget. Good Hope was rounded once and for all 500 miles beyond its geographical location. Leeuwin was really astern when my two porpoises left us after the last dangers of New Zealand, 2500 miles later. And the Horn will be in the wake when the Falklands are too, not before.

A sailor's geography is not always that of the cartographer, for whom a cape is a cape, with a latitude and longitude. For the sailor, a great cape is both a very simple and an extremely complicated whole of rocks, currents, breaking seas and huge waves, fair winds and gales, joys and fears, fatigue, dreams, painful hands, empty stomachs, wonderful moments, and suffering at times.

A great cape, for us, can't be expressed in longitude and latitude alone. A great cape has a soul, with very soft, very violent shadows and colours. A soul as smooth as a child's, as hard as a criminal's. And that is why we go.

I pull on my boots to take a turn on deck. The usual routine. The routine, but also, above all, the religion of nights at sea.

The little cloud underneath the moon has moved to the right. I look. . .there it is, so close, less than 10 miles away and right under the moon. And nothing remains but the sky and the moon playing with the Horn.

I look. I can hardly believe it. So small and so huge. A hillock, pale and tender in the moonlight; a colossal rock, hard as diamond. The Horn stretches a long way, from 50° Pacific latitude to 50° Atlantic. Yet it is that rock, set alone on the sea, alone under the moon, with all the glaciers, the mountains, the icebergs, the gales and the beauty of Tierra del Fuego, the smell of seaweed, the colours in the sky and the serenity of the great albatrosses gliding above the sea, not moving a feather of their immense wings, over troughs and crest, for whom all things are alike.

The whistling of the kettle calls me. I go below, dry off my hands, roll myself a cigarette and smoke it in light puffs with a mug of hot coffee. Thousands of little warm things stir throughout my being. I turn the oil lamp up a bit, and the shadows come to life; I turn the wick up some more, and my little world glows softly.

I wonder. Plymouth so close, barely 10,000 miles to the north. . .but leaving from Plymouth and returning to Plymouth now seems like leaving from nowhere to go nowhere.

Part Four

SEVENTEEN

True Dreams —
and False

Where is Nigel? Where is Loïck? Where is Bill King? And Knox-Johnston? Was he really the one the three Hobart fishermen had heard about? I have been without news of anyone for so long. More than six months without knowing about my comrades of the long way. . .

The Horn is already 1300 miles astern, and in three days *Joshua* will be out of the area where she would be likely to encounter icebergs. But where are the others? I mostly think of Nigel, so vulnerable in his trimaran. Those things can capsize and you can go whistle trying to right them. They can break up, too. Five multihulls were lost in Australian waters last year; fifteen dead, no survivors.

Loïck and I had tried to get Nigel to take along a good sharp saw, with plenty of set to keep it from binding in damp wood. In case he capsized he could cut off one of the hulls and continue on his merry way to land on a sponson turned canoe. A trimaran sponson makes a nice little boat, and she would probably sail very well. Alain Brun and Jean Pellisier had built a small raft in the middle of the ocean with pieces of Eric de Bisschop's big raft, when it was sinking. Pierre Auboiroux had also built a miniature raft out of jerrycans and whisker poles in his cockpit, to save his skin when *Néo-Vent* was on the point of sinking in the Indian Ocean.

Nigel would have none of our large economy-size saw; he thought we were kidding. We weren't: Nigel was our pal and we wanted to see him again. He did wind up buying a wetsuit though, to be able to work in freezing water without dying on the spot. Also, he agreed to take a second liferaft. That way, if the one secured on deck were carried away by a breaking sea, there would still be one below, near the companionway. And if *Victress* were flipped like a pancake, and the outside raft had not torn loose, it would be right at hand, without Nigel's having to dive into the darkness. But where is he now? How are the others doing?

Things are looking up, but I went through a grim period after failing to give word in the Falklands. Already tired by the nervous tension involved in rounding the Horn, I could hardly stand when *Joshua* hove into view of Port Stanley lighthouse at the mouth of the fjord, February 9, four days later.

I wanted to attract attention by signalling with my mirror, and give a message to the pilot so he would radio Lloyds about *Joshua*'s passing through. Family and friends would be reassured right away. But it was Sunday and the lighthouse looked empty; no one answered my mirror flashes. The wind had been stiff all morning, right on the nose towards the end. It was a long struggle, a fog before my eyes at times, just trying to reach the mouth of the sound.

You can or you can't. Sometimes the limit is blurred. I could have. . .but to reach Port Stanley at the very bottom of the fjord would have meant 16 miles in the night and the tidal currents, with gusts to knock you flat and unnerving calm spells as you squeak by the rocks. All that to give word by loudhailer or slingshot to some sleepy guy, maybe dead drunk this Sunday, asking him to please report me to Lloyds. Then getting out of the fjord, vomiting with fatigue. And the moon would no longer be there to show me the way.

Too many risks, and bright spots beginning to dance before my eyes. I know: you stubbornly go on, because the brain is frozen, death-like, in the direction of the spots. You follow them on and on. . .and the beautiful voyage ends on a rock just under the surface. It would be too stupid, after three capes in a clean sweep.

I clearly glimpsed all that in a flash of lucidity; clinging to the flash, I quickly hove-to a mile from the lighthouse, out of danger. Rest a little, gently rocked by the boat, becoming calm again in this crazy wind that's blowing a good force 7 on the stiff chop of the tide-rip.

Heaving-to is really best when one no longer knows what to do: come about without touching the sheets, put the helm alee, stretch out in the cockpit, eyes closed, and then see things as they are. . .the enormous fatigue accumulated these last days with the Horn, the little gale on the Burdwood Bank next day—not nasty, but with the dread of an iceberg stranded in the shallows—watches day and night, making a landfall on the Falklands with a sight pulled out of a hat, fog, the fatigue becoming immense, then suddenly lifting only to send you back to the canvas with stars dancing in your skull.

Heaving-to allows you to look things over while body, nerves and brain relax and get back to the simple rhythm of the sea. After a peaceful quarter hour spent dreaming, everything was clear again. So clear that I slacked the sheets to leave Port

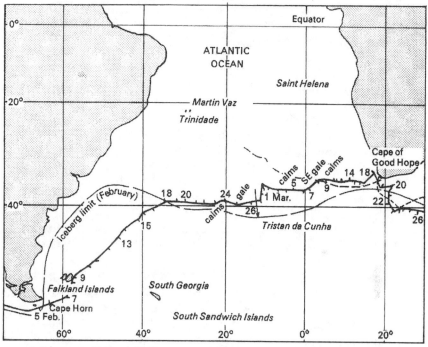

5 February to 26 March 1969

Stanley in the wake and curled up in my berth. I did not even get up once during the night; the big padded envelope with the letters from my friendly Cape Horners would steer *Joshua* clear of any icebergs in her path. Nothing but the sound of the water and the boat, which I could hear deep within me.

Next day, I found out what exhaustion is really like. A great emptiness that makes everything uncertain again. Fortunately, I had to continue NE in any case for ten days or so to clear the iceberg zone. So I let my mind heave-to for the duration. It was by reading Henri de Monfreid as a kid that I learned the trick: stop thinking, stop acting, make no decisions; time will do its work, soothing everything. Noon sights, food—good, carefully fixed grub, talking to the stove and the pans, asking them for all sorts of advice—long naps, good books and falling asleep after a few pages, climbing to the masthead three or four times a day to look for non-existent icebergs and just to look at things, my yoga morning and evening, which I would forget from time to time. . .Thinking neither about Plymouth, nor the Pacific, nor anything. Gradually the fatigue left my brain, and the question of the route to take was no longer a question.

A few more days toward the NE to clear the iceberg zone, and I will be able to steer east toward Good Hope, Leeuwin and the Pacific.

Far from the Horn we are in an area where to encounter icebergs would not be impossible. But the sea has warmed up a lot; the wind has lost its edge since the high latitudes, to the point of being a bit slack at times, and calm today. The temperature was 46° at the Horn, twelve days ago; now it is 77° in the cabin.

I turn the calm to advantage, diving in my wetsuit to check the bottom. The water is not really cold, but it isn't warm, either.

Lots of gooseneck barnacles. They have grown in serried ranks, the size of a finger joint, all over the after part of the hull, and would have slowed *Joshua* quite a bit in light airs. There is also an unfamiliar shelless variety, that measures up to six inches long. I almost feel like eating them in vinaigrette, but am afraid of being poisoned by the antifouling paint which they seem to thrive on. Even the best antifouling has little affect on goose barnacles, I think; at Martinique I found them on all the yachts' bottoms after their Atlantic crossings.

My giant barnacles only proliferate close to the after zinc anodes and on those places under the keel that could not be painted with antifouling. With a putty knife I gently scrape them all off, taking care not to damage the paint.

Today is like half-time in a long game: a special break. I have never gone so long without swimming. It is nice to rediscover this great realm where the body can rest, free of all gravity. The thought of sharks does not worry me. I have seen them occasionally, but never during my very frequent swims in warm seas. I have swum miles in calms or light airs since I first left Indochina on *Marie-Thérèse*. In a light breeze, I used to stay very close to the bow and a little to leeward, ready to climb up by the bobstay if the breath of air increased, or a shark appeared. With my first *Marie-Thérèse* (no bowsprit) I swam along the lee side at the lowest part of the deck, for the same reasons. I very seldom trailed a line astern, because in those days I was a fast swimmer.

A shark bent on mischief can usually be spotted at first glance by his jerky, nervous swimming, which is not at all like his usual demeanor, full of grace and indifference. But the great majority of sharks are timid, frightened by a man's sudden movement (except perhaps the very big ones. . .). I was among them so often, spearfishing at Mauritius, that swimming with 2500 fathoms under the keel does not bother me at all, providing I stay on the alert, ready to climb out quickly.

When I have to work on the bottom, as today, I usually drop the headsails and sheet the main and mizzen flat, to minimize the rolling. In slightly over half an hour of work it is calmly done.

That wasn't the case last night, when the log line got fouled in the trim tab during a calm. I had already lost six rotors since the start (the lines cut by chafing against the lead) and only had two spares left aboard, plus this one, which would be gone before dawn unless I freed it. Impossible with the boathook: I tried for over ten minutes. Two spare rotors would not be enough to keep the log turning for the whole trip, as I had promised Vion. So, after long hesitation, I undressed and dove in. The feeling was horrible: all the sharks in the world were snapping their jaws around me as I untangled the line pell-mell from the trim tab. I was back on deck again in a few seconds, job done, but swearing I must have been completely nuts and would never try anything that crazy again.

The Polynesians would just laugh; they dive for lobsters on moonless nights with waterproof flashlights. Yet they must know sharks prefer to feed at night!

The calm is fine. Calms are always good when you have the time. I drop the mainsail and replace a few stitches that had chafed through against a shroud. It is the first restitching I have had to do since the start. Then I check the slide lashings, several of which have to be changed.

All in all, the gear has held remarkably well for more than six months of constant sailing. Everything is just about like new. Not a single halyard has parted; I climb up at least once a week to oil the nip at the masthead blocks, thanking the little rungs screwed to the masts, which make the job so easy. I only had to change the jib sheet before starting the descent toward the Horn. The bottom, relieved of its four and a half month old barnacles (I had cleaned it in the Atlantic after Trinidad), is as smooth as the day we left.

Joshua is now clear of the broken red line marking the iceberg limit on the Pilot Chart. No more risks, no more watches; just take it easy, heading east toward the Pacific. All the same, I sometimes feel vaguely worried: not a drop of water from the sky in a long time. But the days flow by, and here we are; halfway between the Horn and Good Hope.

I had a strange dream during my nap. Loïck and Nicole Van de Kerchove were at Plymouth. It was Plymouth all right, yet nothing reminded me of the place. We were talking about the voyage. Loïck said his trip around the world was finished, but I could not see his boat, and *Joshua* seemed trapped in the dock. I was trying desperately to get back aboard by climbing over a roof. I was agonized, I shouted to Loïck that my voyage wasn't over. Meanwhile Loïck was going to the station with Nicole.

It seems you can't dream of a dead person; so Loïck must be alive. I am not surprised; he has a good boat and knows how to sail. But where is he? Where is Nicole? When we were leaving Plymouth she was putting the final touches on her steel cutter *Esquilo* and was soon to leave for the Caribbean. Where is she now? Where are Bill King and Nigel? Nigel is the one I think of most often, yet I have never seen him in my dreams. Good Lord! I hope nothing has happened to Nigel. . .

I light the stove and make tea; a nearly sacred ritual after my midday nap. The enamel of the mug is all yellowed with the slow deposits of the leaf from the Orient. I wonder how many thousands of years it took man to discover the soothing qualities of this plant. And there are so many yet to be discovered—or rediscovered—in areas which we seem to ignore.

Some day we will have tiny walkie-talkies no bigger than packs of cigarettes, with a range of thousands of miles. Then pals could communicate without going through the ears of others. . .

Hey old man, eight of our boats are anchored in a really peaceful little spot, five couples have a child each, the other three have decided against having any, but it's as if they each had five kids. And our five only children each have four brothers and sisters. Come join us quick. . .
And what do you do, in your peaceful little spot?
We don't do anything, we just live, we've planted things in the earth and they are growing; potatoes, tarots, all sorts of greens. We've sown seeds of our plant everywhere, the little five-fingered leaves are getting high already! And we have books on a planetary scale, written by guys who really know. Come on, we haven't had to say the word 'cash' since we've been here, it's great, all warm together. Leave the others, don't worry about them, they'll join us someday, the ones who want to, you'll see; come on!

The sun sets on the horizon, neat and clean, red in a completely cloudless sky. Later in the night, I almost see Venus setting, so clear is the sky. I was able to do my yoga in the buff before the meridian. The force 4 breeze was soft and warm, I could feel it entering me with the sun.

Life is wonderful when you can really live it, as animals do when only the present instant counts. I would like to caress the seals and penguins in the Galapagos.

I listen to the sounds of the water, I read, I putter at odd jobs, I sleep a lot. But I listen to the sounds of the water all the time; puttering, sleeping, doing nothing. The barometer is falling but it does not matter, all is well, everything has fallen into place.

A week ago *Joshua* recrossed the longitude she had passed on September 29. She was bound for Good Hope, and wanted to sail round the world. Now she has sailed round the world, and is still bound for Good Hope.

She sailed round the world. . .but what does that mean, since the horizon is eternal? Round the world goes further than the ends of the earth, as far as life itself, perhaps further still. When

you sense that, your head begins to swim, you are a little afraid. And at the same time, what you sense there is so. . .
So. . .I don't know. Further than the ends of the earth. . .

The gale passed well to the south, pretty far away, judging by the swell it sent here. And in our area the breeze remained moderate, force 4 to 5. We are still sailing along the 40th parallel, toward the East. The sun rises before the bow and sets in the wake, as before. The moon has grown.

Nothing has changed. . .Space and time have absolutely ceased to exist, a kind of weightlessness, with the eternal horizon always there.

I do not know yet whether I will try to have myself reported, by approaching Good Hope, or take the wiser southern route, far from everything. If I take the second choice, family and friends will be worried and without word since Tasmania. But I took such a beating last time; in the collision with the black freighter, the damage, fatigue, delay.

Don't think about all that, it depends on too many things I do not know yet. *Joshua*'s buoyancy makes me think. She has got a lot lighter, with only 40 gallons of water in a tank that normally holds 100, and all the stores eaten over six months. Food is no problem, I have plenty left. But water?

I hope I won't have to stop in Australia for lack of water. I often think of Alain Bombard[1] these days. He really pushed his guts to the limit. I try to imagine him at times, in his little open rubber boat, drinking seawater, collecting a little rain in the squalls, spearing dorados to squeeze out their juices and keep from starving to death. All that for more than two months of suffering and anguish, borne by his faith and his truth, whereas those on the *Pamir* nearly all died, despite a discipline and technical organization that might have seemed perfect at the outset. Nearly 80 dead in a few days, some a few hours after the training ship sank. Dead of despair. Yet the 28 guys of the *Endurance,* crushed by ice in the Weddell Sea, all came through because they rediscovered that which joins the spirit to the essential, beyond exhaustion and freezing cold. Henri and José Bourdens pulled through as well, on their raft, with bits of string. . .and something more.[2]

[1] *Bombard's Voyage* (Methuen)

[2] *Cruise to a Cruel Shore* by Henri and José Bourdens (Souvenir Press)

Thousands upon thousands of Cape robins have been flying in the vicinity since yesterday. I have never seen so many before; they make real clouds at times. If I were not sure of having left the iceberg zone long ago, so many birds in sight would keep me awake because I would suspect ice not far off. I look to see if there are any penguins. Not a one. The sea would be too warm for them. If there were any, it would mean icebergs. Come on, go to sleep, there isn't any more ice!. . .

Seeing an iceberg in fine sunny weather. It must be the most beautiful sight a sailor could lay eyes on, a thousand ton diamond set on the sea, glittering beneath the southern sun. It might be enough to last me the rest of my life.

The wind eases. I spend a lot of time trimming the sails, to make the most of it. My ear has become so attuned to the boat's language that I am able to pick up tiny differences in speed. The season is well advanced, autumn will soon replace the fine summer of these last months. Better hurry if I do not want to be late for the Tasman Sea and then New Zealand. Because from there, it will be several more weeks in the high latitudes before I can put north in my east, for Tahiti or the Galapagos.

Which of the two? Tahiti or Galapagos? When you have long skirted vast expanses stretching to the stars, beyond the stars, you come back with different eyes. So I hesitate between Tahiti, and its solid quay for mooring lines, and the Galapagos, where there is nothing. Where there is peace. Where I could very gently get back in touch with men, without being brutalized, without my brutalizing them.

Everything says Galapagos, with the seals and penguins you can caress. . .everything says Tahiti, where there are good friends I can pick an occasional fight with, to keep my hand in.

The warmth of friends. . .the limitless trust of seals and penguins who express themselves in a secret language. Where is the truth? Where is *my* truth.

Two-thirds of the Atlantic are covered. On the chart, the Horn seems tiny, almost unreal in the sounds of the water, that become muted as the wind eases further. At times barely a murmur, especially at night. And the moon continues to grow.

I throw myself into a big juggling session between the aft cabin and the galley, to concentrate all weight amidships one

last time. Two hours of quiet work. The air is mild, yet I am
sweating more than usual. I find I am tiring a bit quickly. Lack
of exercise, probably. By doing nothing and taking it easy, the
least little effort wears you out. I once told a friend with a boat
that blue-water cruising was the most beautiful sleep cure I
ever had. He never knew whether I was joking or not. Me
neither.

My hair has grown so long it tangles on top of my head; the
comb has not been able to run through it for several weeks. I
thought I had got tar on my hair when leaning against the

mizzen mast. It took me a long time to realize that it was
tangles, not tar. It doesn't matter.

What is really amazing is that my skin is still perfectly clear
without a soaping for so long. Say. . .I will have sailed around
the world without washing or feeling the need to, since my last
scrubbing dates back to the Atlantic doldrums and we have just
passed the longitude in which *Joshua* was half swamped by
torrents of warm rain nearly six months ago!

Yesterday wind force 7 WSW, but the sea did not have time to
build; it is calm again today. An exceptional summer for the
40th parallel.

The wind drops. I throw overboard the 45 pound jerrycan of
cement and plaster of Paris intended for underwater repairs in
case an iceberg ripped the hull open (see Appendix). No more
icebergs, no need to clutter *Joshua* with useless weight. I
absentmindedly knead the lump of clay, useless as well now
that the plaster and cement are gone.

Strange, this soft, warm thing whose feel I had forgotten. I
raise it to my face. The smell penetrates me slowly at first. . .
and then I don't quite know what happens, the whole earth
enters me like a flash. All at once I see my Chinese nurse again,
teaching me, as a child, to lie face down on the ground when I

had worn myself out, or been bad. And when I was bigger, she told me that the earth gives her strength and her peace to those who love her.

The wind comes back, very gentle, the sea is calm, very calm, and the water along the side sings on a single note. I listen. I have been listening for months and months.

Is the earth alive? Of course, since plants are alive. They breathe, they hear, they feel, they can be happy or sad, just like us. A scientist proved it. He probably used a big miscroscope. But in addition to the miscroscope he must have put in something of himself; otherwise he would never have understood anything.

I listen to the sounds of the water and I knead my lump of clay and I know the earth is alive. She lives at a very slow rhythm, very powerful, very deep, very peaceful. That life has a rhythm too different from ours for us to measure. But she is truly alive.

The sun gently warms my body stretched out in the cockpit. Behind my eyelids I see the earth as I love her, smelling of soil, letting you live. And I remember the most beautiful and most terrible page of *The Grapes of Wrath,* where Steinbeck shows the rape of the earth by a monster, after the monster takes over man.

In my native Asia, people greet each other by joining palms in front of their chests, exactly the way one addresses a divinity. And it simply means 'I greet the god in you'.

And in the tales of the Far East, there is also a monster who tries to kill the god in us. But it can't harm him as long as we love the earth, because the god in us is a part of earth, the whole earth protects him. My Chinese nurse would say that the earth could not protect this god in us unless we respected both the earth and the god. She said we should give offerings to the earth, that it honoured at once the earth and the god in us.

She said many other things. I did not understand very well; I thought they were just stories.

The wind is back, nice and fresh, the bow rumbles day and night; all the sky is mine, all the sea is mine and all the earth as well. I am so happy, I would like to tell it to my friends who stayed back there, not keep it just for me; tell them how it is here, at sea, after so long. So long I hardly remember anymore. And that is what counts, what is left when you hardly remember.

The pictures of my children blur before my eyes, though God knows I love them. But all the world's children have become my children; it is so wonderful that I would like them to feel it the way I do.

I found a little temple from forgotten times, lost in the faraway forest. I stayed near it a long time, all by myself, to learn to read the marks carved on the stone. Nothing was left of what I had brought, and I lived on roots and wild honey, staying near the temple for as long as it took to find out. And little by little the stone gave forth a name that said go on and seek the truth inside of things, further on.

But how can I tell them? How can I tell them that the sounds of water and the flecks of foam on the sea are like the sounds of stone and wind, and helped me find my way? How can I tell them all those nameless things. . .leading me to the real earth?

Tell them and not frighten them, without their thinking I have lost my mind.

EIGHTEEN

Time
to Choose

February 28. Good Hope is two weeks away, if things keep up as they have for the last few days; three weeks at the most. Moderate NW gale and very heavy rain in the squalls, with sheets of spray. I still manage to collect a dozen gallons of water, half by day, half by night, giving me a range of 20 extra days. But my heart isn't in it.

I do not know how to explain to them my need to be at peace, to continue toward the Pacific. They will not understand. I know I am right, I feel it deeply. I know exactly where I am going, *even if I do not know.* How could they understand that? Yet it is so simple. But it can't be explained in words, it would be completely useless to try.

The drizzle has stopped. I have finished collecting water. The sun rises, very pure before the bow. A bad sign in these latitudes.

I am really tired, not a wink of sleep last night. There is something wrong with the sky.

The sky is blue all over now, the wind fresh from the SW, and the barometer well behaved. Dawn's warning was wrong. I should be happy that nice weather has come back so quickly. But I am completely out of it.

Will Françoise and my children be able to understand that the rules of the game can gradually change, that the old ones have disappeared in the wake to make room for new rules of another order? This is something I just can't express: it would take hours and hours by the fireside. . .

February 26. Covered 172 miles. Cloudy sky, grey sea. Nothingness.

February 27. Covered 94 miles. Blue sky, blue sea. Nothingness.

February 28. I am giving up. . .my instinct tells me it is best. For a week, my spirits have been up and down. I felt physically tired. My appetite had fallen off, the fatigue accumulated in the southern latitudes and in rounding the Horn had not really been shaken off.

During the little gale three days ago I had spent the whole day on deck, to recover as much rainwater as possible. It wore me out. It was only a very moderate gale, from astern, not over force 8. Yet my legs felt like rubber, and I remember asking myself, 'Will you be able to last another four months until Tahiti, including three in these cold waters, with two more great capes to round and gales which will no longer be summertime blows? Remember Tahiti-Alicante, that terrific six day gale. . .remember in *The Old Man and the Sea* he asked himself pretty much the same question. And his answer: *Because I went too far.*

I feel my strength ebbing. I need the sun of the trade wind if I am not to get sick. I need to feel buckets of warm seawater flowing on my body, the water of the trades. I need to stretch out on deck so the sun can enter me and give me strength. The sun has to be hot, very hot, to penetrate right to my bones. I need it all.

I need something else as well: to reassure my family. They would be without a sign of life for months if I continued toward the Pacific. I really can't take the risk of increasing my fatigue by closing the land to pass letters when rounding Good Hope or Tasmania. And anyway, what could I tell them, in those letters?. . .

Also, I want to see my mother again. I do not know when I will be able to visit her if I land in the Pacific. The Pacific is so vast. . .time there is on another scale.

I am thinking of *Joshua*, too. Her anchor winch is in Plymouth with Jim and Elizabeth, as well as a pile of other gear necessary for a boat at rest: mooring lines, paint, dinghy, spare sails left off for this trip but which *Joshua* will need later, anchors, chain, zinc anodes, even the little hundred pound engine, so convenient for changing moorings in a flat calm. I had thought I would simply abandon all that stuff, asking Jim to sell it or give it away, and gradually refit in Tahiti. Easier said than done. . .

And I do not even know if I would feel like steering for Tahiti, once in the Pacific. I might continue to the Galapagos,

J'abandonne... — mon instructeur
dit que c'est la sagesse. Depuis une
semaine, j'avais le moral en dents de scie,
car je me sentais fatigué, physiquement.
Mon appétit avait diminué, la fatigue
accumulée sous les hautes latitudes et
au passage du Horn n'était pas vraiment éliminée. Pendant le petit
coup de vent modéré, il y a trois jours
de cela, j'avais passé la journée
sur le pont pour récupérer le plus possible
d'eau de pluie. Cela m'avait épuisé,
~~pendant~~. Ce n'était que un coup de
vent très modéré, pas plus de force 8
~~et~~ au vent arrière, ~~que~~
pourtant, j'avais les jambes comme
du coton et je me suis posé cette
question : pourras-tu tenir encore
quatre mois jusqu'à Tahiti, dont
trois sous les hautes latitudes, avec ~~des~~ encore
deux grands caps à passer, et des
coups de vent qui ne seront plus des coups
de vent d'été ? Souviens-toi de Tahiti-
Alicante, et de ce coup de vent formidable
qui a duré dix jours... Souviens-toi,
dans "le Vieil homme et la Mer", il se
posait ~~toujours~~ une question aussi
semblable, et sa réponse ~~avait~~ était ~~en~~
~~ce qui~~ "peut que j'ai été trop loin".
Maintenant mon instinct me dit
que je vais ~~peut-être~~ me trouver trop loin

borne by my instinct, for the seals and the penguins. But there would not be so much as a can of paint aboard for the basic care to be given my boat; not even a decent mooring, since I got rid of the ¾ in. line before first rounding Good Hope. No dinghy to row ashore, nothing on board with which to build one. And no way to restock my supplies there, at the ends of the earth.

Too much fatigue for me, worry and sorrow for my family and friends, need to see my mother, to take care of *Joshua*. . .I must steer north, toward Europe. There I can get everything fixed up to leave for the Galapagos or the islands of the Pacific, with *Joshua* well equipped, like new again.

I am also thinking about my movie film. Ninety-two 100 ft reels have been shot. I hope they are still in good condition. . . but if I waited too long, maybe they would be lost forever. And there are so many things in those images. So many true things I would like to share with others.

Steer north! It isn't giving up, but common sense: instead of swallowing it all in one gulp and risking choking and choking my loved ones, I'll just swallow it in two!

The wind shifts to ENE, force 3. Another sign from the heavens, this contrary wind for Good Hope. I now have a fair wind to get myself reported to Lloyds at Tristan da Cunha, so close, just 90 miles to the NW. I will be there tomorrow!

No. . .I do not have the large scale chart. It would be too stupid to take a chance with the reefs around the island.

Saint Helena is 1300 miles away. Just looking at the chart, I can feel all the gentleness of the trade wind in the cabin. It caresses me, so soft, so good, I look a bit further north: Ascension Island, 1700 miles, almost on the direct route. In that case, better make it Ascension. If I can work things out with the heavens to catch the trades without delay, I should make Ascension in two weeks at the outside, sleeping twenty hours a day if I feel like it.

Two weeks! What a relief for all my loved ones! And for me!

I feel good now that a decision has been taken that is reasonable for all concerned.

I dream of the trade wind sun, of its warm sea where I will swim on the first calm day. Swim. . .swim. . .I could swim for days and days without stopping.

Maybe Saint Helena instead of Ascension. Maybe even a

long stay at Saint Helena, it is such a beautiful island. I have plenty of time to think about it. But perhaps I will choose Ascension, because of its immense beach, all white and golden at once, full of turtles and sunshine. We'll see, there is plenty of time, no hurry to choose.

To have the time. . .to have the choice. . .not knowing what you are heading for and just going there anyway, without a care, without asking any more questions.

1er mars

J'ai remis le cap vers ~~Antibes~~ ~~Tahiti~~
le Pacifique ... ~~Je pars~~ ~~bajal~~
~~Je reviens~~ ~~jusque~~ ~~à Tahiti~~.
La nuit dernière a ~~été~~ été pénible, je
me sentais devenir vraiment malade
à l'idée de regagner l'Europe, de
~~me~~ retrouver ~~le~~ ~~panier~~ ~~un~~
panier de crabes. C'est terrible
à quel point le physique et le moral
sont liés — j'étais physiquement fatigué
par le Horn, le moral a donc suivi
la même pente, et flanché quand
j'ai décidé hier d'abandonner. Certes,
il y avait des raisons très valables, et
même assez sérieuses, sages. Mais est-ce
la ~~sagesse~~, que de se diriger vers
un lieu où l'on sait qu'on ne vivra
pas en paix. Je revois ~~la~~ l'existence que j'ai menée en ~~France~~, cette
existence de ~~fou~~ dément en compa-
raison de celle que j'ai connue sous
d'autres ~~di~~ civilisations plus sages
que la nôtre. Ce serait folie, pour
moi, de regagner l'Europe maintenant, je n'y serais pas heureux,
on n'a pas le temps de vivre là-bas,
du moins en ce qui me concerne. Les
~~quelques années~~ que j'y ai passées se sont
écoulées à courir, courir, courir.
Courir après des chimères, courir
après le fric, ce fric qu'on fout
en l'air pour ~~les~~ soi-disant besoins
de la vie moderne, qui n'est
qu'une vie artificielle. Je n'ai
jamais eu le temps de vivre vraiment
pendant un mois plein, en France.

Certes, il y a un risque à
vouloir gagner directement Tahiti.
Mais le risque serait bien plus grand,
en fin de compte, à vouloir regagner
l'Europe :

NINETEEN

The Turning Point

I have set course for the Pacific again. . .last night was too hard to take, I really felt sick at the thought of getting back to Europe, back to the snakepit. I was physically tired by the Horn and my spirits sagged, then collapsed after I had decided to give up.

Sure, there were good, sensible reasons. But does it make sense to head for a place knowing you will have to leave your peace behind? Saint Helena or Ascension, yes. . .and I wouldn't have stopped, I would have pushed on in the trade winds, telling myself 'Don't be a fool, you may as well just put in a little effort, try to pick up the *Sunday Times* prize and leave again right away. . .' I know how it goes!

Trying to reach Tahiti nonstop is risky, I know. But the risk would be much greater to the north. The closer I got, the more disgusted I would be. If I can't hold on until the Pacific, there will always be an island so newhere.

Mauritius. . .an island full of friends in the Indian Ocean, just after Good Hope. But I feel I can hold on until the Pacific—and that it is worth it.

My mother. . .her spirits are so high, her inner life so rich! I know she will not worry, I know I will see her again. But I had better not go as far as the Galapagos. Françoise and the children can take it, too.

I am really fed up with false gods, always lying in wait, spider-like, eating our liver, sucking our marrow. I charge the modern world—that's the Monster. It is destroying our earth, and trampling the soul of men.

> 'Yet it is thanks to the modern world that you have a good boat with winches, Tergal sails, and a solid metal hull that doesn't give you any worries.'
> 'That's true, but it is because of the modern world, because of its so-called "civilization" and its so-called "progress" that I take off with my beautiful boat.'

'*Well, you're free to split, no one is stopping you; everyone is free here, so long as it doesn't interfere with others.*'

'*Free for the moment. . .but before long no one will be free if things go on. They have already become inhuman. So there are those who go to sea or hit the road to seek the lost truth. And those who can't, or won't anymore, who have lost even hope. "Western civilization" is almost completely technocratic now, it isn't a civilization any more.*'

'*If we listened to people like you, more or less vagabonds and barefoot tramps, we would not have got beyond the bicycle.*'

'*That's just it; we would ride bikes in the cities, there wouldn't be those thousands of cars with hard, closed people all alone in them, we would see youngsters arm in arm, hear laughter and singing, see nice things in people's faces; joy and love would be reborn everywhere, birds would return to the few trees left in our streets and we would replant the trees the Monster killed. Then we would feel real shadows and real colours and real sounds; our cities would get their souls back, and people too.*'

And I know all that is no dream, everything beautiful and good that men have done they built with their dreams. . .but back there, the Monster has taken over for men, it dreams in our place. It would have us believe that man is the centre of the universe, that all rights are his on the pretense that he invented the steam engine and lots of other machines, and that he will someday reach the stars if he just hurries a little before the next bomb.

Nothing to worry about there, our hurrying suits the Monster just fine. . .he helps us hurry. . .time is short. . .hardly any time left. . .

'*Run! Run!. . . don't stop to think, whatever you do; I the Monster am doing the thinking. . .run toward the destiny I have planned for you. . .run without stopping to the end of the road where I have put the Bomb or the complete degradation of humanity. . .we're almost there, run with your eyes closed, it's easier, shout all together Justice—Patriotism—Progress—Intelligence—Dignity—Civilization . . . What, you aren't running. . .you're sailing around on your boat, just to think!. . .and you dare complain into your tape recorder. . .saying what you have in your heart. . .just wait, you poor fool, I'm going to shoot you down in flames. . .guys who get angry and speak out are very dangerous for me, I have to shut them up. . .if too many of*' *them started getting angry, I wouldn't be able to drive the human cattle as I please, their eyes and ears blocked by Pride, Stupidity and Cowardice. . .and I'm in a hurry to get them, bleating and satisfied, where I want them to go. . .*

The violent things rumbling within me vanished in the night. I look to the sea, and it answers that I escaped a great danger. I do not want to believe in miracles too much. . .Yet there are miracles in life. If the weather had stayed bad for a few days longer, with easterly winds, I would be far to the north by now; I would have continued north, sincerely believing it was my destiny, letting myself be carried by the trades like an easy current with no whirlpools or snares, believing it was true. . .and being wrong. The essential sometimes hangs by a thread. So maybe we should not judge those who give up and those who don't. For the same reason. . .the thread of the miracle. I nearly gave up. Yet I am the same, before as after.

God created the sea and He painted it blue to make it nice for us. And here I am, at peace, the bow pointed toward the East, when I could be heading north with an unsuspected drama deep inside.

The weather is good, the wake gently spins out astern. Sitting crosslegged in the cockpit, I watch the sea, listening to the song of the bow. And I see a little seagull perched on my knee.

I don't dare move, I don't dare breathe, for fear she will fly away and never come back. She is white all over, almost transparent, with a slender beak and very large black eyes. I did not see her draw near, I did not sense the faster beating of her wings as she landed. My body is naked under the sun, yet I do not feel her on the bare skin of my knee. Her weight cannot be felt.

Slowly, I reach out my hand. She looks at me, preening her feathers. I reach closer. She stops smoothing her feathers and watches me, unafraid. Her eyes seem to speak.

I reach my hand a little bit closer. . .and gently start stroking her back, very gently. She speaks to me then, and I understand that this is no miracle. And she tells me the story of the Beautiful Sailboat filled with men. Hundreds of millions of men.

When they set out, it was on a long voyage of exploration. The men wanted to find out where they came from, and where they were going. But they completely forgot why they were on the boat. And little by little they get fat, they become demanding passengers. They are not interested in the life of the boat and the sea any more; what interests them are their little comforts. They have accepted mediocrity, and each time they say 'Well, that's life,' they are resigning themselves to ugliness.

The captain has become resigned too, because he is afraid of antagonizing his passengers by coming about to avoid the unknown reefs that he perceives from the depths of his instinct. Visibility worsens, the wind increases, but the Beautiful Sailboat stays on the same course. The captain hopes a miracle will calm the sea and let them come about without disturbing anyone.

The sun climbs. It passes its meridian, and I have still not moved. Now my little gull is sleeping on my knee.

I have known her a long time. She is the Fairy Tern, who lives on all islands where the sun is the god of men. She flies out to sea in the morning and always returns to her island by dusk. So all you have to do is follow. And she came more than 700 miles to warn me today, though she usually never goes more than 30 or 40 miles out. In the Indian Ocean, as *Marie-Thérèse* was sailing to the reefs, I had looked for her in vain. And I lost my boat in the night.

The truth is, I was sleeping that afternoon in the comfort of my cabin when the Fairy Tern wanted to show me the island hidden behind the reefs.

Just then she awakens and tells me some more about the Beautiful Sailboat. Lots of the men are still sailors. They don't wear gloves, the better to feel the life of the sails and the lines, they go barefoot and stay in touch with their boat, so big, so tall, so beautiful, whose masts reach all the way up to the sky.

They don't talk much; they watch the weather, reading the stars and the flights of gulls, and watching the signs the porpoises make. And they *know* their beautiful boat is headed for disaster. But they do not have access to the sheets or the wheel, they are a bunch of barefoot tramps kept at large. People tell them they smell bad, tell them to wash. Many have been hanged for trying to trim the after sails and ease the jibs to alter course at least a little. And the captain waits for the miracle to come between the bar and the saloon. He is right to believe in miracles. . .but he has forgotten that a miracle is only born if men create it themselves, out of their own being.

It is a fabulous summer for these latitudes. All the things have been with me from the start, all the miracles, and I dream my life in the light of the sky, listening to the sea. I have been dreaming my life for months and months, yet really living it.

For ten days the breeze remains weak, with calms at times, aside from a moderate SE gale, taken hove-to at first, then closehauled when the wind eased. Then more calms and light airs. Very often the sun sets red.

I had a long talk with my friends. A few tape cassettes full of things. All of the things. The good and the bad, the gales, the setting suns, the seagulls, the porpoises, the Horn, the loneliness and love as well. The simple things of the sea, where I include all men, and refuse everything. Without denying man.

Two more days perhaps, and we will be off Cape Town, with Table Mountain rising straight above us. I listen to the note singing in the bow. There is another muted, rumbling one, because of the light SE swell left by the last gale. I do not listen to the rumbling note, I hear only the one that sings like a clear stream, I have chosen the best part.

Table Mountain is in sight, about 30 miles away. Radio Cape Town forecasts fog tonight. Meanwhile, the sky is clear, with the light SSE breeze on the point of dropping. I feel it will gently shift to a soft NW wind during the night, and then the fog will come.

Cormorants and gannets converge toward the land. They will be back to their nests by sunset to feed the little ones. I think of my children. I know they will understand. Françoise too. And I am here, all alone, with that great peace, tender and warm. And all of humanity is here, friendly in the cabin where the oil lamp is just lit.

Everything is in place. I feel a great strength in me. I am free, free as never before. Joined to all nonetheless, yet alone with my fate.

Dawn. The fog has lifted. The houses of Cape Town can be easily seen, so close and so distant. Great breaths of warmth come across the bay from all those homes. Then cold sets in; the indifference. . .then warmth again. Like waves.

I carefully close the 3 gallon plastic jerrycan. It contains the cassettes, ten reels of 16 mm colour movie film, and two good handfuls of stills, including the log. If anything happened to me, my publisher would then have all the material for writing the book in my place, and my family would be safe about the future.

Suddenly a great burning wave comes over me, pressing with all its might. An irresistible urge to stop at Cape Town, to rest up for two or three months in that friendly yacht club where I had previously spent a year with Henry. Just stop.

A long, long time ago, the Indians killed the whites who came into their forest. But the white trappers went on deeper and deeper, even if they were fated to fall some day, shot by silent arrows. Some of them were spared. They did not know why: nobody knew why. The Indians let them leave with the precious furs they had come to get in the heart of the deep forest. And people spoke of miracles or treason.

They did not answer. They had learned silence listening to magic signs on the secret trails of the forest. At times, though, they were afraid of going too far. But their lithe and silent steps took them further and further toward the deep heart of the forest.

Of course I will continue toward the Pacific. I can't remember who it was who said, 'There are two terrible things for a man: not to have fulfilled his dream, and to have fulfilled it.'

Maybe I will be able to go beyond my dream, to get inside of it, where the true thing is, the only really precious fur, the one that keeps you warm forever. Find it, or perhaps never return.

The launch is coming. I called it with a ray of sunshine caught in the little mirror I used in Tasmania. From a distance, I thought she was black; she draws near, and is blue. I heave-to, sails aback and helm down. I get the loudspeaker ready, to ask her not to come to close. The water is flat in the bay. . .but rigging is easy to rip loose if you rub it with a few tons of launch.

I throw the jerrycan. A sailor catches it on the fly. The skipper is a ship's chandler. I ask him if he can take the package to the French Consul. He promises to do so right away. I ask him if there is any news of those of the long way. He answers that four have been wiped out, but does not know their names. Anything about a trimaran? He doesn't know.

There, it's over already, the launch is heading back to the breakwater entrance. The Consul will send the jerrycan on to my publisher.

I bring the sheets over to the right side and head for a tanker riding at anchor in the bay. Snap! . . .onto the bridge flies a slingshot message to be cabled to Robert of the *Sunday Times:*

> *Dear Robert: The Horn was rounded February 5, and today is March 18. I am continuing non-stop towards the Pacific Islands because I am happy at sea, and perhaps also to save my soul.*

The message is hardly out of my hands when doubt hits me: will they understand back there? Don't worry, even if you don't quite understand. . .don't worry, you can't all understand how happy I am right now, watching my boat beating at 7 knots with a big rainbow in her lee, heading toward Good Hope.

Good Hope is rounded amid the sounds of the water, the sounds of the wind, the singing of all the stars and all the suns and all the moons together, the struggle and the love of the boat with the old ocean on waves so high and magic signs that come from the deep heart of the deep sea.

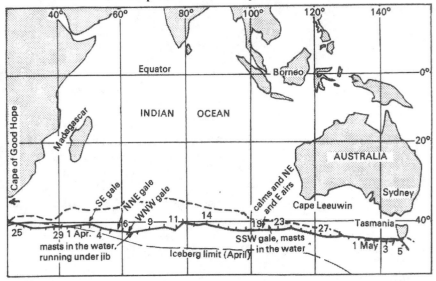

25 March to 5 May 1969
Dotted line: Joshua's first passage, 21 October to 30 December 1968

Now it is a story between *Joshua* and me, between me and the sky; a story just for us, a great love story that does not concern the others any more.

Land is far, far away. . .farther than the ends of the earth. A beautiful story just for us amid the sounds of the boat sailing for the horizon on the sounds of the sea and the light of the sky. So worry no more, back there, even if *Joshua* should go on her way beyond the capes, far beyond, led by a seagull.

But you, back there, when you meet seagulls, share some of your warmth with them; they need it. And you need them too; they fly in the wind of the sea, and the wind of the sea comes back over the earth, always.

TWENTY

Listen, Joshua . . .

Exhausting gales, dangerous waves, dark clouds scudding across the sea with all the world's sadness and all its despair.

Continuing anyway, perhaps because you know you must, even if you no longer understand why.

Clear skies, sunsets the colour of blood, the colour of life, on a sea sparkling with power and light, giving you all its strength, all its truth.

Then you know why you are continuing, why you will go right to the end. And you would like to go still further.

Sounds of water. . .sounds of water. . .sounds of water. . .

In olden times, the Alchemist would shape his matter and re-shape it, and shape it again, for a long, long time. A very long, long time. And people thought he wanted to find the Magic Stone, the one that turns Things into Gold.

What the Alchemist was really seeking was not the Magic Stone but to change himself, through time and patience, and still more time. And sometimes he went too far.

Sailing in these waters, if man is crushed by his feeling of insignificance, he is borne up and protected by that of his greatness. It is here, in the immense desert of the Southern Ocean, that I feel most strongly how much man is both atom and god.

And when I go on deck at dawn, I sometimes shout my joy at being alive, watching the sky turning white above the long streaks of foam on this colossally powerful, beautiful sea, that tries to kill at times. I am alive, with all my being. Truly alive. And perhaps you must go further still, watching the sea.

One can watch it for hours and days and weeks and months. And perhaps years. And one can travel fast and far with the sea and in it. All you have to do is catch sight of a wave, one neither too small nor too big; just right. And then it takes you to its beach, and you come back to the boat whenever you like. One can choose, telling the wave to break on white sand or black. Or even onto coral of any colour you like, or onto smooth rocks green with seaweed. Anything you like.

You can stay on top of the wave or within, and even right inside, rolling ten times around the world, just watching the clouds and the sun and the moon and stars above the clouds, with the wave and in it, just watching and feeling. You can also hop on a moonbeam as it reflects off the sea, and have it drop you on the land to wander through the countryside, breathing in trees and things of the earth, and come back on board to watch the sea, just watching it and thinking while still breathing the smell of the earth and the sky.

It's easy. All you have to do is watch the sea and pick just the right wave, and take the time to look in the sea.

And so I nearly went too far after New Zealand. I kept looking toward the Horn, where there are waves and still more waves. I looked at the long, long curve on the little *Damien* globe, and was fascinated by the waves and the globe. And I held it in my hands and remembered nothing at all.

Nothing but the sea and the globe with the waves in the sea. And sometimes I tried to think in front of the sea. And I knew even less what to do.

But I felt very clearly that there was something *Joshua* was trying to say. So we headed north together. And I sensed that was the way she wanted it to be.

And together we found the trade wind of the Pacific, to seek the Island in the trades.

The beautiful voyage is almost at the end of the long ribbon of foam. And I have almost reached the end of myself. And *Joshua* too.

Down there in the south it was fall, then already winter. Eight gales since Good Hope, in three months. Two knockdowns in the Indian Ocean, before Australia. Two more in the Pacific after groping past New Zealand in the dark, without porpoises this time.

No damage, beyond four sails burst in the last knockdown. And also three shrouds that parted right where the wire curves around the thimble. That really doesn't count, as they were easy to repair with cable clamps and pieces of chain to make up the length.

But the shrouds are generally tired, and *Joshua* too. As for me, I don't know whether I am tired or not; it depends on how you look at it. I must give my boat her eyes, when we reach the peaceful Island in the trades, where you have time to do the things that count. And there is no more risk of going too far, or not far enough. Because the dream first went to the end of the dream. . .and then beyond it.

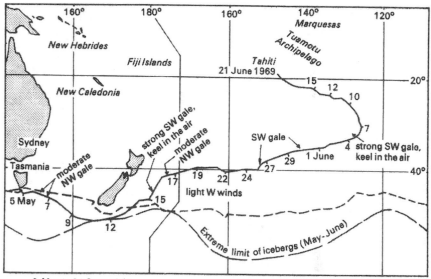

5 May to 21 June 1969
Dotted line: first passage, 17 December 1968 to 4 February 1969

The Fairy Tern glides above the mast, playing with the eddies behind the main. She stays there a few moments, turning her head left and right, shifting around the better to see me, the already low sun glinting in her large eyes.

Those eyes are the most beautiful of any bird I know. In the Cargados Carajos archipelago, you can hold fairy terns in your hand, without their stirring. They gaze at you with their immense eyes as you stroke them. Then you put them back on their nests between the twigs of the bush they have chosen near the beach. And still they do not stir, watching you motionless.

They simply trust men, and that is why they come so far to us out at sea.

My Fairy Tern leaves for a moment, then comes back to fly around the boat. She comes back three times, then flies off WNW, to tell me where the Island is. Tonight she will sleep with her little ones. Me too, tomorrow, perhaps.

The wind shifts in a very black squall. I heave-to. It rains as it can only in the tropics, and I lather myself from top to bottom under the cascades of water pouring off the main. Then I stretch out on deck to breathe the rain. My entire skin and body shivers with deep pleasure, and my hair becomes fine silk under this water straight from the sky.

The cloud is past. A little pale blue thing lies on the horizon to the WNW.

The Island. . .

With ten months of sea and its Fairy Tern. Everything is in place, as it should be. And the sun goes down to rest after giving me all these things.

And *Joshua* will lie hove-to on the port tack, to near the coral at the end of the night.

The passage, shining white. There it is, close already, with the coral to right and left. And above the coral, the sun sparkles on the crests of the long blue-green rollers that mark the boundary between Sea and Land. Between the great free expanses of wind and ocean is this other world, the world of men I am returning to after so long at sea.

The shining pass. . .I would like to feast my eyes on the colours of its coral; the coral of passes is the most beautiful of all, fed by both current and swell. But I must pay attention, carefully taking the middle of the pass, watching only the sails and the middle of the pass.

The reef rumbles very loudly to right and left. And then astern; the pass is cleared. The rumble of the reef is friendly, it says 'Goodbye, I'll see you soon.' The warm trade wind that brought *Joshua* to the pass, and through it and beyond to the inner harbour, says goodbye as well. So *Joshua* sails in little tacks on the land breeze, looking for that quiet spot where she can sleep in peace. She is like a seagull, a little exhausted, but happy to be landing among other birds of her own kind, who will watch over her sleep and protect her.

The anchor is down. A long mooring line snakes toward the quay. I recognize familiar silhouettes. Then faces of old friends. They stand in a motionless group, a little apart from the others.

Rummaging through the atom, a scientist may someday reduce joy and inner peace to mathematical formulae. It would be interesting, but surely too complicated for me. And with his cleverness he might spoil something essential. I prefer what Romain Gary says: *'What man needs most of all is friendship.'*

'How goes it, old man?'

'I'm OK. . .'

'Not too rough?'

'Not too; nice of you guys to be here. . .'

'Nice of you to come. . .'

Not a sound. Not a movement.

It's weird. . .a little unreal. Even in the flattest calm, things speak and answer each other.

I suddenly remember. *Joshua* is in Tahiti, since this morning.

I stretch and wait a bit. Something tremendous fills my chest. I go back to sleep for awhile. Then I get up to make coffee, as at sea.

They left while I was sleeping. All evening long their warmth was with me in the cabin. We talked about this and that, about serious things too. I often dozed off; it didn't matter. What mattered was that they were there, and it was good to be together. I wonder when the last one left. It smells very strongly of tobacco.

I like that smell, of tobacco and friends.

I go on deck. The moon will set in a little while. The night is clear, the stars friendly. . .*we will always be here to show you the way.*

I listen. The coral reef rumbles gently in the distance, pounded by the long ocean swell. . .*I am here, close, I will always stay true to myself.*

And *Joshua*, motionless for the first time in so long, listens to the sky, listens to the sea.

The moon is setting. The town is very, very quiet. And two big trees lie stretched out on the ground, still breathing.

Many trees used to grow along the quay, barely three years ago. But they are building a five-lane highway to replace the quiet little road that runs along the sea. So the trees that made the port so charming and pleasant are being cut down.

The moon has set. The town, left to itself, sleeps peacefully, awaiting the dawn. And a cricket chirps from a hole in the rocks nearby.

I listen. The whole sky sings and the whole earth rests because the cricket is there. If we could save the cricket. . .

Listen *Joshua*. . .listen to the cricket!

TWENTY ONE

Time to choose—
Part II

Another tree, two trees, three. . .a whole row of trees. All that so cars can go through easily. It takes a hundred years to make one of these beautiful trees. It takes the bulldozer half a minute to knock it down.

Man invented the bulldozer and the concrete mixer to work in his place. So they work as they were taught: efficiently, without bothering with details. They really work. And when there isn't any more work for them, they make it up. They can't stay idle, it would kill them.

That they might kill man some day, they couldn't care less. So long as the bulldozer and the mixer don't die.

Construction continues. The destruction goes on. With all the legalities in order. That's their strength: papers. The Law. The Law that says you can wreck everything. Maybe that's what the dinosaurs did, with their enormous stomachs and their brains no bigger than walnuts.

Lots of people believe that the bulldozer and the concrete mixer don't think. They're wrong: they do think. They think that if they don't have any work to do, they won't earn any money, and then their slaves won't be able to buy the fuel and oil they need to go on living and go on thinking serious thoughts.

They think human beings are pretty retarded, still making their babies in joy and love and pain. Their procreation technique is much more efficient: they work flat out without ever getting tired, and that means profits, and their slaves hurry to make more bulldozers and concrete mixers which are born fully grown, ready to work without wasting a minute. And what they think really hard is they had better hurry up and get the robot age going before man catches on. Then the bulldozers and the mixers would never risk running short of fuel, or fail to have more and more gigantic babies to perpetuate the species and multiply right out of sight.

The concrete quay in front of the five-lane highway is finished. Overheated, unshaded except for the shadows of powerful twin street lamps. Concrete, with plenty of red and plenty of black and not a shred of green. Whatever became of the Wise Men's Council of olden times?

There is a little patch of earth left at the harbour entrance. Bare, but earth nonetheless, with rocks along the shore, crabs, the green moss and the green smell of seaweed. There is a world of difference between the lapping of the sea against natural rocks and the hollow noise it makes against a concrete quay. And here, the cars don't pass too close, the street lamps are far enough away not to blind us.

This is where we all got together; an English boat, two Americans, a Spaniard, a German, two Swiss, a Canadian whose wife is Polynesian, three Frenchmen. and Ivo our Dutchman, at twenty the youngest of us all, who sailed in on a boat not much bigger than a matchbox.

Many passports, but just one kind: citizens of the world and friends of things that grow. Three year old Lawrence was practically born at sea. Elodie crossed the Atlantic when she was two. Vaï-Tea and Hina-Nui, Bert the Canadian's children, are three and four. They go fishing with Matuatua and Bert as far out as the atolls behind the horizon.

It is peaceful in our little spot, but the rat raised a few problems at first. Klaus even sent a red flare after him in his crack in the rocks. It was as if the flare had eyes, bouncing and zooming all over the place, trying to get us. In the beginning, most were dead set against the rat. But some of us felt that everybody has the right to live in peace. I felt that way too, because of the old story. After a few weeks' discussion, Klaus suggested we feed him over on the rocks, so that he wouldn't come aboard to help himself. Yves and Babette were the hardest to convince, because the rat often came onto *Ophélie* with twigs and rags which he stuffed into the port cockpit locker, as if to make a nest. Finally. . .we all agreed. So we started breaking our coconuts after drinking from them, making it easy for the rat to gnaw the meat, and put them close to the rock where he lives.

When the weather turns bad, a dangerous swell comes in here, and our boats have to move. Those with engines tow the others. One day, Marc towed four of us, strung out behind *Maylis,* while Julio helped to pull Jory with his outboard. And we all wound up in front of the cement quay at the bottom of the harbour.

We are protected there. Oh yes, 'protected', but it is stifling, without any shade. We are deafened by the cars roaring by five yards away. And at night the big street lamps send their glare right into our cabins. No slingshot in the world could zap them, the glass is too thick. They might even be bullet-proof, for all I know.

As soon as the weather improves, we quickly go back to anchor in front of our patch of real earth. But we know that one of these days the concrete will drive us out or bury us, if we just sit around talking about the good old days.

Since we can't take shovels and plant trees ourselves at the risk of all winding up in the clink labelled 'revolutionaries— vandals', we write a letter to the authorities.

> . . .*It is not too late to improve the inhuman quay that has been imposed on us. . .Planting pandanus would give some shade, and they would grow, since there is earth under the layer of cement. . .they would soften the harsh glare of the street lamps. . .pandanus is a very hardy shrub; two of them are flourishing in front of the Donald department store in spite of the concrete. . .*
>
> . . .*All the work done so far has completely failed to take man's deep needs into account and will have come to no good at all. . .the developer decided to do it that way, but the highway could have been built without wiping out the shade and killing century-old trees. . .crickets and birds need greenery to live as well, and man, even if he does not know it, needs crickets and birds, not just electricity and cement.*

In our peaceful spot we had planted a dozen banana trees, so that there would be some green to rest the eyes, so one's gaze could wander over something cool. So the cricket would not die.

And next to our banana trees, a garden with real grass, tightly laid pieces of turf that we had fetched. We water it morning and evening, and it is doing well. Six feet square, just enough so that pals from the boats can get together to drink coconuts as the sun sets on the island of Moorea.

We are at peace, here in our garden by the sea, close to our boats, right in front of the passage through the reef, which we hear rumbling softly in the evening when the wind drops. It is good to be in front of a pass: you feel free to leave whenever you like or free to stay.

This would be a perfect place to cover with grass and trees. Nearly an acre with nothing but green things, to bring some softness and beauty back to the port. Just a little island of peace to help forget the concrete. Like a seed borne on the wind from the high seas and dropped here at random, some day sprouting into a tree whose restful shade shelters man's troubled heart.

In front of the pass. Coming or going. Freedom between the green and the blue.

But the bulldozer and the concrete mixer are the ones who make the decisions. They don't like blue and they hate green, and getting rusty is what they hate the most. So when they have nothing left to do, they keep busy so as not to rust. And if it turns a little extra profit, so much the better. That's why they decided to build a big parking lot here, with a rocky path running right over the garden.

We are crushed at the news. Right to the last, we tried to stop it, and nearly succeeded. But a sailing pal on the newspaper told us there was too much profit at stake.

The rat saw it all. He did not come too close, still on his guard because of the red fire that had smelled so bad. But he has a keen ear, and you could see him stop gnawing his coconut from time to time, the better to hear.

The banana trees listened, not stirring a leaf. They listened and they felt, and then breathed the air and the time they had left to live. The grass listened too, and could do nothing but be soft to us for the time she had left. And the cricket was there, but his chirping rose sadly from the brand-new little nest he had dug in the grass of our garden.

We. . .a handful of barefoot vagabonds armed only with slingshots not even strong enough to break a street lamp.

Everything was done very fast: the garden was covered over with stones and debris, the cricket died, three boats set sail to find some part of the world that the Monster might have overlooked.

As for me. . .I don't know any more. I feel like vomiting.

Dear Bernard,

I am involved with an organization called 'Friends of the Earth'. Our objective: to protest against the insane civilization that is being imposed on us, to militate for the restoration of a balance btween man and nature. Oppose developers devastating areas that are still nearly untouched and balanced. Rehabilitate not only the concept of nature, but nature itself in the mind of city dwellers, who tend to put it in a museum.

Do not let the word 'Earth' put you off; oceans cover seven-tenths of it, and the oceans urgently need to be saved from the oil spills and dumping that are their lot.

Alain

I slowly reread my old pal Alain's letter. So it is true, all is not yet lost. . .back there as well, men are getting angry at civilization run amok, standing up to the Monster.

I stick my head out of the cabin hatch. I watch our garden being destroyed. The bulldozer is rumbling. Yet a great faith fills my heart. . .I see men walking to the coconut tree, more men, still more. . .we all grab the tree together and shake it and shake it. . .coconuts rain down on us, but the monkeys start to fall!. . .*Hey you, why are you just standing there watching us? You're on our side. . .You say you're ashamed, but you're too afraid to get creamed by one of those big baboons. . .don't be ashamed, we're human beings, not bulldozers. . .you can still plant a tree while the monkeys try to hang on. . . .if every man planted even one tree in his lifetime, it would mean billions more beautiful things on our earth, people would become nicer. . .plant your tree!. . .*

And then something fantastic happens: a really huge monkey calmly climbs down the coconut tree, looks at us and says, 'You barefoot vagabonds don't scare me. . .but from now on, I'm on your side.'

He takes off his monkey skin, and becomes a man again.

TWENTY TWO

The Second
Turning Point

The garden may yet be saved. Men were aroused in the face of shame. Four big trees have been planted and lots more shrubs and greenery. It is said that the rocky path will soon be covered with earth and grass. And the cricket, whom I had thought dead, has come back. We replanted our banana trees, and they are there to this day.

As for the inhuman concrete quay, without shade, without green, without anything at all, there is talk of putting in pandanus. That way not only the garden may be saved, but it may be on the way to becoming a beautiful bit of green.

Yet there are too many 'maybes': it's disturbing.

If *Joshua*, who measures 40 ft, were racing a boat of the same design but 10 ft longer and with a proportionately larger sail area, she would lose every time. Because a 50 ft boat sails faster than a 40 ft one.

Still, *Joshua* would have a chance of finishing ahead of the big boat in an ocean race, if she tried what is called the 'suicide tack': seeking a different wind somewhere else. It either works or it doesn't, but there is no other way out. And if *Joshua* finds a fair wind 200 miles to the right of the bigger boat, for example, while the latter struggles with calms or headwinds, she can finish first. But if *Joshua* does not take the suicide tack, if she stays in the wake of the 50 ft boat, she'll be beaten flat.

That is where we are right now. . .and the big boat is far ahead. She has not yet finished the race, but if we do not take the suicide tack, she will win it for sure. And when she does, the planet will explode, or else man will have become a brainless robot. Or both: robot-man will swarm over the earth, and our planet will rid herself of him like so much scum. A few Tibetan lamas may be left, and perhaps a handful of survivors in the mountains and at sea. And the whole cycle will have to start over again. The Monster will have won, and humanity lost.

Unless we understand in time where our last chance is; the

last door left ajar in our age of nuclear devices and general decay of body and soul.

I dream of the day when a country of the modern world has an intensely simple president and barefoot ministers. I'd ask for citizenship right away.

Christ and the Apostles were barefoot vagabonds and I'm sure it helped them work miracles. They were remarkably simple too, just like Buddha and all the saints. And our times have never seen a man as great as Gandhi at the head of a nation.

The automobile manufacturers and munitions makers will call it an outrage to Freedom and Everything We Hold Sacred when they hear our anthem. . .but our earth would find herself again, and men as well. Just men, with no capital letter. Our nation would not collect gold medals at the Olympics, but the gold medal supermen would listen to our anthem. And they would seek citizenship so as not to be superior any more. Then the manufacturers of cars, and oil, and super giant planes, and bombs, and generals, and all-the-rest would gradually begin to feel that the turning has been finally taken, that it is a thousand times truer to have men guided by heart and instinct than the twisted gimmicks of money and politics.

The Monster has arranged things so that the hippies are accused of lots of crimes. Their crime is feeling deeply that Money is not the ultimate goal in life. It is refusing to be accomplices of a society where anything goes so long as it is legal. It is disagreeing with the physical and spiritual depradations of the race for Progress. That so many understand this is a great hope for us all.

Many are hippies without appearing to be. There are many more than we think, fortunately. Lanza del Vasto, Jean Rostand and his team of World Citizens, the Friends of the Earth, men like Ralph Nader, who take on the biggest corporations of America and force them to stop wrecking everything for Money, men like the thruway builder who turned around and burned his car, to ride a bicycle, after he realized where thruways lead and what surrounds them; Charles Reich who wrote *The Greening of America* and shows thousands of people how the Corporate State really works, Aldous Huxley with his book *Island* who shows how things could work if we only wanted to open our eyes. All these men are fighting the Monster, with the simple, human way of life of hippies, kids and adults; their search for peace, respect for nature, feeling of brotherhood without borders, renewed awareness that we all belong to the same big family, their communion with things around us. All the beautiful and good the human soul can do, these true things we can't live without.

The hippy president has not come yet. Many of us have been waiting for him. We have been waiting for two thousand years. And sometimes you feel a little tired, and say 'What's the use?' So then you do some thinking. You think of your friends too. . .

They left, one after the other, like seagulls answering the horizon's call. But we agreed to meet here in a few years, in our garden, with the cricket and the rat. He is completely tame now, and draws near as soon as he hears me breaking the coconut shell. Sitting crosslegged in the grass, I put the meat down next to my feet. He comes to eat it, unafraid, and looks at me, telling me the old debt is wiped away. There is another debt, though, a very old one. It was in Singapore, 20 years ago.

In the harbour, my junk *Marie-Thérèse* started making an alarming amount of water. I had left Indochina penniless. If I had wanted to leave with money, I would never have gone, or else left many years later exhausted by Money. And there I was in Singapore, with a boat that needed a complete professional caulking job, and no means of earning money in that foreign port. So I had already reached the end of my voyage, barely 600 miles from the start. And I could see no way out.

A guy came to see me. I did not know him. He brought a crew of professional caulkers. He paid for everything, and he wasn't rich. Then he said, 'Pass this on to a stranger as I did for you. Because I got it from a stranger too, who helped me one day, and told me to pass it on to another in the same way. You don't owe me anything, but remember to pass it on.'

Now, I believe this whole book is in the scales. If it were otherwise, the route we have followed together would be nothing but words.

Cricket chirps clearly in the garden. Rat looks at me gravely. And I dream that the unknown hippy of Singapore goes to see the Pope, and says,

'A friend is finishing his book, and has asked that his rights be paid to you. He hopes you'll use this drop of water to help rebuild the world by fighting with all the weight of your faith in man at the side of the barefoot vagabonds, the Friends of the Earth. They all know that man's destiny is linked to our planet, a living creature like ourselves. That is why they walk the paths of the Earth and want to protect her. They sense that through her, mankind of all churches will rediscover the Source of the universe from which the Monster has cut us off.'

The Pope is really surprised. He wonders how the barefoot tramp got into his well-guarded palace. Just then, he sees a little white seagull perched on his armchair, and understands that she helped the tramp slip in. The Pope feels glad; he was a little lonely this evening. And he offers his guest a chair.

The barefoot tramp prefers to sit crosslegged on the floor, and he says,

'Because of the Monster, men are destroying each other and destroying our Earth for very low motives. In addition, they're multiplying like rabbits: there will be twice as many of us swarming here in just thirty years, and four times in seventy years if things go on the way they have. How will our children and grandchildren make it, if we're suffocating already? How will they make it, if we don't find the Source in time by all of us getting together fast to fight the Shame and Insanity of the modern world?'

The Pope smiles. He likes barefoot tramps and vagabonds; they remind him of the beginnings of Christianity, when it was simple. So he offers him a cup of tea.

The tramp sips slowly, without talking, blowing on his tea because it's hot and good. He too likes this Pope, who symbolizes the little flame of spirituality which still flickers in corners of the West.

When he finishes his tea, the barefoot tramp gets up and says,

'Holy Father, we trust spirituality, not any particular religion, and we trust you. If your religious beliefs keep you from joining us in our fight, pass our rights on to the Friends of the Earth; it is for everyone's garden, all churches rest on her, she's the one who carries them all.'

The Fairy Tern comes and lands on the Pope's knee. He strokes her very gently. She looks at him with her immense eyes. And the Pope asks the barefoot vagabond whether she can stay with him for a few more days, in his palace. The vagabond says yes, of course. Then he joins his hands before his chest to greet his host, and leaves.[1]

My book is finished. In a manner of speaking, since I don't yet know what it's like on the banks of the Ganges. And it may not be necessary to go that far. The Ganges is everywhere, and especially within each of us.

Oh! One more thing before I pack up. It is from Steinbeck's *East of Eden*, a book I like very much, a fine companion on a voyage. In one chapter, Lee the Chinese and old Samuel discuss a Bible verse where a word is translated differently in the American Standard and the King James versions. The word was so important that Lee consulted his Chinese community. And the Chinese got so interested in the exact meaning of the verse at issue that they learned Hebrew to try to part the veil. At the end of two years, they were ready. One of the accepted translations said 'Thou shalt rule over sin' (a promise). The other equally accepted translation said 'Do thou rule over sin' (an order). The Chinese had found that it read 'Thou mayest' (a choice). And they knew their two years spent working and meditating on it had not been wasted.[2]

> *Samuel said, 'It's a fantastic story. And I've tried to follow and maybe I've missed somewhere. Why is this word so important?'*
>
> *Lee's hand shook as he filled the delicate cups. He drank his down in one gulp. 'Don't you see?' he cried. 'The American Standard translation* orders *men to triumph over sin, and you can call sin ignorance. The King James translation makes a promise in "Thou shalt", meaning that men will surely triumph over sin. But the Hebrew word, the word* timshel *– "Thou mayest" – that gives a choice. That says the way is open. That throws it right back on man. For if "Thou mayest", it is also true that "Thou mayest not". Don't you see?'*

[1] Excerpt from a letter to my publisher: 'Please pay all royalties due me from the sale of this book (French and foreign rights) to the Pope.'

[2] *East of Eden*, by John Steinbeck (The Viking Press, New York and William Heinemann, London)

Appendix

The west to east route in the vicinity of the 40th parallel was chosen for this circumnavigation because of the dominant westerlies in these latitudes. East winds are sometimes encountered there, but they are unusual and of short duration, as they represent an anomaly in the general wind pattern.

In the south, summer lasts approximately from the middle of November to the middle of February. December–January is midsummer. In that period of the year gales are less frequent (but sometimes more severe) than in winter, and the days long. It is the best period; or the least bad, if one prefers. For *Joshua* it was good, with very few gales. But there can be very bad summers too. The clipper captains expected one bad summer out of three.

For yachts of our size, it is better, during preparation, to consider the season as always bad. As I said, December–January is midsummer in the southern hemisphere, yet December was the month *Tzu Hang* pitchpoled in the South Pacific. It was also in December that *Joshua* ran into the most dangerous gale of her career, during Tahiti–Alicante. In January, Robinson's *Varua* (50 tons displacement) surfed over incredible distances, trailing warps, bowsprit under water. So midsummer can be very hard. A boat leaving Europe to sail around the three capes will in any case have to round Good Hope too early in the season if she does not want to find herself in the Horn waters too late. And the smaller and slower the boat, the sooner she will have to be off Good Hope. Knox-Johnston's *Suhaili* had to leave England in June so as not to reach the vicinity of the Horn too late, and therefore had to round Good Hope in early spring when the gales are stiff, and then continue across the Indian Ocean out of the best season. But Knox-Johnston had no choice, as his boat was smaller, and therefore slower, than *Joshua*.

Is it better to round Good Hope too soon, or the Horn too late? Vito Dumas picked the end of May or early June to round the Horn from west to east. In his book, he considers that that was the best period. Being Argentinian, he was well informed. I believe Chichester rounded in March, as did Alec Rose at about the same time the following year, in a 32-ft boat. In his trimaran *Victress*, Nigel rounded on March 18 or 19; *Joshua* on February 5 on this trip, and January 16 during Tahiti-Alicante.

As I write these lines, I learn that my pals from the *Damien* rounded the Horn from east to west against the wind on March 4, 1971. They then called at Ushuaïa on the Beagle Channel in Patagonia, and headed for the South Shetlands, South Georgia Island and then Cape Town, by way of the South Atlantic. Knox-Johnston rounded the Horn west to east in January, a few weeks before *Joshua*.

I am under the impression that Good Hope is more dangerous than the Horn, because of the areas of convergence of the warm current from the Indian Ocean and the cold Antarctic current. But it is anybody's guess. Loïck Fougeron and Bill King both more or less pitchpoled toward the end of October in the South Atlantic, around the 40th parallel, before Good Hope. On the same day, Knox-Johnston was nearing Tasmania, after rounding Good Hope and crossing the Indian Ocean much earlier in the season, under very difficult conditions (capsize, self-steering out of commission, leaks). And while *Captain Browne* and *Galway Blazer II* were being pummelled by the heavy weather in the South Atlantic, *Joshua* had already rounded Good Hope and was sailing with a nice force 5 to 6 wind in the Indian Ocean, making a little northing. She then encountered calms and light airs until Cape Leeuwin, with only one westerly gale for the entire Indian Ocean crossing. A matter of luck. How would *Joshua* have compared to *Captain Browne* and *Galway Blazer II* in the gale that put those two boats out of action? Nobody can tell. In the high latitudes, you're in the hand of God.

For the Indian Ocean crossing I had selected a calmer zone, between the 37th and 38th parallels, to be in good physical shape on entering the Pacific, whereas Knox-Johnston tore along south of the 40th parallel so as not to be late rounding the Horn. He was racing time and seasons, far more than other boats. A sailor is always racing in those parts. And if *Joshua* had beaten *Suhaili* to the mark (it is by no means sure that

Joshua would have finished first), it would have been a grave injustice, as Knox-Johnston's boat was much smaller, and much less sound.

Whatever the size of a sailboat, this route is dangerous. And the smaller the boat, the more dangerous, especially if she is a traditionally built wooden boat and far from new. Yet of the fifteen who have sailed in the area (including Nigel's *Victress*), I believe only one has been lost—blown aground during her stop at Tristan da Cunha without loss of life. Four others, *Tzu Hang, Ho-Ho, Galway Blazer II* and *Captain Browne*, had to give up after major damage. The only one to be lost with all hands was Al Hansen, after rounding Cape Horn from east to west (against the wind) far offshore, under much more difficult conditions than on a west–east passage, which is downwind. *Tzu Hang* next rounded the Horn from east to west, far offshore, in January 1969.

Anyone who has sailed in the high latitudes knows they can be extremely hard on equipment, and considers the technical preparation to be of major importance. I will not venture to give advice, as I have too much yet to learn. I will only describe what I noticed, the way I solved various problems, and my observations and thinking at the present and considerably limited state of my knowledge. The sea will always be the sea, full of enigmas and new lessons. And when I happen to mention a supplier or manufacturer, it is never out of gratitude for services rendered. I received assistance for this voyage, and am grateful to those who helped me to fit out and prepare. But I will never speak well of this or that piece of gear if I am not able to recommend it sincerely to my sailing pals.

All that follows is written with cruising in mind, not racing. For a racing sailor, a good sail is one that keeps its shape perfectly and draws to the limit for one season, even if it is worthless when that season is over. For us, a good sail is one in which the material can last ten years, even if it loses its shape a little. Good cruising sailmaking will often be bad for racing, because a sail built to last will be reinforced by chafe patches and extra stitching that impair the efficiency of a racing sail, where a tenth of a knot means the difference between winning and losing. Racing masts, also, must be as slender as possible—if they break sometimes, it's too bad—the blocks as light as possible, even if they have to be replaced more often. In cruising, the mast has to be above all strong, even if somewhat oversized shrouds increase windage. And one should be able to climb the mast easily to look for reefs or change a halyard or fix something in the middle of the ocean. So we screw rungs to it, something a racing sailor would not even consider. Because *our problems are not the same*. Racing thinks: *performance at all cost*. Cruising thinks: *simple, cheap, strong, durable*. This is true not only for the high latitudes, but for all types of cruising.

Sail

Strength and chafe resistance
I said earlier that for those of us who cruise, whether coastwise, on long ocean crossings in the tropics, or in high latitudes, a good sail is one that lasts a very long time. It must be borne in mind that the thousand square feet of a single set of sails for a boat the size of *Joshua* cost approximately $2000, $2 a sq. ft being about the minimum for a well reinforced sail. That does not include spare headsails, or a genoa, apart from a storm jib, which is really essential. To be properly outfitted, one should really have spare headsails, if only in case of damage (headsails being the most vulnerable). And aside from the risk of damage, it is nice to have a good wardrobe to make the most of a weak breeze by putting up a genoa and big staysail. As for the main and mizzen, a cruising boat can get by with a single set for a trip round the world in the trades, and even in the high latitudes. The earlier trip from France to Tahiti, returning by way of the Horn, was made with the original main and mizzen. Few are the boats with a spare mainsail: the one being used is enough; in case of chafe or accidents, one repairs it. The mainsail on David Lewis's catamaran *Rehu-Moana*, which called at Tahiti after passing the Straits of Magellan and the channels of Patagonia, displayed hand stitching from one boltrope to the other, made between gales; 30 to 50 ft of stitching, at least. But a decently heavy mainsail seldom rips to shreds; it can always be repaired. In addition, a mainsail is protected from the seas. Once furled on its boom in bad weather, nothing can happen to it

except under unusual circumstances, which is not true of the much more exposed headsails.

This doesn't mean that one can't sail without spare jibs and staysails. *Joshua* did two years of cruising school with a single set of sails. Yves Jonville's *Ophélie* has only one set, as does Roger Rey's *Heurtebize*, Henri Cordovero's *Challenge*, and many others. It calls for a little more caution so as not to have one's feathers plucked in a gust. And in light airs one goes more slowly, dreaming of a genoa and a big staysail. But those can come later; the main thing is that one can put to sea and go very far with a single set of sails if one wants to.

By 'a single set of sails' I imply that every boat has a storm jib as well. After all, 50 or 70 sq. ft of sail is not that expensive, especially since one can cut and sew this heavy weather sail one's self; the quality of the cut is not too important for a storm jib. Raised in place of the jib in a fresh wind, a storm jib adds years to the life of the working headsails.

I use No. 16 sail needles (the smallest I know) or even ordinary round needles for repairing Tergal [similar to Dacron and Terylene], so as not to damage the fibres. For repairs involving several layers of material (head, tack or clew), I use the heavier No. 15 or 14 needles, as smaller ones would not go through. A sewing palm is essential, as is a supply of fairly heavy Tergal [Terylene or Dacron] thread and a good piece of beeswax to wax the thread.

For a sail to last a long time it should be triple stitched with the heaviest thread possible. With only two rows of stitching, the occasional flapping, and especially the continual shivering of a sail closehauled, tends to cause the panels to work very slightly: this chafes the thread in the needle holes, because synthetic sailcloth is hard, sharp material. With three rows of stitching, the panels are more tightly held together and work less, and this prevents or limits the cutting of the thread in the needle holes.

This is easier to understand if the stitching of two panels is compared to two thin metal sheets held together by two rows of loose, small diameter rivets: the holes will be enlarged and the little rivets will shear off. If there were three rows of bigger rivets (three rows of stitching with heavier thread) the two sheets would be more tightly held together, they would work less and they would not shear the rivets; also the larger diameter rivets would not enlarge the holes.

I am not making anything up, because I have looked at sails made in New Zealand (the land of wind): they were sewn with heavy thread in three rows of stitching. Sailmakers do not like to use heavy thread—one reason for their reluctance is probably because they have to refill their thread bobbins more often, and this slows the work down.

I had two complete sets of sails for this trip, plus a good number of jibs and staysails, all cut from material used in racing. It was to be a trial for a friend who manufactures Tergal. He gave me the material free, and I sent him the sails after the trip so that he could examine the material in his laboratory, to see how it had stood up. With two complete sets, I was not taking any risk, and gladly agreed to the experiment. Otherwise, I would never have dared set out on a trip this long with sailcloth I was not personally familiar with.

It is not easy to recognize synthetic sailcloth that meets cruising requirements. One can make a reasonable try by feeling the material. If it is very supple and does not crackle at all under the fingers, it ought to be all right. A sail needle (triangular in section) should go through it without the slightest sound from parting the fibres. But if the material is already 'a bit stiff' even before being made into a sail, if one can hear the needle push through; then it is more than likely that the material does not meet cruising requirements, because durability is put well ahead of the extra tenth of a knot on a close reach.

A sailmaker usually knows what distinguishes racing from cruising; he will have materials designed specifically for each. And I think that the best credential a sailmaker can show is to be a sailor himself. Being right in a gale helps one to grasp many things about reinforcements and eyelets. A flat calm with a swell lets a sailmaker see where a sail rubs against the shrouds, and to understand what steps should be taken to keep them from chafing the stitching. These are details that will allow a sail to last *much* longer, and to take a few mistakes by the crew without complaining.

Sail track

Whether coming into port or lowering canvas in a fresh wind, it is important that sails come down easily. A well lubricated

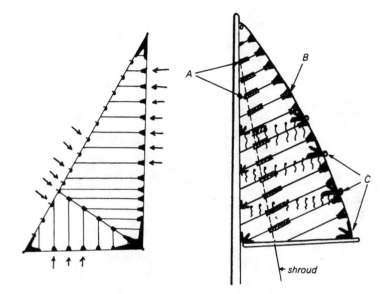

shroud

Headsail reinforcement

The black spots in the drawing indicate all the places that should be reinforced; arrows indicate the areas which suffer the most. As well as patches sewn over the seams at the leech and foot (see detail) it is very useful to sew a patch next to each hank. In calm weather the hanks tend to chafe and split the canvas when the boat is rolling, and in fresh winds the pull on the hanks causes great strain around the eyelets.

Main and mizzen reinforcement.

A The dotted line shows the wear caused by contact of the shroud and the sail. Baggywrinkle on the shrouds is good, but is inadequate in certain conditions. The patches serve to limit chafe against the shrouds, and they must be long enough to be effective when the sail is reduced by reefing, because the area of contact is then altered.

B When a sail gets torn, it is almost always from violent flogging, which can split it along the whole length of a seam, all the way from the leech. The highest seams are the most exposed, for it is the top of the sail which flogs the hardest when tacking in fresh winds, or when lowering sail. (See detail.)

C The reinforcements at the leech cringles are subjected to great stress and it is advisable to distribute the strain. The detail sketch shows how these patches are sewn on Joshua's sails.

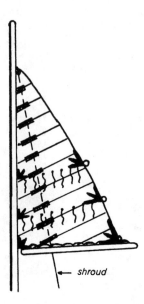

shroud

Seam patches when sail area is reduced
The sail is shown with the first reef tied in. With the area thus reduced,
the sail is a different shape, and the shrouds touch on a different line
across the patches. If a further reef is taken in, these patches will be just
long enough to still protect the seams.
The reef bands should be angled slightly upwards towards the leech, to
prevent the end of the boom sagging. The stronger the wind, the higher the
waves, and the end of the boom should naturally be higher in extreme
conditions than in fine, to avoid being plunged into the sea during a
heavy roll or extreme heeling.

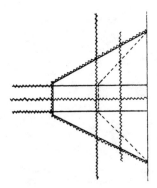

Seam reinforcement at the leech
The triangular shape allows the edges to be cut on the bias across the
weave, for better strength. The patch is sewn 'astride' the leech. it should
extend more on one side than the other, to distribute the thicknesses of
canvas.

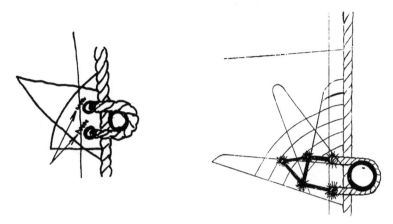

Reinforcement at cringles
Weaknesses that will lead to tearing (on left):
Insufficient thickness of the reinforcement, which is only two layers of canvas.
The two eyelets take all the pull of the thimble, without being backed up by extra help. Tearing will occur next to the eyelets, as shown on the left.

There are seven layers of reinforcing patches. The extra eyelets spread the pull on the thimble over more of the reinforced area near the cringle, which is where the pull is strongest and tearing the most likely and worrying.

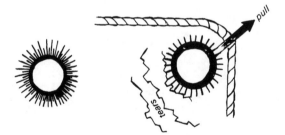

Eyelets
The principle shown (left) is good, for the stitching forms two circles, of which one is well away from the edge of the hole. In the old marine tradition, all eyelets were made in this fashion.
The needle holes on the right form a single circle too close to the eyelet. Under a strong pull the canvas will tear in spite of the number of reinforcing layers: even with ten layers of cloth, such an eyelet will never do the work it is meant for.

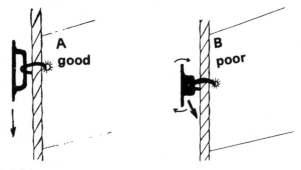

Sail slides
Slides which have an open flange are a good design: when the sail is
hoisted or lowered the siezing or shackle pulls upward or downward along
the axis of movement of the slide, and it does not jam in the track.

Poor slide design: the seizing or shackle works in a fixed point at the
centre of the flange, and thus tends to twist the slide so it jams in the
track. The large arrow shows the direction of pull when lowering sail, and
the two small arrows show the direction in which the ends of the slide tend
to lift or dig in.

track makes things easier. I have used tallow, but it tends to get
sticky after a month or two. Vaseline in a tube has given
excellent results. Two-stroke motor oil also suits me, but it
does not last as long as vaseline.

Joshua's sail slides are of the large becket type, shown on the
left of the diagram; the one drawn on the right, with the small
hole in the centre, always tends to jam.

Blocks

Before leaving, the sheet and halyard blocks had lasted 35,000
miles with their original pins and sheaves. For this voyage I
therefore used new ones of the same type. They are very
traditional wooden blocks with nylon sheaves, taking $\frac{1}{2}$ in. to $\frac{5}{8}$
in. diameter line ($1\frac{1}{2}$ in. to 2 in. circumference) without friction
against the wooden cheeks. They are strong, and not expensive
compared to modern blocks.

Lines: chafe

I was perfectly satisfied with the braided Tergal line manu-
factured by Lancelin. It resists chafe well, and a $\frac{1}{2}$ in. ($1\frac{1}{2}$ in.

circumference) line used as a sheet for a 40 ft boat will never part unless it is worn by chafing somewhere.

It should be noted that tallow, petroleum grease, or any oily substance gives synthetic line considerable chafe resistance. I have always carefully lubricated the nip at the sheaves by vigorously rubbing tallow into halyards and sheets at those points.

The mizzen and staysail halyards, pre-stretched Tergal, were deliberately measured about 5 ft too long. This allowed me to cut off a few inches every week at the sail head end, so as to shift the area bearing on the sheave. In that way, the working part of these halyards was always new. Tallow in addition, of course. I never had to replace a halyard during the entire trip. Still, as a precaution, there were spare halyards for the jib and staysail in place along the shrouds. I did not use them, but felt better knowing they were there.

The jib and mainsail halyards were flexible $\frac{3}{16}$ in. stainless steel wire, rove through stainless steel blocks made by a friend, with very large sheaves (3 in. in diameter). It is important that stainless halyards run through large diameter sheaves, so that the wire is not bent too sharply. Stainless steel is much more susceptible to work hardening than galvanized steel; the stainless strands fatigue and break if the sheave diameter is not as large as possible.

To wind up the problem of lines chafing, I have got excellent results by soaking my reef pendants with oil at the nip of the cringles. As the Tergal pendants are only $\frac{3}{8}$ in. (1$\frac{1}{8}$ in. circumference) line for the mainsail and $\frac{5}{16}$ in. (1 in. circumference) for the mizzen, chafe is rapid in the reef cringles because of the constant motion of the leech of the sail. Once soaked with oil (I had a can of two-stroke motor oil along), the three-strand line stood up far better. I only had to replace the reef pendants twice in ten months; without oil, it would have been five times.

Henry Wakelam got the idea of oiling lines after noticing the chafe resistance of a nylon mooring line full of diesel oil that we picked up in a harbour. I have heard that fatty substances reduce the strength of synthetic lines. But traction resistance is not really a factor when compared to the problems of rubbing and chafe. Line makers may have run tests on the subject: so what if a sheet treated for chafe resistance had its breaking strength reduced to 3300 pounds, for example, against 3700 for untreated line? What cruising people want is for the gear to last a long time, because it costs and weighs a lot.

Mast rungs

For cruising, near or far, it may be necessary to climb up the mast to change a halyard or block, to look around for a lighthouse, or to check the entrance of a pass or harbour. The rungs I screwed on as alternating steps on the main and mizzen masts are invaluable. They were designed by Guy Raulin, a sailing friend, using $\frac{1}{4}$ in. steel rod. Mock spreaders 3 ft below the main masthead let me sit down to work comfortably.

Masts and rigging

Joshua's masts are slightly oval, solid wooden poles, shaped with adze and plane. They are solid for economy, although a hollow glued mast would be lighter and perhaps just as strong, while putting less strain on the rigging. When pitching, the momentum of a heavy mast puts great stress on the rigging.

Shrouds are $\frac{5}{16}$ in. and $\frac{3}{8}$ in. diameter stainless steel wire for the mainmast, and $\frac{5}{16}$ in. diameter for the mizzen. I prefer to use oversized shrouds on the mizzen, because the mast is a heavy one, and poorly supported fore and aft, since it can't have forestays or fixed backstays. I do not use a spring stay (a wire joining the two mastheads, sometimes found on ketches) because if one mast comes down, the other almost always follows.

There are no splices in my shrouds, but cable clamps instead. I prefer three cable clamps to a splice, as the strands of a splice in stainless steel wire tend to fatigue and harden, and can then become brittle, particularly in the taut wire used in standing rigging. Clamps make repairs much faster and easier. When cable clamps are used, the lowest one (nearest the thimble) should be tightened moderately, the second more, and the third all the way; this avoids straining the wire just after it rounds the thimble. I always put the U-shaped part of the clamp against the shroud's 'non-working' short end (see diagram). Otherwise it could put unnecessary local stress on the shroud proper.

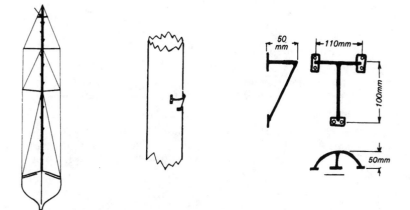

Arrangement used on Joshua
False spreaders, for sitting on while working at the top of the mast.

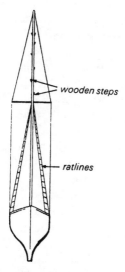

Arrangement used by Inaé and Gerard Borg
Above the spreaders, reached by way of fixed ratlines on the lower shrouds, there are wooden steps screwed to the mast.

Thimbles

Whether clamps or splices are used, the usual thimbles are not designed for stainless steel. Stainless is fragile when bent, and the usual thimbles have too small a radius of curvature; the wire suffers and tends to harden. That is how a *new* mizzen shroud parted just under the thimble at the point of greatest curvature (see diagram). With galvanized wire the problem does not arise, since galvanized does not readily fatigue, and tolerates a much smaller curvature radius than stainless steel. Good thimbles for stainless steel should be very big: I could easily see them 3 in. wide and 4 to 5 in. high.

As for the system used on airplanes, where the shroud is swaged directly into the end fitting of the rigging screw, without bending, I instinctively distrust it. Sure, it should never slip. . .but if the stainless steel shroud gradually fatigues, it will part without warning, level with the terminal fitting. On the yacht *Solo*, calling at Tahiti, I saw two shrouds, about $\frac{7}{16}$ in. in diameter, which had parted right where they entered the end fitting, after 30,000 miles of sailing. With a thimble, you can see what is happening; a few strands beginning to part under the thimble will give warning, and start you thinking about a remedy. Mine consists of shortening the shroud, putting another thimble on the unbent part, and making up the length with a bit of chain (see diagram). No problems at the mast end of the shroud: the eyes go around the mast with a wide radius of curvature, and there is no fatigue at that end.

I take this opportunity to reiterate the mental process that guides us all in cruising: between a simple thing and a complicated one, we choose the simple, because it is cheap, quickly made, and can be repaired at sea with what we have on board in some out of the way place, without problems, expense or having to write away to Australia, Europe or America for spare parts. This permits us to cruise with peace of mind, going where and how we want, and in safety. Meanwhile, I will have to find some good thimbles. . .or make them myself, cut from solid metal.

Spreaders

On *Joshua* the spreaders are mounted flexibly. They weathered a collision before rounding Good Hope the first time, then five knockdowns when the masts were in the water, four of which

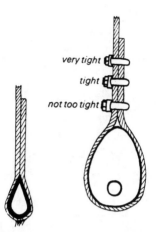

Small thimble (left): the stainless steel wire rope can fracture due to hardening around the small curvature of the thimble.
Large thimble (right): no such hardening of the wire.
The U-shaped parts of the cable clamps should always be placed around the short end of the wire rope.

Repair of a shroud which has broken under the thimble and been shortened. The length is made up with a short length of chain, or half a dozen shackles.

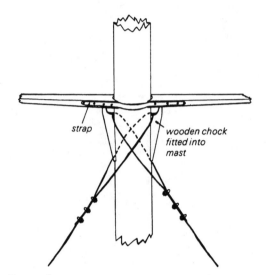

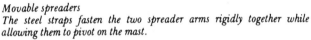

strap

wooden chock
fitted into
mast

Movable spreaders
The steel straps fasten the two spreader arms rigidly together while
allowing them to pivot on the mast.

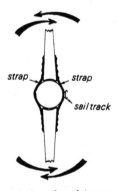

strap   strap

sail track

The wooden chock on which the sail track is screwed is interrupted by the
metal straps linking the spreader arms. This permits movement back and
forth under the track as the spreaders swing. During a heavy gybe, the
spreaders will feel happier if they are allowed to swing.

were very serious, when crossing the Indian Ocean and the Pacific the second time.

If the spreaders had been rigidly mounted with immovable metal fittings I am *positive* that *Joshua* would have stopped before Tahiti, and very probably before the first passage of Good Hope, as a result of the collision with the ship.

Not only is the flexible mounting very safe, in my opinion, but it is easy to install, cheap, and quickly done, without expensive metal fittings (see diagram).

I am still a fan of galvanized rigging screws packed with a 50/50 mix of tallow and white lead. I have seen threads protected in this way unscrewed by hand 8 years later. The same treatment works for shackles.

Remember to put a shackle between the chainplate and the rigging screw; it acts as a swivel and in certain cases keeps the shaft from being twisted. This 'swivel shackle' precaution is essential for the rigging screws on headstays; otherwise the shafts will eventually break because of the continual torsion to one side then the other, created by the strain and movement of the headsails.

Under way

From the high latitudes on, I used the following sails:

mainsail: 269 sq. ft, with three reef bands
mizzen: 150 sq. ft, with three reef bands
staysail: 194 sq. ft, with three reef bands
jib: 161 sq. ft, without reef bands
storm jibs: 54 and 75 sq. ft, with reef bands
staysails: 107, 65 and 54 sq. ft, all with reef bands. These small staysails were cut so that they could also be used on the bowsprit.

All these sails were of 9 oz. Tergal, a reasonable weight in my opinion and not too heavy. But the 161 sq. ft jib was of light 5 oz. Tergal. A further test for the maker was involved: 'How will such light material stand up during an extended trial?' For me, the question was, 'For the same sail area, is it worthwhile to have one very light headsail, easy to furl and carry?'

This light 161 sq. ft jib turned out to be so convenient that it went right around the high latitudes for six months before giving out shortly before rounding Good Hope the second time. I was very sorry to lose it, as it handled easily, furled very tightly, and was easy to carry from the end of the bowsprit to the forepeak when the weather worsened. When the wind eased it stayed well filled. It would never have lasted as long as it did, though, without all the reinforcements shown in the diagrams.

I prefer to reef the big 194 sq. ft staysail rather than change sails. I find it far less complicated. When the weather improves a reef is easily shaken out—quickly taken in again, too.

To reef the main and mizzen, I use a 'jiffy-reef' system which involves a running reef pendant. This makes it possible to reef without dropping sail to secure the reef pendant to the end of the boom. With this system *it is easier to haul on the leech pendant before the luff pendant*. Without running reef pendants, it is the other way around: the luff pendant has to be taken care of first.

It took me no more than a minute to reef the mizzen, and two to reef the main. No need to luff up: it was easy, even with the wind aft. As my pendants worked both ways, to either port or starboard, I could always stand on the *windward* side of the boom, which makes it *much* easier to reef. This detail is very important. All it takes is a cleat on either side of the boom for each pendant (i.e. for each reef band). The pendant runs from its port cleat, is rove through the port cheek block screwed to the boom directly under the appropriate reef cringle, runs up to that cringle, goes through it and down the other side, is rove through the starboard cheek block, and runs back along the boom to its starboard cleat. You can therefore haul on either the port or starboard end of the pendant. Standing always to windward of the boom, a good idea in foul weather as you can see breaking seas coming, you are unlikely to be caught by a roll which, standing to leeward of the boom, could send you overboard. The harness is there, of course, but that is no reason to take chances.

A small winch on either side of the main boom makes the leech pendant easy to haul taut, saving time, since the last inches are important, spelling as they do the difference between a well set sail and a bag. No need for a winch for the luff pendant, as the halyard will be hauled up taut after reefing.

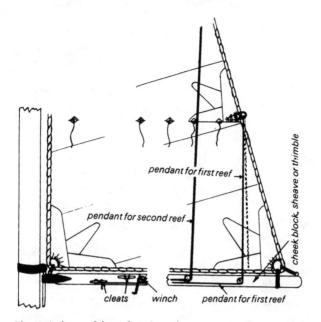

The vertical part of the reef pendant where it passes behind the sail on the starboard side is indicated by a dotted line. (Where it leads along the boom on that side is not shown in this sketch.) There is one winch and a few cleats on each side of the boom.

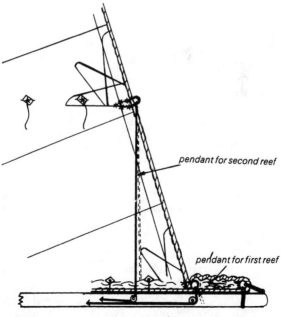

to winch and cleats on boom

The first reef has been tied in. The slack in the second reef pendant is then taken up. It is already rove.

No need for a winch for the mizzen pendants either; one good heave is enough to get them taut.

The whole system therefore consists of a small winch and four cleats on each side of the main boom, and three cleats on each side of the mizzen boom.

Reef points

To tie in the mainsail reef points with the wind aft, I harden in the sheet to be able to work without leaning out of the boat. In a strong wind, I start by tying every second reef point, and then tie the ones in between. I use a reef (square) knot rather than a slip knot. A reef knot may seem hard to untie, once pulled tight. In fact, it is very easy (see diagram) but the reef knot will not come undone by itself in foul weather, as the slip knot often does. The reef knot is particularly necessary for the staysail reef joints, because if they came untied when you are asleep at night under the impact of seas, the mass of loose canvas hanging like a big pocket under the sail could cause problems.

Loosening a square knot in small line

On the bowsprit

The system for changing the jib on the bowsprit is simple: a $\frac{3}{32}$ in. steel wire stretched horizontally between a mainmast shroud and the jibstay allows me to clip on all the sail hanks one after the other. The entire sail can then be slid out along the $\frac{3}{32}$ in. wire to the end of the bowsprit (or back in) without wind or sea being able to rip it out of my hands.

Sail areas

The big lesson learned from the earlier Tahiti-Alicante trip was the need to be able to adjust the sail area in all weathers. *Joshua* was then not really prepared on that score, as her smallest sail (the storm jib) was .86 sq. ft, and the close-reefed main 194 sq. ft.

For this trip the close-reefed mainsail covered 65 sq. ft, the close reefed mizzen 54, and I had everything I needed where headsails were concerned, with tiny sail areas if necessary. This allowed me to sail with peace of mind during the whole trip, never over and rarely under canvased, and always able to adapt sail area to changing weather conditions.

The diagrams illustrate the importance of this set of small sails and all the adjustments made possible by having plenty of reef bands, the last of which were placed very high.

Self-steering

In ten months at sea, I steered for an hour before the island of Trinidad, about the same at the entrances to Hobart and Cape Town, and then for the second half of a night following the last capsize in the Pacific when the wind vane broke and I did not dare go on deck to replace it. Finally, I steered to take the Papeete pass, and anchor.

The following diagrams show different types of self-steering rigs, designed according to the shape of the boat's stern. The guiding principle, always the same, corresponds to the cruising spirit: simple and strong. On Henri's moulded ply Frégate *Challenge* and Ivo's *Vlaag*, the vane acts on the auxiliary rudder by a system of cross-links. The main tiller is then lashed amidships, and the auxiliary rudder corrects the boat's heading. On Yves Jonville's *Ophélie*, and *Joshua*, the vane acts directly on the trim tab, which then controls the main rudder, with the tiller left free. Julio Villar's *Mistral* (a stock Super Mistral) uses a combination of auxiliary rudder as on *Challenge*, and a vane mounted on the trim tab head, as on *Ophélie* and *Joshua*.

These diagrams are not definitive; each could be modified as appropriate to suit the boat. *Joshua*'s is good, but not perfect

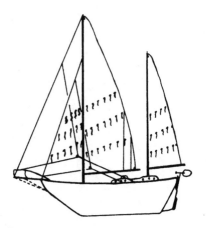

In the trade winds:
Mainsail 376 sq ft, three reef bands
Mizzen 215 sq ft, three reef bands
Staysail 194 sq ft, three reef bands
Large jib 237 sq ft, or small genoa of 376 sq ft

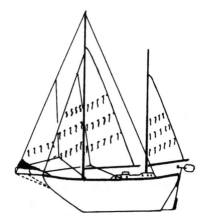

High latitudes (good weather):
Small mainsail 269 sq ft, three reef bands
Small mizzen 151 sq ft, three reef bands
Small jib 161 sq ft, lightweight Tergal
Large staysail 194 sq ft
The storm jib is furled and lashed to the end of the pulpit.

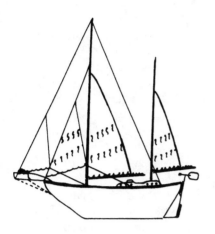

High latitudes (fresh breeze):
Small mainsail with one reef in, 194
sq ft
Small mizzen with one reef in, 129
sq ft
Staysail with one reef in, 129 sq ft
Small jib, reefed to 100 sq ft
I prefer not to reef this 161 sq ft jib,
but to wait until the wind freshens to
lower it and raise the storm jib in its
place.

High latitudes (strong winds or
moderate gale likely to abate):
Mainsail, double reefed, to 129 sq ft
Mizzen, double reefed to 86 sq ft
Staysail, double reefedm to 65 sq ft
Storm jib 54 sq ft

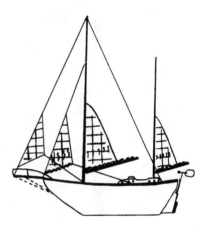

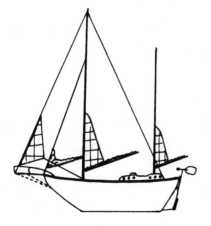

High latitudes (strong winds or
gales likely to strengthen):
Main, triple reefed (last reef) to 65
sq ft
Mizzen, triple reefed to 54 sq ft
Storm jib 54 sq ft

because the trim tab protrudes beyond the main rudder and can catch on other boats' mooring lines in port, or snag the log or fishing lines at sea (it has never caught seaweed, which floats on the surface). *Ophélie's* works on the same principle, but the trim tab is some distance from the rudder, which gives the trim tab greater leverage and probably makes it more effective in light airs. In addition, it will not snag moorings in port or the dorado line at sea.

Note especially that when the vane is mounted directly on the head of the trim tab (*Mistral, Ophélie, Joshua*) it is essential that the pivot point of the vane be at the convergence of the rudder and trim tab axes. Otherwise the rig will not work; the boat yaws and will not stay on course. The last diagram shows a badly designed self-steering rig.

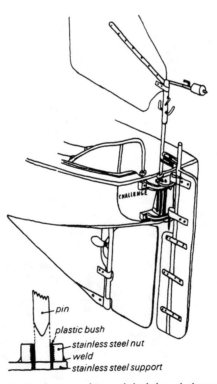

The two wooden brackets A *and* B *are bolted through the transom and braced by thin rods of stainless steel.*

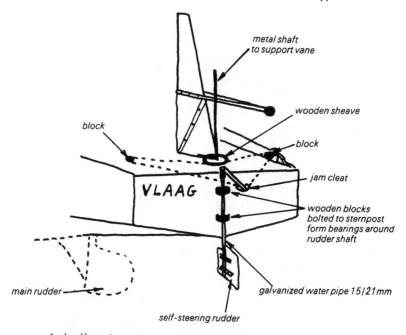

Ivo's self-steering system
The cable (dotted line) goes over a wooden sheave fixed to the vane and then through the two blocks to the end of a short tiller on the rudder shaft, where it is made fast with a jam cleat. The line is ¼ in. diameter Tergal.

High latitudes

The total trip amounted to 37,455 miles between noon sights, in ten months. Of that, there were about 29,000 miles in the dangerous area of westerlies for eight consecutive months. By way of comparison, *Joshua* only spent one and a half months in the high latitudes (December 10 to January 28) during Tahiti-Alicante, a fifth of the time taken for the long way, and with only 5000 or 6000 miles in dangerous waters. But whereas the sea had rumbled continuously in the high latitudes during the previous trip, it stayed relatively quiet, and even beautiful at times, for more than a complete trip around the world: an exceptional summer, without a doubt. Only during the second passage of the Indian Ocean did it become constantly dangerous for nearly two months, with winter coming on.

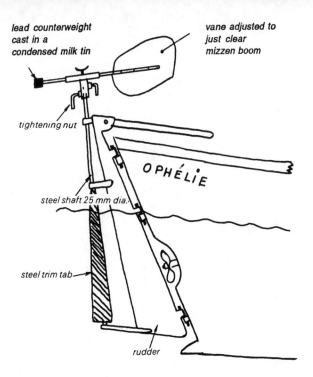

lead counterweight
cast in a
condensed milk tin

vane adjusted to
just clear
mizzen boom

tightening nut

steel shaft 25 mm dia.

OPHÉLIE

steel trim tab

rudder

The vane is adjustable up or down to allow the mizzen boom to pass over it. In bad weather there is less risk of touching the water in the high position. If the mizzen is reefed, the end of the boom will be higher than in the unreefed position.

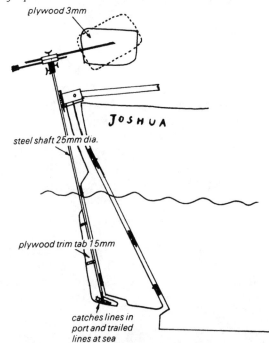

plywood 3mm

JOSHUA

steel shaft 25mm dia.

plywood trim tab 15mm

catches lines in
port and trailed
lines at sea

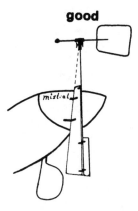

good

Here the principle is good, as the pivot of the vane is on the axis of the pintles of the auxiliary rudder. The fittings supporting the auxiliary rudder are in fact much stronger than is shown in this sketch.

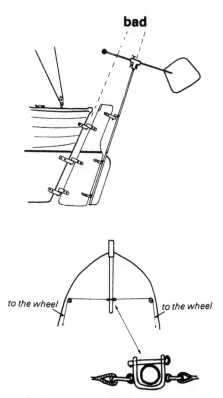

bad

to the wheel   to the wheel

The linkage to the tiller used on Ophelie and Joshua allows instant connection or disconnection.

Tahiti-Alicante witnessed a terrific prolonged gale linked with two lows, but only one knockdown, when the masts were just below the horizontal. That gale's main danger came from the secondary SE seas raised by the first low after it had passed. These secondary swells were about the size of a truck, and were mixed in with a confused sea coming from more or less every direction. The second low then kicked up extremely high westerly seas on which *Joshua*, under bare

Gale on the Tahiti-Alicante voyage
At A Joshua *risks digging in and pitchpoling into the secondary SE swell.*
At B Joshua *takes the main W swell 15° to 20° on the port quarter, thus meeting the secondary SE swell at an angle that is less likely to cause the bow to dig in or be struck directly by it. The risk of surfing is less. The more the boat surfs, the greater the danger of pitchpoling.*

poles, tended to surf. She then risked plowing into the secondary SE swell raised by the first low, and pitchpoling. It nearly happened twice before we started steering so as to take each westerly sea 15° or 20° on the port quarter. That tactic had a double effect. Firstly, by cutting the secondary SE swell at a distinct angle, we were less likely to plow into one, and thereby possibly pitchpole. Secondly, taking the main seas 15° or 20° on the port quarter caused *Joshua* to heel as she tore down the slope. The starboard part of the bow then pressed against the water somewhat like a ski, or the rounded side of a spoon. This prevented the bow from entering the secondary swell (see diagram).

On this trip, there were no comparable fantastic gales, but in exchange, three knockdowns with the masts horizontal or a little below, and four serious ones, well below the horizontal, with the keel 30° and once probably 40° above water. These last four knockdowns occurred during the second crossing of the Indian Ocean and the Pacific. The first two of this last series occurred ten or twelve days apart, in the Indian Ocean, *because of the boat's excessive speed for the very steep sea that was running at the time.* The last two, in the Pacific, were caused by *erratic breaking waves.* In all of these cases, *Joshua* was under way with shortened sail, doing better than 6 knots. The boat always righted herself in two or three seconds. It is of these four knockdowns that I am going to speak now.

Indian Ocean

The two knockdowns occurred at night, in gales from astern. I was awake in my bunk. That is what usually happens when something is up: you are in your bunk, not really tense but somehow expectant. The body rests as the mind roams the deck, observing, comparing, weighing wind and sea. The first time, *Joshua* was running downwind at 6 knots under the small 75 sq. ft storm jib and 54 sq. ft staysail, with main and mizzen lowered.

When she went over, I was certain it was not because of a breaking sea; I would have recognized the sound and felt the dull impact. There was no such thing: the boat hove down, lots of things went flying in the cabin. I did not understand how it had happened.

The second time, ten or twelve days later, the same thing again. This time, *Joshua* may have been moving a little faster, at the end of another gale, and before the longitude of Cape Leeuwin. Still no breaking sea. I couldn't understand it.

A few days later, I think I found the answer: I was on deck, wind force 6 to 7 full aft, speed 6½–7 knots, a winding wake due to the yawing. Suddenly the boat accelerated on the advancing face of a sea and luffed, heeling quite a lot. The windward deck dipped 6 or 8 in. into the water, and I distinctly felt the braking effect as the heel increased. Nothing happened, the heel did not exceed some 30° and the wind vane put the boat back on course, but I felt very clearly that it would not have taken much for us to go further.

When the sea is steep, I now think it better to reduce speed considerably under self-steering, leaving just enough sail for the rudder to respond instantly, but slowing enough to limit the risk of surfing on a steep sea. If the boat luffs while yawing, and is hove down as well, it can spell serious trouble for the masts.

It should be noted that the boat cannot start surfing unless she has already reached a certain speed: a board floating amid very large seas will stay at the same place. But if you push it a little at the right moment, it can start surfing. As a boat is not designed like a surfboard, she can stay under way without risk of surfing so long as she does not exceed a certain speed, which varies with the steepness of the waves. This threshold depends on the boat and the sea. Under 6 knots (and rather 5 than 6), *Joshua* is usually safe. It is likely that a boat with a long keel is less inclined to luff under these conditions than one of the same length with a short keel. But the more I see, the more I learn, the more I realize how little I know and to what extent everything can change according to the sea and the boat. The sea will always remain the great unknown. It is sometimes enormous without being too vicious; not as high a week or a month later, it can become very dangerous because of either a few cross-swells, or an unexpected or completely new factor. The person who can write a really good book on the sea is probably not yet born, or else is already senile, because one would have to sail a hundred years to know it well enough. Just the same, K. Adlard Coles' *Heavy Weather Sailing*[1] is a real accomplishment: he does not flatly affirm anything, but presents lots of *facts*, letting each reader weigh them in the light of his own observations.

Heavy Weather Sailing by K. Adlard Coles (Adlard Coles Ltd and John de Graff)

Pacific knockdowns

None of the gales of the long way exceeded 36 hours. Each time an isolated low was involved. When it had passed, another might come along, but after a sufficient interval for *Joshua* not to be affected by two lows at once, as had happened during Tahiti-Alicante.

I am going to speak of these gales in general; tell what I know of them, what I see, what I feel, what I usually do. First, a general picture of a typical gale.

1. High latitude lows move from west to east. In the southern hemisphere the wind turns clockwise around the centre. This low pressure centre moves eastward at 10 to 20 knots, and sometimes much faster near the Horn.

2. Most of these lows travel south of the 50th parallel. Small sailboats such as ours would normally always be north of the low's path, since we rarely stay below the 43rd parallel, except when rounding the Horn.

3. The further one is from the centre, the less violent the gale. The approach of a low is announced by a falling barometer, or by the needle's jumpiness: one can tell something is up.[1] So I put a little bit of north in my east (steering 075° or 080°) to stay as far as possible from the low's centre.

4. The low approaches. It is now fairly close, to the SW. The wind, which may have been hesitant from the north, goes to NW and freshens. In a few hours it is blowing a gale. The sea builds up, but is not dangerous for a 40-ft boat, and I try to keep some north in my east so as not to get too close to the low's path.

5. The low continues eastward. Soon it is due south and closer than before, although my course tends to take me away from it to the extent possible. Still, I am a little further from the centre than I would have been if I had continued due east since yesterday or the day before.

Now that the centre is due south, the wind blows very hard from the west and the main westerly swell, which has been circling the globe since the beginning of time, builds up

---

[1] Alan Watt's little illustrated book *Instant Weather Forecasting* (Adlard Coles Ltd, Dodd Mead) helped me tremendously to feel things faster, by observing the advance clouds. It also spared me needless worry. To my mind, this book is a masterpiece. I recommend it to all sailing people.

tremendously. In addition, the NW swell raised by the first phase of the gale (blowing from the NW before shifting to west) crosses the big westerly swell, provoking sometimes enormous breaking seas. That is where it really starts to get dangerous: the main westerly swell breaks in long sections in addition to the breaking seas from the NW. These NW breaking seas are often very powerful, and they frequently change direction somewhat as they break, hitting from almost NNW. That is why, when the gale enters its westerly phase, I prefer to alter course and steer ESE, so as not to risk being rolled over by one of these erratic NW seas.

When the NW phase of the gale has been moderate and short, these erratic breaking seas do not last long, and are not really big. Once the wind goes to west, the boat is in no danger of getting closer to the centre, since the low is continuing eastward, moving faster than the boat. I therefore think it wise to alter course to ESE at this time.

6. The low is still south of the boat, continuing eastward. The wind shifts to WSW and then it generally blows hardest. The sky clears and the sea is very heavy, sometimes enormous. It lasts a few hours, 3, 6, 8 or more, depending on the speed at which the low is travelling, its strength and other factors. It will have been wise to take the other tack and put a fair amount of south in my east, because if the residual NW swell is large, the erratic breaking seas coming from the port side can be very big. Obviously, these NW seas can hit far ahead or far astern of the boat, but they can sometimes break right on top of her. That is how the last two knockdowns happened in the Pacific, with the masts under and the keel 30° or 40° above the horizontal.

The first Pacific knockdown was not my fault: I had rounded New Zealand and was heading NE with Chatham Island about 60 miles on my right, when the gale entered its westerly phase. I therefore could not alter course without running a serious risk with the reefs, especially as the sea was too dangerous to go on deck with the sextant and so I was not quite sure of my position. It was on the 44th or 45th parallel, and I was in a hurry to reach milder latitudes, having rounded New Zealand south of the 49th parallel a few days earlier.

The last knockdown was even more severe, in only 34° south two weeks before Tahiti. And that time, it was entirely my

NW swell, but not very big

The low is to the SW and there is a NW gale in the boat's area. The NW swell is not dangerous for the moment, and the boat makes a course ENE, in order to get a little further away from the centre of the low, which will pass to the south. NB: In the high southern latitudes one views a chart with the South Pole at the top. In this sketch S is accordingly at the top, N at the bottom, E to the left and W to the right.

A *Enormous breaking waves are sometimes provoked by the over-lapping of the main swell from the NW with the residual swell from the NW gale.*

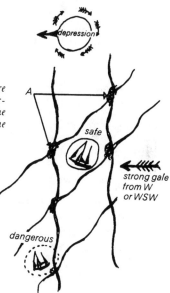

The low is now to the south of the boat. The gale has gone into a W or WSW phase and blows really hard. The upper boat has wisely altered course to ESE to avoid taking breaking seas on the port beam. The lower boat has made the mistake of not heading ESE and runs the risk of being struck on the port side by a rogue breaking wave. This is what happened to Joshua during the last gale we met before arriving in Tahiti.

fault: considering the very moderate latitude, I thought that the gale was just another one. Being in a hurry to catch the trade winds, I therefore did not alter course when the gale went into its westerly phase. And *Joshua*, continuing NE, found herself with her keel at least 40° above the water; a big erratic NW breaking sea, lots of noise and things on the ceiling, storm jib and small staysail stove in, wind vane broken. I quickly went on deck to connect the steering wheel, and steered from inside until dawn.

Heaving-to in the high southern latitudes

In the high southern latitudes, a gale from the *east* will seldom raise an exceptional sea, even when it blows like hell. I therefore think that it is always possible to heave-to without danger of being rolled over by a very large breaking sea; these remain of moderate size, and the boat can take advantage of her dead water to windward. *Joshua* usually heaves-to with close-reefed main sheeted flat and a little staysail aback, helm down. The dead water calms the breaking waves just like an oil slick.

The picture would be very different with a gale from the *west* quadrant, blowing in the same direction as the big westerly swell always present in the high southern latitudes. Under the stress of a stiff wind, this swell can very quickly become enormous, with gigantic breaking seas that no dead water could subdue, at least as far as a heavy displacement 40-ft boat is concerned.

In the northern hemisphere, breaking seas kicked up by a gale from the west are normally smaller, thanks to the barrier of the land masses (America and Asia), and yachts lying hove-to rarely suffer too much (rarely does not mean never. . .). In *Heavy Weather Sailing* one can see breaking seas that no yacht could ride out hove-to. Yet the pictures were taken in the Atlantic, between 30° and 35° north latitude.

Freak waves

It is strange but true: in the high southern latitudes, where the seas can be 50 feet high and 2000 feet long, they roll forward in endless procession, with occasionally one sea of abnormal size towering above the others, its approach visible from a considerable distance.[1]

[1] From *The Cape Horn Breed*, by Captain W. H. S. Jones (Jarrolds)

All sailors have occasionally noticed certain waves much higher than the others. They can even be encountered in the Mediterranean. I suppose these abnormally high seas are caused by the overlapping of several waves moving at different speeds. There is a little of everything in the sea: main swells, residual swells from an old gale, or those sent by a very distant low.

A wave passed under Tzu Hang *and she slewed slightly. Beryl corrected her easily, and when she was down in the hollow she*

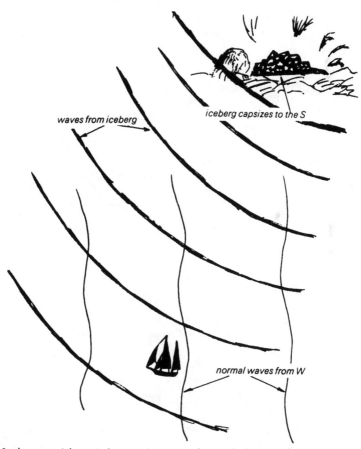

In the upper right, an iceberg capsizes. It can then send a big sea as far as the boat. If the sea is already heavy where the boat is, and the iceberg's sea overlaps another sea at just the wrong moment as it passes under the boat, it could create a freak wave.

looked aft to check her alignment. Close behind her a great wall of water was towering above her, so wide that she couldn't see its flanks, so high and so steep that she knew Tzu Hang could not ride over it. It didn't seem to be breaking as the other waves had broken, but water was cascading down its front, like a waterfall.[1]

How was this liquid wall formed, that plowed into *Tzu Hang*, sweeping both masts and the doghouse away, to leave a half-swamped boat on the point of sinking, with a 6 ft opening where the cabin had been? Coincidence of several seas crossing just at the wrong time? I would be inclined to think so. But freak waves could possibly have a completely different origin: perhaps the enormous surge from an iceberg capsizing far to the south. It is only a hypothesis, of course, but so many strange things happen at sea. And icebergs can capsize, it's well known...Also there are glaciers, which can calve, dropping huge blocks of ice into the sea.

It should be noted that *Tzu Hang* pitchpoled in 98° west longitude and 51 20' south latitude, just inside the extreme iceberg limit, according to the American Pilot Chart for the months of December–February.

This hypothesis remains fairly unlikely for small yachts such as ours, which generally pass well clear of the iceberg area. But I do not think it can be completely discarded, particularly since the ice area is fairly close to the south when the boat is rounding the Horn.

Problems under way

Celestial navigation

I used the English AP 3270 tables (the equivalent of the American HO 249). Three volumes cover the whole world (two for sun, planets and moon, and one for the stars). A position line is quickly worked out with HO 249: a single entry for the stars, two for the sun and planets. The 1963 reprinting of HO 249 explains how you can use it without a nautical almanac until the year 2000. HO 249 is put out by the US Navy Hydrographic Office.

[1] From *Once is Enough*, by Miles Smeeton (Adlard Coles Ltd)

It is good if the sextant telescope can be easily removed to allow aiming with both eyes open when the sea is heavy, or for star sights. At dusk, one can make out the horizon much more easily with both eyes open.

For this trip I took only three star sights in all, as the sun was enough, navigation being simple on the high seas. I was content to draw a position line in the morning and a meridian sight at noon, except when nearing land, when I drew further position lines in the afternoon. It must be kept in mind that the afternoon lines sometimes involve errors due to greater refraction, particularly in warm regions. Using stars, there is no refraction and fixes can be incredibly accurate (to less than half, sometimes a quarter of a mile), which is invaluable when nearing a low coast or an atoll. Then night fixes can be excellent, but the sextant observations must be good. Without the telescope and with both eyes open, I often took very accurate star sights on moonless nights during my previous sailing. It would have been impossible using the telescope.

Time

A 4 second chronometer error means a 1 mile error in a fix; 1 minute means a 15 mile error at the Equator and about 12 miles in the temperate zones. Since the advent of radio there are no more problems; one could navigate with an alarm clock.

For time signals, I use Station WWV, which gives Greenwich Mean Time every five minutes, 24 hours a day, on 5000, 10,000, 15,000 and 20,000 kc/s. I was able to pick it up during the whole trip on my Technifrance radio, which has been aboard for eight years.

As far as chronometers are concerned, I use the big Fred wall clock which is powered by a little mercury battery. It is regular, losing three seconds a day, and its battery lasts six months. I liked this big clock a lot because I could read the seconds from the cockpit, thanks to its large hands. I also had a waterproof self-winding Rolex which did not leave my wrist for the entire trip; the strap never broke, as I feared it might. Very accurate and regular, it was the watch I used most for sights, as I could read it any place on deck that I happened to be at the moment of observation.

A relatively recent watch mechanism exists, the Accutron, using an electronic resonating 'fork' instead of a balance wheel. It is guaranteed accurate to within one second a day.

Compass

The compass on a steel boat is strongly influenced by the metal mass. Even if well compensated for a given region, the compass readings could be way off in an area where the magnetic variation is different. Adding or subtracting degrees of variation is not enough to straighten things out; the entire compass compensation has to be redone. And to make matters worse, heeling throws it all off. So I have preferred to simplify everything: aboard *Joshua* there is a compass at the foot of the berth (it is wrong, but shows course changes) and a Vion hand-bearing compass in the cockpit. Neither is compensated; I even threw the magnets away. Standing in the centre of the cockpit, with the compass held as high as possible, the reading is correct. In addition, I check my course frequently against sun and star azimuths, especially when nearing land. It is child's play with AP 3270 or HO 249 (no sextant needed): just a glance at the clock, one entry in the table, and half a minute later you have the sun or star azimuth.

I admit that all this has a 'do-it-yourself' quality. It is far better, however, than relying on a compensated compass on a steel boat. And also it suits my temperament, which leads me to prefer reading my course in the sky and the signs of the sea, rather than on a magnetized needle. If I were to sail regularly in the Channel, though, or any similar place full of fog, rocks and current, I would adopt Jean-Louis Martinet's solution: he mounted his compass on *Ia Ora Na's* mast (30 ft steel cutter), far from the metal masses, with an electronic repeater compass in the cockpit. He managed a perfect installation very inexpensively, with quality work.

Weather reports

For the Channel, the Bay of Biscay, Good Hope and Australia, I taped the radio weather reports on my recorder. I was thus able to repeat them and get a better feel for the general trend, since I did not erase the previous days' reports.

After a certain period of time, a tape recorder can lose its sound quality, and give the impression that the speaker is dead. This is because the recording head (the metal knob that rests against the tape) has gummed up. I learned later that all one has to do is gently rub the head with tissue paper to revive its tonal qualities. There are also 'cleaning cassettes', which remove the particles deposited on the recording head. Also to be remembered: a 60-minute cassette is normally more robust than a 120-minute one.

Equipment made by Goïot

The Goïot winches and sail hanks were completely satisfactory. I took the winches apart after the trip to look inside: they were like new. Also, the mechanism is simple and strong. Despite their price, these winches are considerably less expensive than many others. They were given to *Joshua* by the manufacturer, but I repeat that I am not writing this out of gratitude: if I could not recommend these winches to sailing friends, I would not mention them. I think it essential to be careful when mounting them to isolate their light alloy bases from the steel of the boat, to avoid any risk of corrosion. I used Bostik, a black rubber-based adhesive, for coating the four mounting bolts. The same precaution would apply for bronze winches mounted on a steel boat.

The Goïot sail hanks surprised me. Those on the big staysail, almost continuously in service thanks to its three reef bands, did about 35,000 miles almost without a trace of wear (the staysail ripped before the end of the trip). Traditional yellow metal hanks would probably not have lasted a third as long; I had seen some give up the ghost just during an Atlantic crossing on the preceding trip. Calms really put sail hanks to the test: they get the most wear then, rubbing against the stays. For those who use Goïot hanks, I recommend soaking them in oil for a few days before securing them to the sail. They will be a little oily for a week, but the treatment keeps them working perfectly for a very long time. I prefer to have Goïot hanks one size too big; that way the sail slides more easily. Sail hanks that just fit tend to jam on the way down; $\frac{3}{8}$ in. hanks for a $\frac{5}{16}$ in. diameter stay are about right.

Stainless steel keyhole toggle shackles

I used these during the whole trip for tack and head on the jibs and staysails ($\frac{5}{16}$ in. shackles), and was completely satisfied. These shackles, made by the Vichard firm, always opened without a shackle key, and never failed. In addition, there is no risk of losing the toggle, as it can't come all the way out—one less worry.

In my opinion, the stainless steel keyhole toggle shackle is a solution midway between the usual slow-to-operate threaded galvanized shackle and the rapid-action model, where a press of the thumb releases the catch: the latter has earned its spurs in racing, but is made of yellow metal, which I distrust for really prolonged use.

Lights

In the shipping lanes I used a small dioptric lens kerosene (paraffin) lamp. Its glass lens concentrates the light from the wick instead of allowing it to scatter as would an ordinary shade. The light of this lamp carries much further than that of a large hurricane lamp, for an insignificant consumption of kerosene (about four tablespoons per night). Wind never blew it out, and I have only heard it praised on that score. I had it mounted quite low on the aft cabin hatch, and it was not hidden by any of the sails as the jib and staysail have relatively high tacks. So positioned, the lamp was visible from any direction; it was only slightly hidden by the mizzen mast, which was $2\frac{1}{2}$ ft aft. With the slight yawing, however, its light was probably also intermittently visible from astern, which ought to attract the attention of a ship. (But I normally never quite sleep while in the shipping lanes; I just stretch out in the cockpit to rest from time to time. And I try to cut them at right angles, to get through faster.)

When the weather is not fair, and a sea is running, I prefer to use a 250 candlepower Coleman pressure lantern, which is visible from very far away, and also makes a halo. It consumes a bottle of kerosene per night.

Movies and photography

Though this is not properly a part of sailing equipment, it should be mentioned here. I was equipped with the Japanese Nikonos underwater camera given to me by the *Sunday Times*. Good pictures and no worry about spray. My movie camera was a 16mm Beaulieu R16. It was highly recommended to me by Irving Johnson, who had made seven cruising school trips around the world on the famous *Yankee,* and has considerable experience with the problems of filming at sea. I am not sorry to have followed his advice: this very light camera allowed me to take difficult shots, especially from the bowsprit and the masts. I hardly missed a picture, though I was completely inexperienced, thanks to the very high quality lenses (75-25-10mm) and the built-in light meter, which obviates diaphragm errors.

To take the place of the little nickel-cadmium battery, which has to be recharged from an electrical outlet or a generator after 15 reels or so, a case was made out of an underwater flashlight for me, housing five standard batteries. Five 1.5 volt leakproof Wonder batteries lasted for 10 to 12 reels at 24 images per second. This gave me nearly complete autonomy, since the batteries left from the supply put aboard three years earlier still work perfectly.

Boots
All-rubber boots can be easily wiped dry inside with a rag. Wool or canvas lined ones stay damp.

Wool socks
Plastic bags over the socks, fastened at the ankles with rubber bands, let one move around the cabin comfortably when the floor is wet—which often happens upon coming below after handling sails or spending time on deck. Loïck also suggested taking a bundle of newspapers: a few sheets spread on the floor soak up the water, and one can walk on them without slipping. The result is excellent, and they can last a day before being replaced. On occasion, I even kept the sheets for several days before having to change them.

Jean Rivolier gave me some nylon-type lined slippers with very supple leather soles, used during the Paul-Emile Victor polar expeditions. They are pleasant to wear in the cabin, and very warm; no need for plastic bags.

Gloves and mittens
I had leather gloves for outside and mittens for the cabin. Even when soaked, the 'outside' gloves kept my hands warm.

Inside heating
None: warm clothes instead. It should be said that a metal boat really is as watertight as a tin can; what goes into a closet dry will come out dry.

Chapping

The state of one's hands is very important. With chapped, painful hands, one hesitates to make useful adjustments, and the going is slower. In addition, the hands almost always get worse. A few years earlier, during a cruising school season in the Mediterranean, a chapped middle finger caused me a lot of pain, to the point of making me practically unable to trim a sheet.

For this trip, I therefore kept a careful watch on my hands, using adhesive tape at the slightest sign of trouble. I took it off for the night, rinsed my hands well in fresh water, and rubbed the places that were beginning to chap with a stick of Dermophile Indien, after trying two other brands of cream I liked less well. I had no problems during my ten months at sea, but I kept a wary eye on my hands.

Fresh fish

As I was continuously towing the Vion patent log as a test for the equipment, I could not always troll, for fear my fishing line would snarl the log. But generally good sea conditions during the first passage around the world allowed me to troll a line for a third of the time, and for the entire first crossing of the Indian Ocean. Yet I caught only two dorados in the Atlantic trade wind and two 15–17 pound tuna in the high latitudes. The fresh fish rations would have been better if I had been able to troll with two or three lines, as I usually do, but one should not count too much on fishing at sea in these latitudes.

Fresh water

One usually figures an average of $2\frac{1}{2}$ quarts per day per person; probably a little more in the tropics. Two and a half quarts a day over ten months (303 days, to be exact) represents a consumption of 200 US gallons. As I left with 100 gallons, I therefore must have collected at least another 100 gallons of rainwater, with the buckets hung under the main and mizzen booms, in point of fact I collected much more, since *Joshua* arrived with her tank still half full, and I used a fair amount of fresh water to rinse clothes along the way. I could have reached Tahiti with my original hundred gallons if I had wanted to. So there is nothing to worry about in these latitudes on this score; a fact I had already noticed during Tahiti-Alicante.

On a long cruise in the tropics a boat will remain much freer

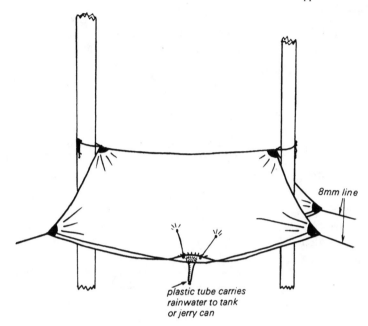

plastic tube carries
rainwater to tank
or jerry can

if she has an awning rigged with a very simple device which allows large quantities of rain to be collected when at anchor in out-of-the-way places. The system used on *Joshua* allowed us to subsist for months on rainwater.

Emergency watertight tanks

For this trip, only one 100 gallon tank was used for water. The other three contained food, clothes, blankets, socks, mittens, batteries, a spare radio, lined jumpsuit and sleeping bag. All this gear was 'extra', so if the boat had pitchpoled and smashed all of her ports, winding up half full of water, I could have got dry clothing and other items intact from these tanks.

Food and health

The grapefruit lasted three months, and I ate one a day or every other day for those first three months. Then I started on the lemons; individually wrapped in a sheet of paper, they lasted nearly seven months. I used one a day squeezed in water, half in the morning, half in the afternoon.

I took a single tube of vitamin C tablets during the whole trip, and a vitamin B-complex tablet every day, from the third month until my arrival. I drank about half a glass of seawater per day, putting a little into my rice water in place of salt; I drank some twenty bottles of wine and no liquor.

Cooking was done on a two-burner Optimus kerosene stove, without gimbals. I put a little asbestos in the cup, so the alcohol used to pre-heat it would not spill out when heeling; it acted as a wick, soaking the alcohol up. I also used a tiny butane stove to make tea, Ovaltine, bouillon or coffee, and was always able to cook, even in foul weather. The pressure cooker saw a lot of use; it has the advantage of not spilling. Little steel springs held it and the other pots on the stove.

I ate all I wanted and chewed well, to make the most of it. Yoga, which I discovered on this trip, helped me a lot on that point. I paid little heed to the lipid-glucid-protides proportions. My basic staple was white rice (I had not found any brown rice, which has more vitamins) and dried potatoes. I would then add canned or dried vegetables (peas, green beans, carrots, sometimes asparagus). The dehydrated products were produced by Professor Griffon (France) and by Batchelors Foods Ltd (Sheffield, England). I had a fairly heavy consumption of sweetened condensed milk (a can a day, or more), and Marvel powdered milk (England) mixed into the dried potatoes.

I always fixed two generous hot meals, plus a 'breakfast' of oatmeal, condensed milk and Ovaltine two or three times a day; two little snacks during the night. In short, there was a little of everything, including spices (curry, chutney, *nuoc-man*, soy sauce), a few cans of smoked oysters and mussels, jars of shrimp and salmon paste, etc.

All in all, I ate well for the first eight months, and less well during the last two, as I had finished up all the most appetizing things. On leaving Plymouth, I weighed 139 pounds; on arrival, 143 pounds, without oedema, gaining 4 pounds during the trip. My normal weight is 145 to 147 pounds, and abnormally low weight on setting out was no doubt due to fatigue and nervous tension related to the preparations.

Shortly after rounding Good Hope the first time, I was distinctly sliding downhill; not to the point of considering giving up, but on the wrong track: tired, still underweight, with no punch. I was no longer at all sure of reaching the Horn, and I felt that even if I managed to round it, I would probably drag myself across the Atlantic like an exhausted animal.

Yoga, which I started practising then, thanks to Desmond Dunne's little book *Yoga Pour Tous* (Les Ecrits de France)[1] allowed me to round four more capes without such a prolonged effort pushing me to my limits. It is both a physical and mental discipline, which took me a half hour to an hour each day. The results were surprising and very quick. The overall balance I derived from it allowed me to reach a far higher energy potential than I had had on leaving Plymouth. My ulcer had begun to give me pain after first rounding Good Hope. Yoga swept all that away: no more stomach pains in spite of canned goods and food that grew less and less appetizing as the trip wore on. No more lumbago in spite of damp blankets (they did get damp, finally). No nervousness despite the foul weather of autumn and winter in the Indian Ocean and the Pacific, and the four knockdowns of that second period.

I did my yoga regularly until the Horn, but thereafter in a less continuous and regular fashion, I must admit. I would not want to be thought of as any different from others, unfaltering or with a will that never wavers: I am like other men. I also did some gymnastics every day, particularly for the abdominal muscles.

After crossing the longitude of Tahiti, I continued eastward for about ten days, to be able to sail in the trade wind, taking it easy without any worries and resting up before getting back to land.

Seven days after arriving, I had a very thorough medical examination at Tahiti's Jean Prince hospital. All of the test reports were normal, except my stomach X-rays, which showed as usual the duodenal ulcer I have had for a dozen years.

At the beginning of my stay in Tahiti, the change of pace tired me out. At sea, you often sleep during the day and awaken several times at night to take a look around, and go right back to sleep. On land, I could not take those little daytime naps as I had things to do—visitors, invitations—and at night I did not recuperate as well, because I kept waking up out of habit, as at sea. Everything settled down in two or three weeks.

[1] based on Dunne's writings, and in particular his *Yoga for Everyone*. He is also the author of *Yoga Made Easy* and *Yoga: the Way to Long Life and Happiness*—Translator's note.

General remarks on cruising life

I am convinced that a strong boat, even a very small one the size of a 19 ft Herbulot Corsaire, could be sailed single handed non-stop from Tahiti to the Falklands by way of the Horn without mortal danger, provided she was made of metal. If a well-plugged bottle is loosed in the middle of a cyclone, it will normally float. For a boat, the main point is the same: if made of metal, well sealed, well designed, breaking seas could roll her over ten times in a row without her sinking. The rest is just a matter of details, of adaptation.

A small boat has the advantage over a big one in that she costs much less to buy and keep up. My intention is not to drum up business, but those who are really interested in cruising as we understand it would do well to read the technical appendix of my first book, *Sailing to the Reefs* (Hollis & Carter). Written more than ten years ago, with far fewer miles in my wake, the conclusions I drew then on the conception of a cruising boat are still valid. Replace 'wooden boat' by 'metal boat', read between the lines a bit, and the main points are all right. Details are up to the individual.

Ferrocement boats

Several have been built in France, many in New Zealand, and in the United States. I saw three in Tahiti, whose owners were very satisfied. Right here, the 34 ft cutter built by Alain Brun and Philippe Sachet is on the point of being launched. For the concreting, Philipe and Alain scoured the quay; a dozen of us came, and everything (hull, deck, cabin roof and cockpit) was mortared in a day. But I can't go into details, having only a very superficial notion of this type of construction, which requires careful precautions if the job is not to be botched.

In any case, what little I have seen has convinced me that ferrocement is by far the cheapest way to build a boat. The only thing that would give me pause would be the risk of hitting a reef: once seriously holed, I doubt that a ferrocement hull can be properly repaired. Wood can be nailed, caulked, glued; steel can be welded or riveted: cement? In any case, if I wanted to go sailing, and could not afford a steel hull built in a shipyard, I would not hesitate to build a ferrocement boat: it could be finished in less than a year, perhaps in several months, five to ten times faster than the same boat in steel or wood, and far more cheaply.

Maintenance of a steel boat

Joshua is nearly ten years old. Her bottom does not show a speck of electrolysis. Yves Jonville's *Ophélie* and Michel Darman's *Santiano* are likewise intact. Our three hulls are protected by the same Dox Anode zinc silicate paint, made by Omexim, 1 Rue Lord Byron, Paris, and by zinc anodes from Zinc & Alliages, 34 Rue Collanges, Lavallois Perret (Seine), France. These anodes should be welded to the hull by their attachment points, and not bolted on; Zinc & Alliages is very explicit on this point. I have seen several steel boats with bolted-on anodes whose hulls were eaten up by electrolysis.

I find there is no problem when a rust spot appears above the waterline: I scrape it and then apply Rust Killer, a phosphoric acid based liquid made by Steel Cote (US). Rust Killer destroys the rust and bares the metal. If the metal does not appear completely cleaned by the product, apply some more. In ten or twelve minutes it should be clean. Rinse with fresh water, and when dry, put on the first coat of anticorrosive primer. For really perfect work, precede the primer with an application of Rustoil, a kind of anticorrosive oil that leaves a thin protective film.

The two best anticorrosive paints I know are Minium Gris, made in France by Julien, and the American primer made by Steel Cote; both are remarkable. A second coat of anticorrosive paint goes on when the first is good and dry, followed by five to six coats of enamel.

For routine maintenance, I give the exterior two coats once a year when the boat is not sailing, and two coats twice a year if she sails a lot. If the owner of a steel boat were conscientious enough to automatically put on two coats of paint a week before each ocean crossing, and one or two coats after arriving, after rinsing everything down with fresh water, I think the boat would never have a speck of rust, particularly if the entire hull, deck and cabin roof had been painted with Dox Anode before the boat were first put in the water. This complete Dox Anode treatment is often as good as hot-dip galvanizing. But the steel must always be sandblasted first, or thoroughly cleaned with a product of the Rust Killer type, if the Dox Anode is to hold well. To repeat, Dox Anode is the first coat of paint to go on the steel: it is never removed, or at least not before ten years. All other paints go over it.

The first paint to go over the Dox Anode should be a zinc chromate. But Dox Anode must be left to air for about two weeks after it goes on; this gives the zinc time to oxidize very slightly and to return to a neutral pH, which will allow the chromate to hold well. If there is no time to wait, if you are in a hurry to get off the merry-go-round, spray the Dox Anode painted surfaces with a 2 per cent solution of phosphoric acid, and rinse with fresh water a few minutes later. You can then put on the zinc chromate without delay.

As far as the interior is concerned, there is no problem provided the paintbrush can reach every nook and cranny. If one has taken the precaution of giving everything seven coats of paint, one will be able to rest easy for a long, long time. Flat steel ribs welded on edge make much more sense than angle iron; with flat steel, there are no hiding places for rust, as everything is visible.

The water tanks, if built into the hull (and therefore not galvanized) should be fitted with an easily acessible inspection hatch, large enough for internal maintenance. Michel Darman had some problems with his built-in fresh water tanks at first, so he scraped the paint down to bare metal, and cement-washed them (cement mixed with water, like whitewash). He recently opened the hatch to check, and called me over: after two or three years, the inside was like new. And it is really cheap.

One more thing: locate the head overboard valve above the waterline, and the intake quite far away and connected to the head by a tube of reinforced rubber. That way there is no possible contact between the bronze head fittings and the steel hull, eliminating an eventual risk of electrolysis.

It is commonly thought that a steel boat can't be under 30–33 ft, because she would otherwise be too heavy, as the steel plate must be at least 3mm thick (approx. $\frac{1}{8}$ in.) so as not to corrode through too quickly. The hulls of *Ophélie, Santiano, Joshua* and many other 40 ft boats destined by their owners for blue-water cruising are made of 5 mm steel. If 4 mm had been used, they would be noticeably improved from the standpoint of speed and heavy weather sailing. If I were building *Joshua* over again, I would use 4 mm steel for the hull.

After nearly ten years' experience with *Joshua*, and my very favourable observations of other steel boats, I would not hesitate to build a 23 ft boat out of 2 mm ($\frac{3}{64}$ in.) steel if, for plenty of perfectly valid reasons, I now preferred a very small boat whose upkeep would be much cheaper than *Joshua*'s. In my opinion it would even be possible to go to 1.5 mm ($\frac{1}{16}$ in.) for a 20 ft boat. Corrosion and electrolysis are no danger if proper precautions are taken.

What about aluminium alloys for small boat construction? The first problem is that a boat made of light alloy is very expensive, because of the cost of materials and skilled labour. I once saw a 30 ft hard-chine boat built by an amateur with 2 mm galvanized steel plates riveted to the ribs with $\frac{1}{4}$ in. rivets. She is now some twenty years old. The same amateur would have been faced with almost insurmountable problems if he had tried to build his boat out of light alloy: one must be highly skilled and very well equipped to machine and weld aluminium alloy. As for riveting, I saw rivets on an old, apparently intact seaplane fuselage which crumbled when scratched by a fingernail; with time and fatigue, the rivets appeared to have undergone a molecular transformation. I think that *long-lasting* light alloy construction is not yet perfected; in my opinion there are still too many unknown factors with this material as far as hardening and electrolysis are concerned for the very long-term use we have in mind.

How about fibreglass for small boats? Take a tin can and a plastic container, and just kick them along a stony path for a couple of miles. No need to say more; the choice between metal and fibreglass is up to the individual. But those who pick fibreglass will be especially careful around rocks. And if they have read books on sailing, they will recall that very great sailors like Slocum, Pidgeon, Voss, Bardiaux and Vito Dumas found themselves unintentionally on the rocks or aground. During our four months 1965 stay in Tahiti, four yachts hit coral in the Tuamotus. Three were total wrecks within a few hours; the fourth escaped with major damage thanks to the keel bolts breaking on impact, which allowed the boat to ride high on her side as far as the coconut trees, after passing over the reef. More recently, a fibreglass trimaran being sailed from Tahiti to Hawaii hit a cliff on arrival. Within a few hours the biggest piece of the wreck was not over five feet long. This doesn't mean that a steel boat would have survived under the same conditions, but it would make a big difference in less drastic circumstances, on a reef, for example. Nevertheless, fibreglass boats have one fantastic quality; they need practically no maintenance compared with steel or wooden boats. For that reason, I must agree that fibreglass boats can be really welcome, especially when small. And a small boat is easier to handle among coral reefs and in narrow entrances.

Repairs

So as to be able to save *Joshua* in case she accidentally ran aground, her removable ballast is composed of 50 to 60 pound pigs of iron in the hollow keel. These pigs are locked in place with detachable bars. That way, nothing can move in case of a capsize.

It would be a serious mistake to think that the hull of a steel boat with 5 mm plate is necessarily safe from holing: a steel wreck hit in shallow water, or a nice sharp rock with swell and a little bad luck. . .

So in addition to the ballast and a lot of other gear, the hollow keel contains several 1.5 mm galvanized steel sheets, and glass jars (they don't rust) filled with $\frac{1}{4}$ in. rivets. About twenty metal-piercing drill bits are also sealed in with the rivets, and the whole soaked with oil, to keep them in perfect condition. In that way, *Joshua* is ready for eventual major repairs on a lost atoll; it also allows me to remain completely independent wherever I may be, with just a friend's help to assist me with repairs, if necessary.

I have never done riveting with professionals, but I know from experience that amateurs can do strong, watertight work. Helping Henry Wakelam, the two of us riveted a dozen thin metal patches on the damaged parts of *Shafhaï*, a 28 year old steel boat. She was made completely waterproof by placing $\frac{1}{4}$ in. rivets about an inch apart, after inserting a sheet of newspaper painted with red lead between the patches and the hull. The patches totalled 27 sq. ft, and the two of us did the job in about ten days, using what we had on board. The holes were made with a hand drill, and the patch temporarily held in place with four small bolts. We then finished the holes (a little under an inch from centre to centre), drilling through patch and hull at the same time. The holes done, we countersunk the exterior end of the holes with a ⅜ in. drill bit, removed the patch to file off the burrs, glued the newspaper against the hull with red lead and put the patch back, held by its four temporary bolts. Then came the riveting, me inside, Henry outside. I pushed the rivet through, held its head against the hull with a dolly (a heavy iron weight), signalled with a kick that everything was ready on my end, and Henry riveted with a small hammer, smashing the rivet until it was well countersunk. It was cold riveting; that is, without first heating the rivet. Not a single drop of water came through.

A big hole in a wood, plastic or metal hull can be temporarily patched underwater with an Asian technique, using a putty composed of one part ordinary cement mixed with one part clay; it hardens under water in about 12 hours. Big leaks in *Marie-Thérèse's* bottom were plugged that way in the Indian Ocean. Thereafter, Henry Wakelam perfected the process considerably. Our tests together resulted in this recipe: mix equal parts dry plaster and cement. In another container, mix water and clay (not kaolin) to make a very runny mud. Pour this mud on the plaster-cement mix and knead into a putty the consistency of modelling clay. You now have to move fast, since it will not stay malleable for more than 2 or 3 minutes. This plaster-cement-clay is applied under water and hardens in less than a quarter of an hour. At Plymouth, Loïck found quick-setting cement, which is even better than the ordinary kinds.

Here in Tahiti, I heard of an amazing result with another product, Underwater Patching, which comes in two tubes; it is made by Petit Paints Co., San Leandro, California. To use, mix the two substances in a dish (like epoxy), then put the putty on by hand, rubbing on the damaged parts on the hull under water. It sticks to damp wood. In the present instance a section of the bottom the size of two hands had been scraped bare against a coral head, and the wood had to be protected against teredo worm. The boat had just been hauled out, was about to leave on a long charter in the Tuamotus, and could not wait for the slip to be free. It came back seven or eight months later and was hauled out. I did not see it with my own eyes, but three trustworthy friends told me that this underwater repair job held amazingly well; after the protective plastic patch was ripped off, the bare wood did not show the slightest trace of teredo. It is my feeling that Santofer and similar plastic preparations should also give reasonable results, provided one takes the precaution of putting a few nails (as an armature) in the damaged part of the hull, to help the putty hold. The same applies to the plaster-cement-clay mixture: small nails in the right spots will ensure its holding to the wood, if the place to be protected is too smooth.

Teredos (shipworms)

It might be thought that teredos die very quickly once a boat is hauled out. This is not true: teredos can live for several weeks, perhaps even a month, in wood taken out of the water. Do not believe that a coat or two of antifouling paint over wood already attacked will inconvenience teredos in the least. The boat has to stay out for a good month to be sure no teredos are left alive.

Do not blindly trust the protection afforded by copper sheathing or fibreglass over the wood, either. If a teredo manages to get to the wood through a small crack, it can do serious damage without your suspecting it. I have seen it happen several times on copper-sheathed boats, and once on a moulded ply glass-covered boat.

Undiscovered leaks

A bag of sawdust aboard an old wooden boat can prove invaluable in overcoming a multitude of leaks. Fill a can with sawdust and dive about six feet below the keel, holding the can upside down to prevent the sawdust from escaping and getting wet. Then turn the can over, so that its opening is upward; the sawdust will float up to the hull in a cloud (shake the can to disperse it better). Once against the bottom, the sawdust particles are sucked in by the leaks, get stuck, then swell up in a few minutes. I periodically used this ancient procedure on *Marie-Thérèse's* hull during her Indian Ocean crossing. The result lasted from a few hours to several days. At anchor the boat does not work, and waterproofing obtained this way can last for months.

One more bit of information before leaving this inexhaustible subject of repairs and do-it-yourself work: I have seen ripped sails that had crossed at least one ocean after being temporarily repaired—but in a quasi-permanent way—with patches glued on with Texticroche, without needle or thread. I have also seen a Tergal sail repaired with Formica glue, a kind of rubber cement, also without sewing. Naturally it is makeshift, but can prove useful. Having watched the operation, I will describe it. A nasty snag in a Tergal sail was involved. The owner cut a patch the right size, and brushed the glue on one side of the patch and the corresponding part of the damaged sail. He waited about ten minutes for the Formica glue to become barely tacky to the touch, then he put the patch on, glue to glue, being careful not to make any wrinkles. It held for nearly a year.

Aboard *Joshua*, during cruising school, the old jib, badly ripped along a seam, was glued together with tape of adhesive material laid over both edges of the rip; one of my crew regularly used the technique on his own boat. I have unfortunately forgotten the name of this emergency repair material. The jib held until the end of the season, with some care, of course, but despite several *mistral* blows. I would not go so far as to recommend this method, but it has helped more than one sailor.

Charts

The set of Pilot Charts covering the whole world is not expensive. They contain all sorts of information on weather, currents, ice, etc. on a monthly or trimesterly basis. These charts are put out by the US Navy Hydrographic Office in Washington, DC.

Nautical charts proper, both large and small scale, are very expensive everywhere. In all countries, I think these precious charts are destroyed by the local cartographic services once they are out of date. If some official body could get hold of them before they are destroyed, and sell them to us at pulp value plus handling charges, we could correct them for the areas which interested us by checking them against the same charts on ships.

Food

Jean Rivolier's recommendations, based on Arctic, Antarctic and mountaineering experience, were as follows.

For an ocean voyage like the one I had in mind, the body requires about 3000 calories a day maximum. Some people eat more than others. One should not go against one's nature of habits.
    It is essential that the food be a balance of glucides, protides and lipids. Glucides (sugar, cereals, potatoes and rice) provide the greatest energy output. Protides (meat, eggs, fish and certain starches such as soybeans) help to recover from weight loss. Lipids (fats, vegetable oils and butter) increase resistance to cold, and also provide energy.*
    Beware of dehydration, which can go unnoticed and have serious consequences. A few mouthfuls of seawater, in addition, also provide mineral salts.
    Eating only canned goods entails no risk of vitamin deficiency, provided one eats something of everything. Analysis of certain canned fruits and vegetables often shows a higher vitamin content than the same produce eaten fresh in urban conditions (when fresh vegetables spend too much time on display, for example). The great tragedies of the past were linked to exclusive or nearly exclusive consumption of dried or salt food, without variety.
    There is no point in taking additional synthetic vitamins, unless it gives peace of mind. In any case, vitamin dosing, which consists in taking synthetic vitamins as medicine, does not improve man's performance with regard to adaptation to heat, cold, altitude or effort.

In some ports of call, unhoped-for opportunities arise to get provisions at a bargain, that is, for nothing: sea turtles, lots of fruit and fish in the Galapagos, lemons, oranges, grapefruit, wild goats and sheep in the Marquesas, tuna and dorado at sea when you sail over a school and they all start biting at once, eggs and turtles on Ascension Island, etc.
    In the days of *Wanda* and *Marie-Thérèse II* Henry Wakelam and I regretted not having the equipment for canning:
    'Can you imagine how sorry we'd be if we came across a nice, fat, ownerless donkey some day all to ourselves!'
    'But we couldn't kill it just to eat curried donkey for a few days,'
    'Whereas if we could can it. . .'
    Our teeth were long and sharp in those days, it should be said. They are probably not as long now, but a simple canning

set-up could still prove very useful. I have heard of little household devices for sealing cans, but do not know them myself, and imagine they must be a little cumbersome on a small boat. Also, the stowage problem posed by the empty cans would be considerable.

In the Galapagos, the De Roys used special glass jars that took very flat metal lids; a big supply of them would take up very little space, an important detail on a boat (the big traditional glass jars with hinged lids would be far too bulky, not to mention their weight). A good-sized pressure cooker is suitable to sterilize the food to be canned.

William, the translator of this book, stocked up on wild goat when he called at the Galapagos in the ketch *Tiki*. Apparently the best parts are the fillet along the spine and the heart and liver. Here is his recipe for salting the rest: cut deep slits in the meat a half inch apart to spread it out as much as possible without removing it from the bone. Rub rock salt into the meat and put the flayed pieces in the sun. Pour off the juices each evening and store the meat out of the dew; two or three days should do the trick. To cook, rinse in at least one change of fresh water for a few hours; the *cabron* tastes best in curries and risottos. In the Galapagos, rock salt can be found in open natural crevasses.

You can also smoke sea turtle and goat meat. It is a fairly long process, taking at least a day and a night of patient work to do right. You will need an old 50 gallon drum, wire hooks made on the spot, and green mangrove wood, cut with a machete near the shore. Those who stop in the Galapagos can ask the settlers for the recipe.

Drying bananas is useful, because the whole stalk ripens at once, and the bananas can't be eaten before they go bad. Peel the ripe bananas and cut them lengthwise into thirds. Dry in the sun four to six days, covering at night to protect them from the dew. Very nourishing; they keep for several months.

In his very interesting doctoral thesis on Polynesian plants, Paul-Henri Petard gives us some valuable information. The quotations are from this thesis, published in 1960 at the Marseilles School of Medicine and Pharmacy. On the big arboreal ferns known as *mamau* in Tahiti, *aki* and *aki vivi* in Rapa, and *tuku* in the Marquesas, Doctor Petard writes:

The heart (the core of the trunk), the terminal and the lateral buds are rich in starch, and may be eaten when cooked. This is a survival food, which saved hundreds of natives from starvation before the coming of the white man. It is still used today by the inhabitants of Rapa, and those of the Marquesas on rare occasions. A person lost in the woods and short of food can generally survive for some time on the fronds of most ferns, if picked very young before they unfold and put out leaves, and cooked carefully. Poisonous species are extremely rare.

Discussing the Pandanus (*fara* in Tahiti, *ha'a fa'a* in the Marquesas, *hala* in Hawaii, *tina* in the Tuamotus) Paul-Henri Petard informs us that:

The fruit of the pandanus plays a major part in the nourishment of the natives of certain islands. On recently formed atolls, where the Pacific food plants such as taro, bananas, potatoes and breadfruit are hard to grow, and even coconuts sprout with difficulty, the pandanus grows wild and is an absolutely reliable food source. The pulp is not eaten raw, even in times of want, as it strongly irritates the mucous membranes. . .

For immediate consumption, pandanus fruits are boiled in water, or baked in a Tahitian oven. If they are to be used later, the pulp is taken out, mixed with freshly grated coconut, and made into cakes; these cakes are sun-dried and will keep indefinitely, to be cooked when needed.

Paul-Henri Petard gives some very interesting facts about coconuts:

On some of the waterless Pomotu islands, i.e. all of the atolls, the inhabitants drink coconut milk when the rainwater cisterns are dry. This massive daily intake causes no problems. . .

Coconut milk is usually sterile: it can be injected subcutaneously, intramuscularly or intraveneously, without ill effect. It advantageously replaces glucose solutions or the various artificial saline solutions, actually flushing out the kidneys. . .

The meat of the coconut—fresh albumin—can be eaten at any stage in the nut's growth. Nia coconuts (ripe but not dried; they must therefore be picked from the tree) have soft meat, similar to curdled milk; it is given to babies as well as weaned piglets. According to J Lepine, the meat contains (per 100 parts):

sugars	1	cellulose	4.30
gums	0.33	mineral salts	6
albumin	1.46	water	84
oil	2.40		

Further on, Paul-Henri Petard speaks of the *ti*:

> *a shrub with an unbranched, straight flexible stem, ending in a clump of long, dark green leaves, which grows in hedges around most of the huts. The* ti *belongs to the lily family. In native life, its many uses make it as important as the* uru *(breadfruit) and the pandanus. . .The* ti *has a long pivoting root, often branched; in a 20 year old shrub, it can grow to 6 ft in length and the thickness of a man's thigh. . .A 10 pound root contains more than 2 pounds of saccharose. Young roots are very poor in sugar, and are not used for food. The sugar content increases with age, and the natives always use roots more than 5 years old, weighing over 10 pounds. The root must be cooked in a* himaa, *or Polynesian oven.*

This oven is built approximately as follows: dig a hole 5 ft across and 18–24 in. deep, and build a wood fire in it. When you have a bed of coals, put in stones and let them get red hot. Cover the stones with a layer of banana leaves. Put the food in, and cover with more banana leaves to keep the dirt out. Finally, cover everything with earth or sand, and cook slowly. Most foods take one or two hours. The *ti* requires 24–48 hours, according to Paul-Henri Petard.

> *Until about 20 years ago, cubes of* ti *cooked in a* himaa *could still be found on the shelves of Papeete's street vendors. The Tahitians were very fond of this treat and sucked the pieces of* ti *as candy, or used them to sweeten their tea. . .When the natives of Rapa do not have the time or energy to lay a* himaa, *they merely slice the raw roots very thin and boil them in water for several hours; the result is a sugary extract, which they strain and use to sweeten their drinks and foods. . .*

In places not always well supplied in greens, like the Galapagos coast and the Tuamotu atolls, it would be nice to sprout wheat, soybeans, and watercress seeds on board. I did not persevere along these lines during the trip largely because I am not a very gifted cook, and knew no good recipes for fixing the sprouts.

Beware of fish in the atolls and coral islands of the Pacific:

some fish are perfectly edible at one spot, whereas at another, two or three hundred yards away, the *same variety* can be very poisonous. Fatalities are believed to have occured. Always ask a native whether a fish is all right to eat. He will ask you where you caught it.

As a general rule, fish that hunt, caught in coral waters such as tuna or jack trevales (members of the *Caranx* family), are seldom poisonous. But it can happen: I met two people laid low by a tuna (they were sick for a month). On the other hand, it seems that the soldier or squirrel fish (*'i'ihi* in Tahitian) can always be eaten. It is bright red with large, very black eyes, and scales almost as sharp as a razor. No bigger than a man's hand, it sticks to dark cracks in the coral heads and lives in schools, easy to shoot with a speargun. All of the Tahitians, Marquesans and Paumotus I have asked affirmed that this fish never poisoned anyone.

In the parts of the Indian Ocean that I know (Chagos, Cargados–Carajos, Mauritius) poisonous fish are also found, but the effects are much less serious than in the Pacific. You can pull through with a bad night or two.

One hears suspicious rumours in the Galapagos: all the fish are supposed to be edible, except the *tetradon* (puffer fish); it is said that it can be fatal in all waters. The fish is easy to recognize: it blows up, and grunts when caught on a line. Yves and Babette Jonville ate a lot of them during their stay in the Galapagos, but took great care to remove the skin and head, and especially the innards. An oceanographer friend had told them the puffer is a very tasty fish, once those precautions had been taken.

In mid-ocean, one can sometimes harpoon trigger fish during calm weather. They like to hang around the rudder. They are the size of a man's hand, with a leathery skin and a large spine on their back, which becomes and stays erect— hence their name. I have eaten about ten in my life, but on re-reading Bombard, I just learned that trigger fish can be poisonous to the point of being fatal.

A friend of mine mentioned a book on the subject which he considers very good: *Dangerous Marine Animals*, by Bruce W. Halstead, MD (Cornell Maritime Press, Cambridge, Maryland). In Tahiti, I consulted Dr Christian Jonville, a sailing pal who sailed around the world and knocked about the Pacific quite a lot. He is therefore able to see things from our point of view, and here is what I noted: A state of intoxication produces headaches, pain behind the eyes and in the joints, diarrhea and eventually vomiting; then very intense itching. In 1971, Dr Jonville recommended the following treatment in the event of poisoning in some out-of-the-way place:

> *For pain: two intramuscular injections daily of Novobédouze dix mille (hydroxocobalamine, 10 mg per injection), long-acting vitamin B_{12}, plus four tablets daily of Bétrimax (made up of thiamine chlorhydrate 100 mg, pyridoxine 100mg, and hydroxlobalamine 1 mg), a vitamin B_1, B_{16}, B_{12} complex. Keep to these doses for two to four days: do not exceed them. Reduce the injections to one a day as soon as possible.*
>
> *For diarrhea, if present: in addition to the injections and tablets above, take an intestinal antiseptic such as Ercefuryl (nifuroxazide 100 mg), Ganidan (sulfaguanidine) or Talidine, for three days.*
>
> *For vomiting, if present: add Primperan (metoclopramide 10 mg) to the treatment as drops, injections or tablets, as desired, as long as the vomiting lasts.*

In any case, try to reach a settlement to get medical help or hospitalization. There is no sense in fooling around with something like this unless there is no choice.

Christian Jonville found the writings of the old Tahitian sorcerer Tiura'i, long since dead, and with the help of Professor of Tahitian Maco Tevane translated two recipes of interest:

1 tablespoon vinegar
1 tablespoon brown sugar
1 green (unripe) *nono* fruit (*Morinda cyclifolia*)

This fruit grows on a shrub, and has pineapple-like nodules; its size varies from that of an egg to a tennis ball. It is found on many islands of the Pacific, and on the atolls.

The recipe is as follows: crush the entire *nono* fruit (skin, seeds and all), extract the juice (by squeezing it through a cloth, for example); mix the juice with the vinegar, pour it in a glass of water, add sugar, and drink. Repeat next day; *no more*.

The second recipe is used when one has nothing else on hand. Take the bones of the fish responsible, grind them to a powder, mix with water, boil, and drink. Sorceror Tiura'i's text does not specify the amount of water or the length of time to boil it.

Money

Alas yes, money. . .for all our picking up butts and living with
a reasonable amount of brains, more or less money is necessary, depending on one's temperament. In any case, one thing
is certain: one can go very far and lead an interesting life with
very little money to start, because one always makes out once
underway—provided one *is* underway.

There are various ways of propping up finances. Chartering
or cruising school has helped plenty of people out in the
Caribbean or Tahiti. The boat's kitty will not overflow, as it
can in the Mediterranean, but it is undeniably a decent way of
bringing in enough to keep going.

Here in Tahiti, a good number of sailors work ashore or on
other yachts, and their boat's finances stay healthy. Jory used
his sewing machine to mend sails and make awnings for rich
yachts. Christian, who crewed on a visiting boat and arrived
without a penny, left for Holland two years later to buy a 27-ft
steel cutter; he had earned the money by taking Polaroid
pictures of tourists on arrival at the airport or on shipboard,
and in bars at night. Jack made money writing business letters
in English for the Chinese importers here. If you speak a
foreign language really well, there is money to be made doing
translations, as William and another long-hair found out.
Klaus asked us to look after his boat for a few weeks so he
could skipper a wealthy businessman's 82-ft yacht from the
Caribbean to Tahiti. It was a real coup, because that kind of
delivery pays well. Of course, you should not count on jack-
pots like that too often, but you can always make out. I
remember giving French lessons during a stopover in British
territory in the Far East a long time ago. True, it brought in
just enough to feed me, and I don't know if my victims learned
anything, but my English made a lot of progress, and it came
in handy later on.

You can also write a book. Just tell the story. Also, sailing
magazines are often glad to get articles on passages and life at
ports of call. It would not pay for life ashore, which is
expensive, but living on board is another story. During my
previous trip from France to Tahiti and back, we lived for two
years without touching our savings, thanks to a rigging and
self-steering job on a neighbouring yacht at Casablanca, some
chartering in the Canary Islands and the Caribbean, a few

articles for a yachting magazine, and a one-week boat delivery.

Making movies while sailing can be fascinating, and showing them at stopovers feeds the kitty. The risks are considerable, unfortunately, and the investment a big one, since 16 mm colour is called for. But if you can take the chance, the cruise will probably be more interesting and more alive; you notice things that would otherwise be missed. And if you can get the investment back by showing the public a film you like, and live on the proceeds, it isn't stolen money. If you still wind up making more than enough for your reasonable needs, you can always spend part of it on things that don't hurt anyone, like planting trees.

Glossary

This glossary is intended for non-sailors who want to follow the story. I have therefore written it as simply as possible. Sailors do not need it, and will forgive me if my explanations seem a bit superfluous at times, or not always written in nautical language.

ABACK A sail is aback when it is set on the side that the wind is coming from (the 'wrong' side). This is done when heaving-to (q.v.).

ANCHOR WINCH A kind of capstan used to haul in the anchor chain. The smaller the boat, the less necessary an anchor winch, since the anchor can be raised by hand. Many racing boats, even big ones, prefer to do without an anchor winch, since they have large crews, and the winch would be heavy, and could get in the way of sail handling. In cruising, the situation is quite otherwise.

Beat A boat is beating (or sailing close hauled) when she is sailing into the wind at an angle of about 45°. As the angle increases beyond that, she is successively on a reach (60°), a beam reach (wind at 90° to the boat's axis), a broad reach, and a run (wind directly astern). A boat performs better on a reach than on a beat; she pitches less, heaves less in the seas, and goes faster. But she does not sail as close to the wind on a reach. One chooses according to sea conditions.

BOBSTAY A wire or chain guy used to steady the bowsprit vertically. Many boats, including *Joshua*, prefer to use chain for the bobstay, rather than steel wire, as it is much less subject to corrosion or damage from the anchor chain.

BONNET An additional fair weather sail that can be set beneath another sail to increase its area.

BOOM A horizontal spar (long piece of wood or metal) along which the bottom of the sail is attached. A boom can be made of wood or metal, such as aluminium alloy. *Joshua*'s booms are wood, as are her masts.

HEAVE (or **HAUL**) **TAUT**   To pull a halyard as tight as it will go, to pull the sail up tight.

HEAVE-TO   This is hard to explain in a few lines. Heaving-to is a heavy weather tactic which lets the boat look after herself when the sea is very rough. One can heave-to in various ways: for example, one can lower all the sails, lash the rudder tiller alee (on the lee side; to starboard, for example, if the wind is blowing from port), and go below. The boat will then float along like a cork without making any headway, until the weather clears. But it can sometimes be dangerous not to carry any sail when hove-to, so one carries some mainsail, sets the staysail aback, and lashes the tiller alee with rubber shock cords. In this way, the boat drifts a little, creating a protective eddy on the windward side which prevents waves from breaking. Since man started sailing, however, reams of paper have been devoted to heaving-to, and it has not always kept boats from being overturned by breaking seas. If the boat has a weighted keel, though, she will right herself before filling up—which is the main thing.

JIB   Triangular sail set ahead of the main mast. (See sketch, page 11.) In descending order of size, jibs include the big genoa, small genoa, working jib, small jib, smallest jib, and finally the storm jib. All these sails, from the genoa to the storm jib, and including the staysail, make up the headsails, i.e. the sails located forward of the mainmast.

LANDFALL, TO MAKE   To sight land, a beacon, or an island. Sailors are almost always nervous before a landfall, for fear of errors in their navigation.

LIE-TO   To be hove-to. See 'heave-to'.

LOG   A device used to record the distance covered, as does a car's odometer. A small rotator (propeller) is towed on a line astern, and turns a pointer on a meter mounted on the rear of the deck. In racing, a much smaller, more advanced type of log is used, consisting of a tiny rotator an inch or so in diameter mounted on the bottom. This does not slow the boat down at all. In fact, many cruising boats use this second type of log, which shows both the speed and distance covered.

LUFF   A boat is said to luff when she alters direction, coming up into the wind (coming closer to the direction from which the wind is blowing). When she turns the other way, she is said to be falling off.

BOWSPRIT A spar which extends forward of the bow. (See sketch, page 11.) Few boats have bowsprits nowadays, but I find one quite useful, as it allows me to set more sails. On the other hand, a bowsprit is sometimes in the way when in port.

CLEW The lower aft (rear) corner of a sail. The sail is trimmed (adjusted) with lines called 'sheets' which are attached to the sail's clew.

CLOSEHAULED A boat is closehauled when she is sailing close to the point from which the wind is coming. This is also called 'beating'.

COAMING The vertical abovedecks part of the cabin. Also, the vertical edge of the cockpit, which protects the helmsman from spray and wind.

COCKPIT A sort of open pit in the deck behind the cabin, where one can sit without being too exposed. One usually steers from the cockpit.

COME ABOUT To turn the boat so as to bring the wind from one side to the other, across the bow. When a boat comes about she goes on the other tack (q.v.), or 'tacks'.

FORESTAY Steel wire running from the bow, usually going two-thirds of the way up the mainmast. It steadies the mast, and is used to set the staysail.

FURL To tie the sail down along its boom after the sail is lowered. It makes no difference if there is no boom, the sail is still furled. Sails are furled with the aid of gaskets, which are short lines or strips of cloth passed round and tightened to pull the sail into a bundle.

GENOA A big jib. The genoa is therefore set when the wind is not too strong, otherwise the mast would break.

GYBE or **JIBE** To pass the sails (accidentally or on purpose) across from one side of the boat to the other, while sailing downwind. When the wind is strong, the boom can break under the impact if the boat is carrying too much sail for the amount of wind.

HALYARD or **HALLIARD** A line (or thin, very flexible steel wire), which passes through a block (pulley) at the masthead, and is used to raise a sail. Each sail has its own halyard.

HEADSTAY or **JIBSTAY** A steel wire running from the end of the bowsprit to the top of the mainmast. This stay steadies the mast and on it may be set the jib, storm jib or genoa. (See sketch page 11.)

became corrupted to 'starboard'. When in port, the oar was protected by tying the boat up with her left side against the wharf, and that side therefore became known as the 'port' side.

TOPPING LIFT   A line which supports the boom end when the mainsail or mizzen are not being used. Jibs and staysails do not usually have booms, and thus no topping lifts.

WHISKER STAY   The whisker stays steady the bowsprit laterally, while the bobstay steadies it vertically. Whisker stays are usually steel wire, but I prefer chain (as for the bobstay), which is less apt to corrode.

WINCH   A little revolving drum with a crank handle, used to tighten the sheets and also for very precise sail trimming. This is why winches are even to be found on fairly small boats. When one has no winch, a block and tackle may be used, but it requires much more time, and is more complicated.

MIZZEN MAST The rear (and shorter) mast on a two-masted boat such as a ketch or yawl (*Joshua* is a ketch). The mizzen sail, or 'mizzen' for short, is the sail that is set on that mast.

PITCHPOLE To capsize forward, stern over bow. Can occur when running before very large seas.

PULPIT The 'balcony' or railing extending out over most bowsprits. It provides a useful support when changing the headsails.

REEF BANDS Horizontal rows of little holes in the sails, reinforced (like buttonholes) by eyelets or grommets made in patches. Small lines, called reef points, are attached to the holes, and are used to reduce canvas according to the wind strength. The third reef band on *Joshua*'s mainsail is the highest, i.e. the one which allows the most canvas to be reduced. Sailing 'triple reefed' or 'close-reefed' therefore means sailing with a minimum of canvas. (See illustrations in the Appendix, showing the various sail areas used on *Joshua*).

SHEET A line used to position the sail relative to the wind, and attached to the sail's clew (the lower, rear corner). A sail is 'sheeted in' when the sheet is pulled close to the boat's long axis; it is 'eased' when the sheet is loosened and allowed to go outside the boat. Obviously, it is much easier to ease a sheet than to haul one in. To ease it, all you have to do is uncleat the sheet and let it slip; the wind pressure does the rest. To sheet it in, you need muscle power, a winch, or a tackle.

SHROUDS Steel wires used to steady the mast laterally.

SPAR Any long piece of wood, such as a boom, bowsprit, etc.

STAYSAIL A headsail located between the mainsail and the jib. Small boats do not usually carry staysails. On a dinghy or small keelboat of the kind you see sailing in sheltered waters, a staysail would be useless and cumbersome, in view of the boat's size. Cruising sailors, however, often prefer to split up their headsails into staysail and jib. This makes adjustments simpler, as the respective sails are smaller, and therefore easier to handle.

STORM JIB A very small, strong jib used in heavy weather. Also called a 'spitfire jib'. One can have storm jibs of various sizes, either small or tiny.

TACK A boat is said to be on the port tack when the wind is coming over her port, or left side, and on the starboard tack when it comes over her right side. The old Viking boats had a long steering oar on the right side; the word for 'steering oar'